media
relations

media
relations

Richard Stanton

OXFORD
UNIVERSITY PRESS

OXFORD
UNIVERSITY PRESS

253 Normanby Road, South Melbourne, Victoria 3205, Australia

Oxford University Press is a department of the University of Oxford.
It furthers the University's objective of excellence in research,
scholarship, and education by publishing worldwide in

Oxford New York

Auckland Cape Town Dar es Salaam Hong Kong Karachi
Kuala Lumpur Madrid Melbourne Mexico City Nairobi
New Delhi Shanghai Taipei Toronto

with offices in

Argentina Austria Brazil Chile Czech Republic France Greece
Guatemala Hungary Italy Japan Poland Portugal Singapore
South Korea Switzerland Thailand Turkey Ukraine Vietnam

OXFORD is a trade mark of Oxford University Press
in the UK and in certain other countries

National Library of Australia Cataloguing-in-Publication data:

Stanton, Richard.
Media relations.
Bibliography.
Includes index.
For 1st and 2nd year undergraduate students.

ISBN 9780195557343.
ISBN 0 19 555734 4.

1. Mass media - Study and teaching (Higher).
2. Communication - Study and teaching (Higher). I. Title.

302.230711

Edited by Sandra Goldbloom Zurbo
Text and cover design by Adrian Saunders
Proofread by Anne Mulvaney
Printed in Hong Kong by Sheck Wah Tong Printing Press Ltd

Contents

Preface

This book explores, investigates, and explains **media relations**. It is interested in the relationships that are built between all types of **stakeholders** within the public sphere, including corporations, communities, political candidates, individuals, governments, and not-for-profit organisations, but most importantly it is interested in the **media**. It explains how media relations theories are derived, and how they are linked to practical applications in the worlds of business and trade, society and community, health and education, politics and government. It advocates a practical application of media relations and shows why theory is important in underpinning practice.

The theoretical focus of the work is on **framing** and **relationship building**, two models widely used in Western and non-Western media relations. It provides an understanding of why relationship building and framing are important, and from where they have travelled, to be considered important. It discusses the valuable contributions made by a number of scholars, including Carl Botan, Robert Entman, Erving Goffman, Vincent Hazleton, James Grunig, and Dean Kruckeberg. The theoretical argument is tied unconditionally to stakeholder case studies and profiles, revealing a wealth of information about how they develop successful media relations campaigns, how not-for-profit organisations—reliant on a finite pool of funds for their important and often life-saving work—construct media campaigns and build long-term relationships, how leading international corporations present an image of integrity and corporate social responsibility, and why some political candidates are more successful than others in getting their messages in the media.

The idea that a book with a focus on media relationship building can find a place in the literature of public relations, political communication, and corporate communication sets the stage for an additional investigation: the two part question of why we need to develop media relationships in both democratic and non-democratic states, and how the development can assist us and those who inculcate mediated messages. To understand

stakeholder
a citizen who has an interest, financial or otherwise, in the outcome of a media relations campaign.

media
a vehicle that provides a means of communication; includes the instruments of communication, viz. newspapers, television etc, and the objects of communication viz. journalists reporters, editors etc.

framing
the act of shaping and forming a story so that it resonates with a particular viewpoint.

relationship building
the development of a connection or association, either emotional or rational.

field

a sphere of action in which actors, agents, and other forces exercise theoretical and empirical arguments that contribute to the existence of the field.

subfield

an area within a field that is taken up by specific theories and practices.

why media relationship building has become important, indeed, crucial, to all types of organisations and individuals, the book begins with an explanation of how media relations fit within the wider **field** of public relations. We will use this as a basis for our understanding of the development of media relations as a **subfield** of public relations. Additionally, we will explore the future of media relations through a simple explanation of the argument put by German philosopher Jurgen Habermas: that the media have altered the shape of society and that the alteration has been advantageous. We will discover that with the emergence of the mass media came the need to present information in such a way that it would be persuasive and, in turn, influence stakeholders beyond the media. Theories of influence and persuasion thus play an interesting role in media relationship building.

The meaning of stakeholder

For the purposes of this book, the media are important primary stakeholders. They are the stakeholders that agents and other forces are interested in influencing and persuading. Beyond the media lie a vast number of other stakeholders, known variously as **publics, audiences, listeners, readers**, shareholders, communities, special interest groups, investors, citizens, and individuals. These stakeholders will be investigated after we have built an understanding of the relationship between our primary stakeholders: clients and the media. Stakeholder publics beyond the media are the reason we seek to build media relationships. **Clients**, whatever the nature of their issues or events, seek first to influence and persuade the media to report the importance of their issue or event. But reporting is not an end in itself. Clients do not invest in media campaigns for fun. They invest in media campaigns so that their stakeholders can form an opinion about the issue or event under discussion. Mediated communication is an important part of the opinion-forming process in democracies. It results in public opinion. Citizens read, watch, and listen to **news** differently than they do to advertising. Advertising provides information, but news and feature coverage **frames** an issue or event in a more influential way. A story appearing in a newspaper or on

public

any number of individuals or citizens belonging to a community or nation.

audience

a collection of individuals who listen or watch some event or spectacle.

listener

one who is attentive to a sound or speaker.

reader

someone who takes in information through observation.

television news has, in the minds of citizens, more validity than if the same material appears in a television advertisement or arrives in their letterboxes as a glossy flyer or leaflet. Glossy flyers and leaflets have their place as elements in campaigns, but they cannot compete with mediated material for validity in the minds of citizens. News captures citizens' imaginations. It reinforces or rejects already formed ideas and shapes them into opinions. Thus we have the term 'public opinion'. Public opinion is the opinion formed by a majority after consideration of an issue or event. It is an attempt to represent a wider opinion about issues and events than the opinion held by an individual citizen. In the twenty-first century, it is most often informed by news and other information received from media sources such as television, radio, newspapers, the internet, and magazines. It is reinforced by personal communication between individuals. Public opinion is thus an expression of social, economic, and political will after the point of **mediation**. It is something that occurs because of, not as part of, media relations and media reporting. For this reason it forms an important part of the consequences of media news reporting and interpretation and, as such, is beyond the scope of this book.

client
a citizen or organisation who uses the services of another in a professional capacity.

news
information, whether published, broadcast or communicated from one individual to another that has some bearing on issues and events.

frame
the preparation of a space so that it has boundaries.

mediation
the act or process of intervening on behalf of stakeholders.

The structure of the book

The structure and content of the book are intended for undergraduate students and, as such, assume no prior knowledge of media relations. But it has the potential to act as a resource for early practitioners and for others intent upon building and running media relations campaigns. It may also be a useful resource for reporters and journalists interested in gaining a deeper understanding of the subfield. The text is structured around the idea of a twelve week undergraduate program. It provides a theoretical theme based on media relationship building and framing. It develops links to additional theories of relevance and argues for a particular approach to theory and practice. An additional theme is the United Nations (UN) examples that appear within the work. The UN provides one of the most remarkable examples of an organisation dealing with widespread and complex issues and events that require even more remarkable and complex media relations strategies. UN examples are included to provide evidence of an organisation whose presence crosses all media relations boundaries.

The book is divided into the following parts:

■ Introduction: Building Relationships, Framing Issues and Events

- Part 1: Theories and Campaign Models
- Part 2: Elements of Media Relations
- Part 3: Organisations and the Basis of Practice
- Part 4: Evaluation and Assessment

Chapter 1, the Introduction, provides the foundation for understanding how theories and practices link in both the pedagogy and the reality of media relations. Chapter 2 introduces the theories and arguments that underpin the actions of media relations. Chapter 3 introduces the reader to the idea of campaign formulation; design and development. Chapter 4 provides one of the most extensive lists of tactics available to media relations with examples of how they can be used in different situations. Chapter 5 provides a broad understanding of the relationship-building process. One of the most important yet underrated aspects of media relations work is the writing process. In Chapter 6 all aspects of this enjoyable occupation are covered. Chapters 7, 8, and 9 elaborate and reveal the elements of media relations that exist in all types of organisations, including government and politics, business and corporations, community and special interests, health and education, trade and fashion. In Chapter 10 the reader is introduced to the difficult and complex topic of budgets and timelines. To make the task more accessible, I have included case studies on how agencies go about constructing budgets for clients based on a fixed investment or on an idea. Chapters 11 and 12 introduce the reader to the darker aspects of media relations: risk and uncertainty, evaluation, and, if conducted properly, the euphoria of success. In Chapter 13, the Conclusion, I have attempted to show where the media relations subfield might be headed and the relative difficulties associated with the climb. The Conclusion also provides a ledge on which to meet and imagine media relations.

objective

the object of an action such as the communication of information.

The book is structured so that cases and examples appear embedded in the text. The **objective** is to provide readers with seamless reference points that relate directly to the argument rather than waiting until the end. Cases and examples are identified throughout as Chronicles. Each Chronicle is a narrative, an account related to a theory or method. For simplicity, I refer throughout the work to all activities as issues and events. Similarly, the terms 'media relations expert', 'media relations counsellor', and 'media relations practitioner' are used throughout the book. In practice, this may not be the case because different terms attract different levels of seriousness.

Nomenclature

We should not spend too long stressing about whether there is a point of difference between the names we apply to media relations: *public affairs, investor relations, community relations, government relations, corporate communication, strategic communication.* While all these names indicate specific areas, they take their existence from public relations. They all have stakeholder publics that they are keen to build relationships with, and they all use the same communication skills (media relations) to do so. What is more important is the ability to identify which skills are best suited to which campaign and how they can be used to the greatest advantage.

If we cannot survive without some differentiation, then the example provided by UN Under Secretary Shashi Tharoor would be a good starting point. For the UN, *public relations* is used to win the support of a target stakeholder, domestic or foreign, for the work or objectives of a specific UN organisation or project. *Public affairs* seeks to encourage domestic public understanding and support of government policies and activities, while *public diplomacy* is used to engage, inform, and influence foreign publics in order to promote sympathy and goodwill for a country and its policies. But according to Shashi Tharoor, the UN itself cannot afford to draw distinctions because it seeks support from a wide range of stakeholders as well as specific organisations for general principles. With this in mind, the book will show that the UN position is that most often taken by many other organisations in the pursuit of ethical models and practice in media relations.

A note on Western-ness

The analysis of the structure of relationships among and between stakeholders in the field of media relations as it occurs in this book is on theories and practices that occur in the West. But globalisation makes Western definitions difficult. There are clear delineations between the politics and governments of what we imagine as the West and their former political foes, the communist East. But the world is now defined by trade relationships and non-trade relationships rather than by the politics of capitalism. The significance of organisation—the European Union, the North American Free Trade Agreement, the Australia–China Free Trade Agreement—is what defines **global** media relations. All the strategies and tactics, all the campaign elements described in this book, can be used interchangeably across cultural, social, and language barriers. The political barriers are obvious. An

> **global**
> embracing the whole world, or a whole group such as a global internet search and replace technique.

goal
the finish of a campaign or action; the desired end to a media campaign, but less useful when considering the relationship building process.

environmental protest campaign against the building of a large infrastructure project in China, such as a dam or a tunnel, cannot exist. Citizen stakeholders in Iran opposed to that country's nuclear arms development are similarly thwarted, while in Turkey, organisations opposed to that country's inclusion in the EU will have difficulty developing and sustaining a strategic media relations campaign in opposition. But that does not mean that stakeholders in countries with suffocating political processes and policies should not attempt to use media relations campaign strategies and tactics to reach their objectives and **goals**. It just means that doing so will be a little more difficult.

Supplements and resources

This book is supplemented by a website: www.oup.com.au/orc/stanton. The site includes additional case studies (*The Chronicle*) in a wider variety of industries and services.

Acknowledgments

There are people, issues and events without whom this book may not have come from me. Conflict is a wonderful catalyst for positioning ideas so that they become real, and researching and writing require long periods of quiescence, something with which I have never truly successfully been able to engage.

If, as I have argued throughout the work, relationship building is the foundation for success in media, it is also in book publishing. Oxford's Higher Education Publishing Manager, Debra James, was delightfully diplomatic when rejecting my original proposal, but equally was delightfully enthusiastic about *Media Relations*. Publishing Editor Lucy McLoughlin provided professional balance, gratefully received, in helping me through the complexities of the publishing process, while Senior Editor Tim Campbell stabilised the production process.

In writing the work I have drawn on a number of inspirational sources, notably Dean Kruckeberg, Vince Hazleton, and Carl Botan. Josh Meyrowitz, Susan Barnes, and Janet Sternberg, without knowing it, provided encouragement.

To all the people and organisations I imposed upon with professional and personal invitations to contribute *Chronicles*, I am deeply indebted. Without you the work would be less. Enduring thanks to Sandra Black, Alice Hocking, Liam Bathgate, Penny Barker, Fran Hagon, P J Cottam, Kate Donaldson, Victoria Tulloch, Allan Ryan and Nick Redmond. I must also thank the anonymous examiners of the early draft for insightful and valuable comments.

For providing access to United Nations spaces and people, Chris de Bono deserves special mention. For a professional and enjoyable relationship in editing the text, I am deeply indebted to Sandra Goldbloom Zurbo.

To the University of Sydney Faculty of Arts, I am indebted for the period of study time that allowed me to complete this work. But most importantly, I am grateful to my undergraduate and postgraduate students for their invaluable contributions. They provided the inspiration. Thanks also to Neil Young and Bruce Springsteen for the music.

About the Author

Richard Stanton has worked as a newspaper journalist, reporter, sub-editor and editor, and on national and international business magazines and journals. He has published B2B magazines and worked as a correspondent for international specialist publications. He has worked in the fields of political and corporate public relations with clients in government, politics, manufacturing, trade, information technology and agribusiness. Richard has a bachelor's degree in political science, a master's degree in English literature, and a PhD in journalism and public relations. His published works include non-fiction and fiction. He is presently a faculty member in the Department of Media and Communications at The University of Sydney.

1

Introduction: Building Relationships, Framing Issues and Events

In late 2005, the International Criminal Court (ICC) announced it was issuing warrants for Joseph Kony, leader of a Ugandan rebel organisation responsible for the torture and death of 20 000 children. In announcing the issue of the warrants, the ICC was presenting its credentials in the **public sphere**; this was its first public act since its establishment in 1998 as a permanent war crimes tribunal. The time between the establishment and delivery of a practical application of its mandate was framed by one of the world's leading newspapers as a 'public relations bungle' (*Economist*, 22 October 2005). For the *Economist*, the issue was even more pointed: the ICC's public announcement had been made after its intentions had been leaked to the media some weeks before.

> **public sphere**
> the space in which citizens are freely able to gather to witness or discuss issues or events.

Earlier the same year, in a one-page account of relations between Israel and Palestine, the same newspaper chose to investigate how both sides were using public relations, which it reported under the heading 'The battle for Public Relations: The Palestinians are not only outgunned but out messaged' (*Economist* 26 March 2005). To highlight the story angle, the *Economist* chose another ruling by another world court, the International Court of Justices (ICJ) ruling against Israel's West Bank barrier as an issue on which the Palestinians should have had a huge PR victory. It suggested the Palestinians were unable to capitalise on such an important issue because there is 'no coordinated message, no systematic media monitoring', and that public statements came from officials who did not have media training or from public personalities who did, but were not in the government. Both stories and their angles reveal a lot about the *Economist* as a global news source and the meaning it attributes to media and public relations. On the one hand, it is suggesting media and public relations ought to play a significant role in framing important global issues, yet on the other, they display an overt contempt for those who apply it badly or at a low level.

Such reporting of globally significant issues raises a number of important questions. If, as the *Economist* points out, the continuing conflict between Israel and Palestine can be reduced to descriptors such as media relations and public relations, what then are these concepts and how do we align them with other definitions that represent them at their simplest level, the distribution of **news releases** and the hounding of reporters for coverage of a **local** 'promo ... on the return of the Brazilian bald seagulls' (Kesey 1992: 321), for example? Does the Israeli government have some secret store of media relations campaign strategies that are known only to governments and global organisations such as the ICC, the International Monetary Fund (IMF), and or the United Nations? Do the media frame stories to subsume a complex array of backplays, knowing that any revelation of **strategy** and **tactics** is not as interesting as the foreplay—the action that is occurring at any given moment in a sociopolitical world filled with action? The answers to these and other questions of importance within the fields of media and public relations are the subject of this book.

news releases
see media release.

local
a sense of place that allows individuals to feel comfortable in their surroundings.

strategy
a plan of action that takes advantage of core competencies to the detriment of competitors.

tactic
the action taken to fulfil strategic intent and campaign objectives.

Why media relations is important

Media relations pedagogy frequently claims that the most important issue is the interlocking of practice with theory. Throughout the world, from North America and Europe (including the UK) to Australia, New Zealand, Singapore, Korea, Taiwan, and Japan, and on through to South American countries such as Brazil and

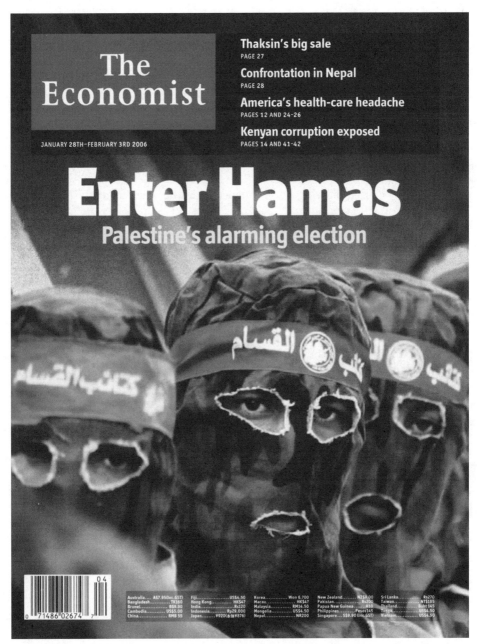

Figure 1.1 'Enter Hamas', front cover, *Economist*, 28 January–3 February 2006

Argentina, there is a belief that the problems within the field will be resolved if theory and practice can be seamlessly locked together. But this is a fallacy. A more important question confronting media relations in the twenty-first century, especially in the area of teaching and research, is how to approach the gap between the teaching of critical thinking and the teaching of applied knowledge. Critical thinking is a central part of the teaching in all fields that surround media relations and from which it has taken much of its theoretical development, particularly social science and political science. Applied knowledge teaching, in which students learn through the application of case material, is a secondary consideration. In the field of media relations, however, the reverse is normative. But the field of public relations and its subfield of media relations are becoming more the subjects of critical analysis as they move towards a position that can offer meaning at all levels. By this I mean they can be understood to have meaning at the level described by a respected medium such as the *Economist*, while also having meaning when debased as **spin doctoring** and influence peddling. Critical analysis is part of the answer to a more meaningful field. So it forms part of this book. But the book is not a critical analysis of the field. Critical analysis informs evaluation and contributes to media relations theory in a meaningful way and to an understanding of the activities and rituals in which media relations are engaged.

spin doctor
an interesting name for a public relations practitioner.

Defining media relations

The *Economist* is one of the most influential media in the world. In general, it reports issues and events in a balanced fashion, relying upon sources that it values and trusts from a perspective that requires them to demonstrate the same level of **symbolic capital** as is demanded of the newspaper itself by its stakeholders. But how much of the material that appears around the globe each week in the pages of the *Economist* is sourced from those who claim to practice media relations? Is every article about governments sourced from governments? How much of the material sourced from governments can claim objectivity?

symbolic capital
the investment in symbols and signs that are as important to an organisation as its financial capital.

A literal translation of media relations is the relationships with and between media, media relations practitioners, and clients. Media relations can have broad implications—such as being attached to a globally sensitive conflict between Palestine and Israel—but at the other end of the scale it can attract attention as the preparation of a popsy bubblehead event as banal as a television song contest. Historically, media relations has attempted to define itself by what it is not—it is not propaganda, it is not lobbying, and it is not advertising. But defining something by saying what it is not is an apological position, because the very being of media relations is to move forward, rather than to defend.

aim
the conscious decision to take a direction and attempt to attain the objectives along the path of the direction taken.

Along the scale—between the extremes of global conflict and popsy bubblehead—lie an enormous number of differentiated activities that are ascribed to media relations. What they have in common is the **aim** that an issue or event shifts from one space to another. This can happen with the application of persuasion and influence upon the media, or it can happen as a communication with stakeholders that does not rely on media for its transfer. The subject of this book is media relations, so the importance of the persuasion and influence that is applied

> **controlled media**
> any publication, broadcast, or communication that bypasses an agent or other force to reach its intended stakeholder.

to all types of media is palpable. But less obvious is the need for media relations to implement other, less direct, types of communication with non-media stakeholders. Media relations is, therefore, not only concerned with building relationships with media, but it is also concerned with the communication processes that bypass media and deal directly with non-media stakeholders. We will discuss the difference between them and why we refer to them as **controlled media** and **uncontrolled media** below.

Governments, global organisations such as the United Nations, corporations, and other elites do not have a secret stockpile of weapons of mass persuasion. Which is fortunate, for if they did, they would have the advantage of what French sociologist Pierre Bourdieu calls recognisable symbolic capital—that is, the ability to trade on reputation—where there would be no need of elaborate media relations campaigns. In the pursuit of their goals and objectives, complex organisations use exactly the same strategies and tactics as do less complex organisations, such as local environmental interest groups. The media relations campaigns that are used by the Israeli government to position its issue within the global are the same in form as those used by the small environmental

> **uncontrolled media**
> news and other media providers who stand between a media relations campaign and the desired recipients of its aims and goals.

action group to position its issue within the local. Media relations strategies and tactics, embodied in campaigns, are the animations of media relations. The scale of the campaign and the choice of strategy and tactics is what differentiates them. And all media relations campaigns have their origin in written and spoken communication. Most often, the writing and speaking are pitched at the media as primary stakeholders in the campaign, thus we have the singular importance of media relations underpinning all other public relations strategies. Practitioners and theorists have always acknowledged the primacy of media relations within the field of public relations (see, for example, Hunt & Grunig 1994; Sriramesh & Vercic 2003; Bains, Egan & Jefkins 2004; Zoch & Molleda 2006).

> **taxonomies**
> classifications, particularly in relation to certain principles.

Media relations may not always be immediately evident, but there are certain tests we can apply to see if it is present. Witness the example above of the conflict between Israel and Palestine. If the *Economist* had not revealed what it imagines to be certain **taxonomies** of public relations displayed by either side, would we be any the wiser? We would if we observed particular activities. Does one side publicly communicate only when it perceives it has had a victory over its competitor, or does it announce everything, win or lose? These are the type of things we will learn about and investigate as we make our way through this book. As we familiarise ourselves, we will discover that global organisations such as the United Nations employ the same structure in media relations as all other organisations around the world, no matter how large or how small.

A very brief history of media relations in Australia and New Zealand

Media relations pedagogy in Australia and New Zealand since the 1980s, when it first appeared as undergraduate courses in colleges of advanced education, has been defined and framed by the work of the American public relations scholar James Grunig. Grunig defined its overarching field of public relations as a function of business, and therefore part of a management strategy in which it played a role as **functional communication**. Public relations was circumscribed by his **symmetry theories** and **excellence theories**. Kruckeberg and Starck (1988) led a shift away from this early frame to investigate the possibility that public relations (and therefore media relations) was not simply about supporting management in its goals and objectives, but also about building relationships across all stakeholders and **stakeseekers**. A little later, Heath (1992) and others attempted to reframe the field in terms of rhetoric. Yet another frame, developed by Ledingham and Bruning (1998), Grunig and Huang (2000), and Kent and Taylor (2002), maintained the position enunciated by Kruckeberg and Starck, but shifted the responsibility of relationship building to a co-creational perspective. More recently Botan and Hazleton (2006) have argued that there is a paradigmatic shift away from symmetry/excellence and that **co-creational theory** has the potential to redefine the field.

functional communication

any communication that can be related to an action or activity rather than to its form.

excellence theory

an argument developed by US scholar James Grunig that relies on four models of communication—press agentry, public information, two-way asymmetrical, and two-way symmetrical.

symmetry theory

the proposition that communication, to be effective, must have as much input from one stakeholder as it does from a stakeholder in an opposing position—for example, a corporation and an environmental group.

Theorists in Australia and New Zealand are generally critical of the excellence theory, yet they continue to use it as a teaching model. Practitioners apply the excellence model because the historical position is one that requires media relations campaigns to act in support of management functions. Like their counterparts in the rest of the Western world,

Australian and New Zealand media relations activities have been traditionally shaped by the needs of organisations to reach ever-widening and more complex publics than could be reached through the application of orthodox advertising and marketing techniques. These technician-type activities included the production and distribution of newsletters and flyers, brochures and pamphlets, billboards and posters—any number of activities that could support management functions and strategies as simple tactics designed to persuade and influence. As far back as the middle of the twentieth century, media relations was absorbed within the advertising departments of organisations. Advertising played a different role in those early days. The front pages of newspapers, even quality broadsheets such as the *Sydney Morning Herald* (*SMH*) and the *Auckland Star*, were still devoted to the nineteenth-century idea of placing advertisements as well as news on the front page. The blending of news and advertisements was much less transparent than it is today.

| **stakeseeker** |
| a citizen who is looking to have an interest, for whatever reason, in the process and the outcome of a media relations campaign. |

| **co-creational theory** |
| the proposition that stakeholders in any communication will work together to achieve desired aims and goals. |

While media relations and public relations around the world draw upon theory and practice derived from the US experience, it must, by its situational nature, adapt to specific social, political, and economic variables and rituals in each individual location (see, for example, Page & Hazleton 1999). Thus the Australian experience will be very different politically to the US experience, despite the similarity of parliamentary democracy, because one is a constitutional monarchy, the other a constitutional republic. In New Zealand, the experience will be different again because of the single-house nature of parliament.

It is difficult to pinpoint an exact location for the start of media relations activities in Australia and New Zealand. Some commentators suggest that historical reference points can be related to events after the Second World War (see, for example, Leitch & Motion 2001), but this supports a positivist or systems perspective in which historically grounded events reveal a particular monologic paradigm. Media relations, even when being considered as a management function, must be seen as **dialogic**.

| **dialogic** |
| being in the nature of dialogue or conversation. |

Others nominate individuals as a way of finding a common reference point. The work of Asher Joel in Sydney is frequently used as a way of historically grounding media relations. Yet this, too, is a less than appropriate starting point given the publicity campaigns of governments before and during earlier wars, or at times of peace or crisis. There is little real value in attempting to find some point from which to construct a perimeter around the field. It would be just as difficult to find the starting points for the fields of medicine or law. What is more important is to be able to define the field as it appears at the start of the twenty-first century and to predict how it might evolve. The history of media relations theory points to all stakeholders besides the agent and client as serving a background role, thus becoming instruments to assist a client to reach goals and objectives.

Why this book is important

Media relations in the Western world, as I have already stated, is dominated by the practice and theory that develops in the USA. Globally, however, practitioners and academics vie for position to present a practical application or theoretical model that will stand out and provide definition for a field that has a poorly regarded history. But practitioners and theoreticians rarely work together in such research. In fact, between the USA and rest of the world there is a marked difference in how one sees the other, and it is usually through the lens of conflict rather than consensus. In Australia and New Zealand students of media relations, upon completing their undergraduate studies and moving into the professional sphere, either as media relations practitioners or journalists, are told emphatically that they should forget what they learnt at university because it will have nothing to do with the real world they are about to enter. This conflict between theory and practice is not justified. It is a hangover from history, from a time when journalists were indentured as cadets to run copy and public relations trainees were used as slaves to make coffee and sweep up. A shrinking number of practitioners continue to pine for those golden days as they are overtaken by history and its definitive changes. Undergraduates in Australia and New Zealand now enter the profession as highly-skilled practitioners with a strong understanding of the role of theory in the development and interpretation of the field. This is not a result of a blind adherence to US theory and practice, but an acknowledgment of its **hegemonic** position combined with the typically rational antipodean characteristic of reshaping something to suit the local conditions.

hegemony
the dominance or influence of one thing over an other.

This book is a contribution to a reduction in the conflict between practice and theory, and a conscious effort to be involved in the reshaping. It attempts to set out how media and public relations work for real stakeholders as diffuse as corporations and their environmental opponents, governments and charities, small businesses and unions, community, special interest groups, and health providers. Its case studies and examples, which I have named *Chronicles*, are locked together by an analysis of relevant theories and how they provide the solid ground onto which practice can be built without fear of tremor, aftershock, or subsidence. The *Chronicles* contribute to the theoretical argument at all levels of achievement, from international, through national and regional to local and community.

Researching, teaching, and practising media relations

Unlike Europe and the USA, where the world's largest advertising and communications corporations own equally large percentages of the business of media relations, the Australian and New Zealand markets are too small to sustain too many large corporate public relations firms. The globalisation of corporations and the media has played a big part in how Australian and New Zealand media relations have developed since the turn of the century. Some large public relations corporations have regional or country offices in Sydney, Melbourne, Auckland, and Wellington to service global clients that have strong interests in the region, but generally, smaller niche agencies account for the type of practice that exists in both countries. Many organisations maintain inhouse public relations and media departments. Practice is divided between small to medium-sized agencies and inhouse. Practitioners range across both, moving between agencies and inhouse because there is a relatively small pool of specialists available at any one time. Practitioners can be differentiated as technicians and managers. For the purposes of this book, they are referred to as counsellors, experts, and practitioners, depending upon the circumstances.

Media relations and public relations pedagogy are more liberal in Australia and New Zealand than in the USA and Europe. (For the purposes of this book, the use of the word Europe includes England, Scotland, Ireland, and Wales as members of the European Union.) There is a tendency in both countries to require academics to have practical experience in public relations or media as well as showing evidence of scholarly pursuits. In this they are similar to the USA and Europe but few professions impose such unusual and stringent requirements. Teaching public relations does not require continual engagement with industry. There is an understanding that there will be some level of engagement through the use of practitioners as tutors or through industry groups such as the Public Relations Institute of Australia (PRIA) or the Public Relations Institute of New Zealand (PRINZ). Public relations courses provide connection with industry by seeking accreditation as a continuing process that is supported by industry. Accreditation provides a measure of the acceptability of a course within the business sphere. It is not a measure of the acceptability or otherwise of graduates. The liberality of public relations pedagogy allows a range of positions to be adopted, from critical to positivist. It also allows a range of theories to be entertained and employed without recourse to efficacy. This is not a suggestion that public relations pedagogy is random selection, simply that such a diverse range of choices creates a canvas that looks more like *Blue Poles* than *Campbell's Soup*.[1]

---

1   I can think of no two images that are of the same genre yet more oppositional: Jackson Pollock's *Blue Poles*, which hangs in the National Gallery of Australia, Canberra, and Andy Warhol's *Campbell's Soup*, which hangs in the Museum of Modern Art, New York.

This book conflates relationship theory to framing theory so that students might develop a broad understanding of what is allowing media relations to acquire a level of respect.

With this in mind, we will march boldly into the field.

Part 1

Theories and Campaign Models

2

Two Theories of Media Relations

CHAPTER OBJECTIVES

- To understand how media relations theories activate practice.
- To investigate why theory plays a role in defining the field.
- To understand framing theory and relationship building.

Media relations as a subfield of public relations

Today we talk about a field of study or activity rather than a **discipline**. We attempt to define a field, in terms best enunciated by Pierre Bourdieu (1977, 2005), because we need to compete with the **agents** or **forces** occupying other spaces who may make attempts to occupy the space (field) we perceive to be our own. A field is thus a site of competition in which agents and **other forces** compete to keep things as they are or to transform things. Bourdieu suggests a field is a space where actions and reactions occur and that the agents within the field have particular views and opinions, shaped by exogenous factors outside the field, that they bring to it. A field must be defined to enable us to identify what lies outside its boundaries as much as we

> **discipline**
> an area of learning or scholarly endeavour.

agent

someone acting on behalf of someone else or an organisation in a matter.

force

power to control or influence some type of effect.

other forces

interests, whether political, economic or social, that are not part of a strategy.

can identify what lies inside. The importance of what lies outside should not be underestimated, given the notion that agents and forces acting upon a field from inside and outside perform the function of shaping the field. Building on Bourdieu's work, Norwegian scholar Øyven Ihlin (2005) provides an image of field that shows how different fields overlap, despite the need to be identified with one particular field rather than another. Ihlin suggests that fields need to be identified at organisational level so that we feel comfortable with them—banks in the economic field, parents' and citizens' associations in the education field, theatre in the cultural field—but at the same time these fields can be identified as being part of larger fields, or can themselves contain subfields. Public relations can be considered to be part of the wider field of communication, but within the field of public relations lies the real subject of this book, the dynamic subfield of media relations.

To understand field more fully, we can investigate briefly public relations' opposing field of journalism, which has been well documented and which will occupy space in this book for comparative purposes. Within the field of journalism there are competing agents—newspapers, television, radio, magazines, internet—and competing actors—News Corporation, Liberty Media, Viacom, Sony BMG, and Disney, for example. Agents such as newspapers and television compete with each other for dominance of the field even when both products are owned by one actor. For Bourdieu and others, television has become the dominant agent in the field of journalism. The decline in newspaper sales across the Western world, particularly in Australia and New Zealand, is best illustrated by newspaper proprietors, such as John Fairfax (the *Sydney Morning Herald*, the *Age*, the *Australian Financial Review*), who compete poorly for market share with television-owning organisations such as Kerry Stokes's Seven Network. This is also reflected in the share price if the organisation is a public company, which is most often the case for Western media. The object of the contest is not destabilisation; it is the valorisation of the **core competencies** that the competitors claim to make them superior. It is a struggle for supremacy based on a platform of economic, social, and political capital. (We will discuss Bourdieu's notion of economic, social, and political capital, particularly the subset of symbolic capital, later.)

core competence

the underlying assumption that an organisation or individual has a central ability and capacity to undertake the professional business they are involved in.

The field of media relations, as a relatively newly constituted arena, is one that is filled with agents and forces who are always operating on behalf of others (clients) who exist in fields other than media relations. While the field of journalism is filled with agents and actors operating as journalists, much the same as the field of medicine is filled with medical practitioners and law with lawyers, media relations is filled with agents and actors theorising about and practising things outside the field, effectively, agents and actors operating overtly, competing on behalf of clients within other fields to maintain a position or to transform a position. And the media are the logical vehicles for media relations agents and actors to use to reach accessible and inaccessible stakeholders within these fields.

The media are acknowledged as being of primary importance to the campaign goals and objectives of all types of issues and events. Rare is the public issue or event that does not require underpinning—or at least minor support—from some form of media. Here we must consider the nature of **public** and **private,** and be able to distinguish them for the purposes of understanding the role of media relations and how it is different to private relations such as lobbying. Within the private sphere we are less likely to engage in media relations because we can resolve whatever it is about our issue or event that requires **mediated communication** as a goal or objective. This is true in the nature of private relations between individuals as well as between organisations. One corporation may communicate with another—a bank with an international defence contractor, for example—without having to enter the public sphere. All communication or dialogue between the two remains private. It is when there is a requirement of the two organisations to communicate publicly that the media are engaged. The media play an important role in reaching additional stakeholders who may not be as effectively reachable as they are through mediation.

> **public**
> any number of individuals or citizens belonging to a community or nation.

Media relations is a subfield of public relations because the media are some of the many stakeholders within the wider public relations field. It is through the media that the diverse range of stakeholders in the public sphere reach other stakeholders and what US scholar Dean Kruckeberg calls stakeseekers. This does not mean the media are supplicant in delivering effective outcomes. The media are generally hostile towards issues and events that seek to influence and persuade them of some virtue that might not normally make a contribution to news. So it is crucial for practitioners to build media relationships in which trust and integrity are the underlying elements. (We are interested in framing issues and events as news so that they resonate with the media we are delivering them to.) The overt hostility of the Western media towards the application

> **private**
> an individual acting in an non official capacity; something removed from public access or view.

> **mediated communication**
> any form of communication that is undertaken by a third party on behalf of two other agents or forces.

of persuasion and influence through media relations makes the job of the media relationship builder and issue framer more interesting.

Media relations in the public sphere

In any attempt to define media relations we must consider its relationship to the concept of a **public sphere**. We will investigate the functions of the public sphere more fully in the following chapters, but for the purposes of understanding the theoretical positions we are about to investigate, we must understand the need for the existence of a public sphere and, within it, the existence of **public opinion** and a general public. To give us a clearer understanding, we can conflate Bourdieu's theory of field with the concept of the public sphere originating with the German philosopher Jürgen Habermas. Habermas defined and conceptualised the public sphere within a social science paradigm (as do most of the theorists who have roles to play in this book). In Western democracies, the public sphere is viewed from a number of competing positions. Habermas's public sphere was defined as a meeting place or public forum—a mediating environment—in which literate and wealthy citizens exchanged information and news about relevant political and economic issues and events openly and with the object of profit.

public sphere
the space in which citizens are freely able to gather to witness or discuss issues or events.

public opinion
an expression of social, economic and political will after the point of mediation.

The existence of a public sphere is central to the relationship building theme of this book. The suggestion is that a public sphere, in which discursive processes in public spaces embody the good in a society, resonates with us as **citizens** (see, for example, Schudson 1999). In creating a persuasive media relationship, we are using a number of theoretical concepts and models that overlap more or less, depending upon what point the campaign is up to. Media relations campaigns have a number of stages between commencement and completion. Any theory overlap can be explained through an identification of each of the stages. Some of the theories that come into play in this book, as well as its underpinning theories of framing and relationship building, are **knowledge gap theory**, **agenda setting**, **dialogic theory**, and the adaptation of Bourdieu's **social contract theory** to media relationship building.

citizen
an inhabitant of a community.

knowledge gap theory
the proposition that interpretation and meaning can reduce gaps in knowledge among individual citizens or groups.

It is important to understand why we are so interested in theory when, in reality, media relationship building appears to be something that is simply instinctive and intuitive: you build a relationship with the media the same way you build a relationship with your partner or your dog. You do nice things for them, and they will respond nicely. But this approach ignores the fact that media is business, and business works in a very different way to personal relationship building. There is very little competition when building a relationship with your dog: you don't have to think about where it might turn its attention, or to whom, other than you, it might show affection because you feed it, take it for walks, and provide it with a warm place to sleep. The dog is easily persuaded that you are the centre of its **universe**. The media, while they have been described as attack dogs (see, for example, Sparrow 1999) are not loyal and obedient because they have plenty of stakeholders willing to feed them better and juicier material and to provide them with warmer beds and better places to walk than you can. Competition for media space means we must be strategic. We must develop a media relations campaign that is competitive. If we are to compete successfully, we need to develop an understanding of a number of theoretical positions and, in understanding why theory is so important to our media relationship building, we must also be in a position to measure the success of our campaigns. A number of measurement models will be discussed in detail in chapter 12.

agenda setting
a strategy that involves the placement of items in some chosen order.

dialogic theory
the proposition that conversation or dialogue underpins actions and objectives.

social contract theory
the proposition that human society relies on mutual agreement for its continuation.

universe
all the objects under investigation.

Framing theory and its application to relationship building

Framing requires us to think about our issue or event in a particular way. It needs us to think about our issue or event as part of a wider **ideology** and to frame it within that ideological position. It also requires us to have some understanding of the ideological position of the media so that our frame matches the **agenda** embedded within the media ideology. Media ideologies come in all shapes and sizes but, most importantly, they are linked to a central position that is the ideological position of ownership. Opinion writers and reporters working for News Corporation, for example, may hold different views to News Corporation's majority stakeholders Rupert Murdoch and John Malone (Liberty Media), and sometimes their writing may reflect this position. But, generally speaking, the ideological position of the ownership or majority shareholding will be paramount. Framing our issue in ideological terms related to the media implies a pragmatism is build into each campaign. It also implies a non-ideological position for our client, who is then seen to be willing to engage in any ideological position to suit the purpose of persuading the media. This is

ideology
an idea or way of thinking that becomes the basis for a political, economic, or social system, and that continues its existence when not in the ascendancy.

agenda
items to be considered at a business meeting.

not the case. The need to understand the ideological position of the media does not translate into a media-relationship-building pragmatism devoid of its own ideology. The need to understand a news media ideology allows the media relationship builder to frame an issue in such a way that it reflects its own ideological position—not a compromised position because it adapts to a particular media ideology. It requires us to:

- measure how much we know about the issue
- measure how much others know about the issue
- evaluate where we obtained our information
- evaluate the validity of the information
- evaluate sources of information other than our own.

What is framing theory?

I have developed a definition of framing theory as it applies in the Australian and New Zealand context. Framing theory is the capacity of a media relationship builder to comprehend and interpret the agenda-setting policies and source selection processes employed by the media. It is the construction of a suitable ground onto which an issue or event can be projected as an elegant story (characterised by grace of form, simplicity, and effectiveness) relevant to specific media stakeholders.

Framing theory requires SGI—**s**trategy (design), **g**round (foreground/background), and **i**mage (story).

Issue framing in media relations takes its lead from work by Erving Goffman (*Frame Analysis*, 1974) in which the idea of what an individual could actually be attuned to at any particular moment was defined by the framework that was built around a particular situation. (The concept of the marketing terms **situational analysis** and **situational variables** in public relations were both developed from Goffman's work.) Goffman began his investigation into framing and frame analysis by asking what it was that an individual did when confronted by any current situation: the 1970s version of 'Wha's happenin', ma man?' or 'Wha's goin' down in da 'hood?' For Goffman, the question required us to be alert to a number of possibilities, chief among them that the answer could be framed in any way that supported whatever needed supporting. (Some critics suggest this is the only reason that media relations exists: to shape and frame responses that match something other than reality.) Goffman argued that the width or narrowness of focus of an issue or event was determined by who answered the question 'What is it that's going on here'?

situational analysis
the investigation of something in relation to its place or position relative to its place.

situational variable
the movement of the position of something in relation to its place.

If we think about the issue of, say, voluntary student unionism in Australia and ask that question, we will get different answers, framed according to the degree of involvement or interest the respondent has in the issue. The federal government will frame its response one way, students another, the federal opposition another. If we consider the issue of an influenza pandemic originating from sick chooks in South-East Asia and ask the question, the answer will be framed as a different response by competing interests. Just as **individuals** must ask what it is that is going on before they can get an answer framed in a particular way, so, too, the media—reporters, journalists, editors, and producers—seek answers to the same question before they can construct and write objective accounts of issues and events.

'individual'
Someone acting alone.

Following Goffman, the media answer the question by investigating the frame in which the issue or event has been presented and try to make sense out of it by matching it to already known frames of reference. These known frames of reference may have been established or entrenched in the mind of the individual reporter for some time, or they may be the product of some sharp occurrence that has had a profound effect on that individual's beliefs or codes of ethical and moral conduct. The reporter may, for example, have had a profoundly moving experience in childhood—the death of a parent—that sets up a frame around the issue of parenthood generally, and single parent families specifically. In the social world (leaving aside for a moment the physical and biological worlds), the organisation of issues and events governs the way in which we see them and the level of acceptance we apply to them. Principles of organisation, Goffman suggests, and our subjective involvement in them causes the principles to be framed in a particular way. If, for example, we feel confident in the government and, by extension, the principles upon which it organises the health system, we are less likely to show panic in the face of the threat of an avian influenza outbreak than if we have less confidence in the government and the health system. We frame our personal response to the threat by remaining calm. If we have less confidence in the government and the health system, we may be more likely to panic. Both responses might be the result of how we frame the issue in our own minds.

The duty of the media relationship builder is to frame an issue or event in such a way that it resonates with the existing or known frames of reference used by the media so that it has meaning. But Goffman, whose work provided a frame for future scholars, such as Robert Entman, among others, was concerned with an additional aspect of framing, one that provides an ethical dimension to the work of media relationship builders. Goffman was concerned that fabricated issues and events could be framed in a certain way or embedded in reality through the use of persuasion so that they took on the shape of reality to the extent that it became difficult to tell the fake from the real. This is the central argument put by the media today about the role of media relations in the embedding process. And it is no coincidence that this process reached a stage where the US Defense Department referred to reporters working in war zones as being embedded with its troops. They are effectively, to highlight Goffman's point, taking up space in the reality of the war, rather than reporting it from an objective sideline.

While the media go about doing good, investigating fake from real, many of them believe media relations practitioners go about doing bad: inventing fake and attempting to embed it in the real. Media reality is organised around the principle of the binary opposite—if you're not with us you're against us, a frame that allows media workers to see media relations itself as a fake, rather than as part of the real.

Goffman suggests that whatever it is about the real that makes us believe in it, those in the business of producing the fake will use the same ingredients, making it difficult to know fake from real. Just ask any Melbourne street vendor with a trolley load of Louis Vuitton handbags selling for $30 each. But this assumes fabrication is the province of public relations and that the building of media and other stakeholder relationships relies on fake. (An award-winning Australian television reporter once told a group of undergraduate student journalists that the important thing to remember in television journalism was to 'fake it till you make it'.)

The importance of interpretation

One of the core and underlying principles of organisation that is used by media relations in representing the real is the act of researching and writing stories in the same way that they are researched and written by the news media. One of the most important reasons that media relations practitioners in Australia and New Zealand have traditionally been drawn from the news media is that they are expert in representing, in print, issues and events in exactly the way the reading and viewing public expects them to be represented. This tradition has now been supplanted by tertiary education institutions. From universities and colleges come trained media relations practitioners armed with writing and other skills that play a major role in the supply of news. But learning how to frame an issue or event so that it appears real requires more than the simple fabrication and embedding of the unreal. All communication, if it is to contain and transfer meaning, must be organised in such a way that it is understood. So the organisation of messages into coherent layers of information requires them to be framed in a certain way. Whether they are then perceived to be real or fake is the risk taken by the media relations practitioner when delivering them to the media.

In our private lives we spend a great deal of time classifying and arranging things within our range of experiences. Without classification and control it all becomes pointless and confusing. We need to make sense of what it is we are engaged in. In so doing we interpret issues and events in a certain way, according to our life experiences, and when we do, we put them into specific frames, just like when we stick a picture in a frame and hang it on a wall, or take a photo of a musician and encase it in a plastic sleeve in front of a music CD, or write a book and divide it into chapters with case studies as examples of experience that we can learn from. Framing not only requires us to interpret and find meaning, but it also needs us to work through a theme for an issue or event. It is not enough that a mediated issue or event may find its place among a chosen stakeholder group that understands the message. It must have a degree of continuity so that the message's meaning can be constructed in a particular way. The threat of an avian influenza pandemic, for example, can be constructed around a number of competing frames (government, health providers, pharmaceutical companies), but for it to have meaning for particular stakeholders, it must carry a theme throughout its mediated life (most news stories run in cycles from a day to a week). So it is unlikely the media will switch themes over the week of its life. They will look for continuity in the story. The *Age*, for example, is unlikely to frame the issue around government inadequacy, then switch to pharmaceutical company competency, then switch again to World Health Organisation support.

Stakeholder picks

When corporations, governments, or individuals (clients) engage a media relations expert (agent) to frame an issue or event, they do it with different stakeholders in mind. Most often, it is the news media stakeholder the client is interested in because the news media can disseminate issue and event information far quicker and wider than any other stakeholder. At other times it might be a specific stakeholder group that the client is interested in, such as community groups or special interest groups. A government, for example, might want to pitch a message to a community of voters in order that meaning can be taken from it. Whatever the nature of the stakeholders being pitched to, we can add to the definition of framing by suggesting that it is the process of imagining, in words and pictures, something that is meaningful to its source, whose meaning can be transferred to others through the construction of issues and events. This is where the media become vitally important stakeholders in the dissemination of messages as issues and events for every conceivable reason. But there is another dimension to this. The media have a duty to investigate the political or non-political context of issues or events so that they can be reported or rejected in an equitable and meaningful fashion. A complex issue or event may have one or more frames. A simple event, such as the launch of a new music CD, may have one dominant frame (**univalent**); a concert to raise money for Africa's poor may have two dominant frames (**bivalent**), namely, the donation of their performance by highly paid musicians and the issue of poverty; whereas an issue with many significant frames

univalent

a story with one subject or theme.

bivalent

the idea that everything is either true of false, but in media relations terms the possibility that two stories can exist simultaneously in one narrative.

multivalent

the possibility that a number of interpretations or meanings can be attributed to one narrative; taking three or more meanings from a single story.

fractured paradigm

a break or crack in a particular view of the world.

independent variable

a thing that has the ability to change and that is not dependent on other actions or factors to make such changes.

(**multivalent**) requires meaning to be applied across a number of levels to a number of stakeholders.

Building on the work of Goffman in general terms that can be applied to media relations, Entman argued in the early 1990s that communication required something to define it in acceptable terms as a field. He chose framing to ameliorate what he termed a **fractured paradigm**. It is here that we begin to draw together the theories of field as they relate to media relations, and the argument for framing as a dominant theory within the subfield. (For the purposes of this book I argue that framing is a theory and relationship building is a process that supports the theory in its shift into practice.) For Entman (1993), frames have four sides. They:

- define problems
- diagnose causes
- make moral (ethical) judgments
- suggest remedies.

Each side of Entman's model has an overlay or outer location in the communication process:

- the communicator (source)
- the text (vehicle)
- the receiver (stakeholder)
- the culture (environment).

This idea is similar to embedding. Each side has an implied frame and, when all four are combined, they provide the theme that is needed to persuade or influence. This model allows us to reflect on each element individually and not to put too much emphasis on the role of the receptive stakeholder (this is where public opinion emerges). If we emphasise the role of the receptive stakeholder, we are left open to the probability of having to deal with an **independent variable** rather than a situational variable. In other words, we may have a situation that is beyond our control or, at least, beyond our understanding of the level of risk we are able to manage in any given situation. By framing each side of the process, including the stakeholder side, we are locking down the risk and managing the communication effectively. For Entman, such a lockdown is the key to understanding the shape of the field of communication (the wider field in which the smaller field of public relations and the subfield of media relations lie).

For our purposes it is the key to understanding communication in the subfield of media relations.

Let's investigate Entman's proposition further, then apply it to the case of avian influenza. If, as Entman suggests, frames focus our attention on some aspects of reality while blurring or avoiding others, they have the potential to provide different stakeholders with diffuse reactions. A passive action to the probability of an avian flu pandemic from normally healthy Westerners—a visit to a medical practitioner for a prescription medication—might translate into an aggressive action if thousands of Westerners reschedule holidays and travel to destinations other than South-East Asia. One aspect of the reality attached to avian flu and its pandemic frame is the increased possibility of death. But the focus on death blurs other frames such as cure or treatment, containment and limitation. When a controversial social issue or event arises, clients (those with some political, economic, or social attachment to the issue or event) frequently attempt to persuade and influence the news media to adopt their particular frame to assist in persuading and influencing other, more diffuse, stakeholders (in this example, medical practitioners are clients, healthy citizens are diffuse stakeholders). Strong emotional rhetoric assists this process but rhetoric alone is not sufficient. It must be bolted to a frame so that it stands out as being more important and more substantial than competing frames. An organisation or interest group can compete successfully if it understands and acts out media relations processes and develops strong media relationships.

THE CHRONICLE: AVIAN INFLUENZA REPORTED

How to build a frame around an issue

For frames to work effectively, they need to have a theme. The theme might be social or it might be biological or physical. A media discourse on avian flu, if it were to be contained to its physical ramifications, might fit well into a magazine such as *National Geographic*, where it can be explained at length relative to the migratory patterns of ducks and geese, for example. It might also be described there in social terms—its effect on human population—but the social ramifications are more likely to be taken up by popular media such as daily newspapers, evening television news, and radio talk-back programs. The frame for *National Geographic* might be:

- source—centre for disease control and prevention
- vehicle—magazine length news feature story
- stakeholders—subscribers
- environment—unsafe farming practices in South-East Asia.

The theme of this case is that there is a likelihood the influenza strain will infect a large human population—that is, create a pandemic. But there is a further implication, one that has economic and political consequences as well as social. In the USA, chicken meat consumption is higher than beef and sheep meat consumption. Australia and New Zealand are still large consumers of beef and sheep meat, but chicken meat consumption is increasing substantially each year. In creating a frame or schemata around the potential for a pandemic based on avian influenza, there is a risk that any number of stakeholders, or publics, might make a link to the consumption of chicken meat and other poultry products, such as eggs, without a true understanding of the level of risk associated with the activity. Cutting consumption of these products may have a devastating effect on an economy (for a detailed discussion of risk see chapter 11).

There are further implications. Governments govern with the consent of the electorate, but in times of distress the electorate allows itself to be governed more easily by those who show leadership. The possibility of a pandemic taking the lives of hundreds of thousands of Australians or New Zealanders might persuade the national governments of those countries to show leadership in both the stockpiling of antiviral drugs and increasing financial support for hospitals and health care infectious disease organisations. The frame for the story may, in fact, be support for raising taxes to increase investment in hospital and medical facilities. It is not new or different for governments as sources to frame an issue in terms of the need to raise taxes, especially when it is seen to benefit the majority. Avian flu is not something that strikes only the poor.

A field of one's own

All the theories employed to define media relations' wider field of public relations have been apprehended from elsewhere: sociology, management, philosophy, and political science, to name a few. How the theories are employed in the comprehension of media relations in Australia and New Zealand is as diverse as the theories themselves. Most, however, adopt an **empirical** position demonstrating the application of strategies and tactics through the investigation and analysis of case material. In the USA and Europe, there is a connectivity between theory and practice that has yet to be realised in Australia and New Zealand. This connectivity has its genesis in the injection of **economic capital** into media relations research. Investment in research in Australia and New Zealand is a relatively small one-way process in which universities compete with every other field of academic endeavour for government research funding. There is very little private investment in research that might expand the field. And media relations is not high on the list of priorities for government funding, the majority of which is shared by those with the highest key economic and social indicators: the so-called hard sciences.

empirical
the act of observation and experiment; the use of experience rather than theory in achieving goals and objectives.

economic capital
the accumulated assets of an organisation or individual from which is derived profit.

Persuasion and influence

It is important to acknowledge Jürgen Habermas's theoretical contribution to the subfield of media relations as it has been the basis from which other world-recognised communications scholars, such as Nancy Fraser, Nicholas Garnham, and Michael Schudson, have drawn inspiration.

Among Habermas's many valuable contributions to the theories of media and communications, his *The Structural Transformation of the Public Sphere* (1989) has been the most discussed. Habermas wrote the *Transformation* in the early 1960s, but it was not translated into English from the original German until 1989. At this time in the English-speaking world, a number of paradigmatic struggles were under way within media and communication fields. Despite being relatively unknown outside Germany for almost a generation, when the *Transformation* emerged it provided the resonance that was needed to focus a number of communication fields. Habermas himself, among others, has since renegotiated his original argument, but the provision of an outline of its idea is important to how we view the theories within the field of media and public relations at the beginning of the twenty-first century.

The initial importance of the work lies in its subtitle: *An enquiry into a category of bourgeois society*. Habermas investigated his theory of public enlightenment through a lens focused on eighteenth-century England. He argued that particular stakeholder publics at that time began to be informed about political, social, and economic issues and events in a way that had never previously existed, and that this informed state enabled them to make decisions and take actions that improved enormously the value of their existence. Published pamphlets provided news and information about trade and commerce as they began their inexorable global spread. In England, journalists and writers, most notably Joseph Addison and Richard Steele, met with other literate citizens—merchants and owners—in coffeehouses and later in clubs such as Button's to discourse on issues and events that were newsworthy and of economic value. (Pretty much the same as journalists, businesspeople, and sports stars get together today at rugby clubs and golf clubs to stitch up deals.)

Today, Habermas's work would be called an extensive case study and might be accorded less praise as it competed for space with other equally important cases, most likely coming out of Africa, South America, or Asia. But the idea that a stakeholder public—even one of an elite or ownership class—had the capacity to discourse about issues and events within public spaces was very attractive to Habermas. So it developed a life of its own. And an important life it has been, for it provided a base on which to build or redefine a variety of communication theories that have human populations as their primary focus. But Habermas was concerned primarily with political awareness, with how literate citizens exchanged information in public places and spaces, and how they used that information. His work has been adopted and investigated more vitally in the field of political communication than that of media relations. Yet it is vitally important to the media relations field precisely because of the argument that professional communicators dominate public communication (Mayhew 1997). But the theories of media relations are no less transparent than other means of communication, most notably, the field of journalism. There is no question that media relations is exercised by all types of organisations to persuade and influence stakeholder publics in all spheres: political, economic, social, technological, legal, and environmental (PESTLE). The reverse is also true: media relations is used by stakeholder publics to exert persuasion and influence as a countervailing measure. In this it is neither a positive nor a negative tool of persuasion and influence. It is a subfield from which can be extracted theories that have the capacity to provide a **competitive advantage** in practice for all organisations and individuals. These can range from a local environmental activist group attempting to persuade a bi-weekly newspaper editor of the value in their framed opposition to land-use zoning changes at the country club in their village, to a global humanitarian organisation attempting to influence a powerful government to cease its military activities in a developing nation. The difficulty for media relations lies in the frequent argument that organisations or individuals with greater access to capital will benefit exponentially from higher investment in the field. This book attempts to reveal how inexpensive strategies and tactics can inform campaigns as successfully as large investments.

competitive advantage
the ability to make an organisation more economically valuable when compared with similar organisations.

The existing paradigm

As I have already mentioned, most of the theoretical arguments that have built the field of public relations and its subfield of media relations have come from the USA. Any number of reasons can be attributed to this phenomenon—contemporary practice was born in the USA, there are more scholarly departments within universities and colleges devoted to media and public relations in the USA than the rest of the world combined, the USA is not as resistant as some parts of the world to the adoption of new ideas (in this, the embrace of the new technology known as television as a strategy in the 1952 presidential election campaign of Dwight Eisenhower proved decisive). New research from Botan and Hazleton (2006), building on their definitive 1989 work *Public Relations Theory*, shows that the USA has played a dominant role in the development of media relations and public relations theory, but evidence suggests the field is becoming more international in its focus, with important contributions being made by Germany, the UK, Australia, and New Zealand, with the possibility of large contributions in future coming from China and Brazil. The value of the theoretical contribution of China and Brazil, I would suggest, will be circumscribed by cultural, political, and language issues. This is not to suggest they will not contribute, but the significance of the contribution will lie in the relationship that stakeholders have with governments, as both countries have very different political and legal systems to those others mentioned above.

Within the field of public relations and the subfield of media relations, the ideas developed by James Grunig in the early 1980s have been hegemonic. Grunig's theories (or models) were adopted from a large study investigating the practices of media relations and public relations in the USA in the late 1970s. As Grunig suggests, prior to the 1970s, there was very little scholarly work done on theory development in public relations (Grunig 2001). His excellence constructions provided a solid platform for scholars to think about the practice of media and public relations, and how it might be linked to the established of a body of theory that could define the field, particularly in Bourdieuian terms, so that what did exist might not be acquired and **asset stripped** by other communicative fields. Between the early 1980s and the end of the first lustrum of the twenty-first century, the public relations paradigm, as Botan and Hazleton suggest, has been defined by Grunig (one of his models, which he called **press agentry**, was the first description of what we now call media relations). For the purposes of theoretical investigation, Botan and Hazleton define a paradigm as being comprised of an existing body of theory mixed with the scholars in the field who contest or agree with the theories, and the body of research that is generated by the theories. They believe that within the field of media and public relations a paradigm struggle is occurring and that the level at which the struggle is taking place—the defining of the field through the survival of the fittest theories—is close to producing the shift required for the field to stand separated for the first time in its history. Botan and Hazleton are supported in this by a number of highly respected scholars notably, Kent, Kruckeberg, Ledingham, Starck, Taylor, Toth, and Walker.

> **asset stripping**
> the aggressive removal of items of value from a core business for the purpose of making a profit.

> **press agentry**
> the action of seeking publicity through media and other sources on behalf of a client.

A future fracture

While Botan and Hazleton suggest the field of public relations, with its subfield of media relations, has evolved to the point where it has paradigmatic stability and may be about to shift, I suggest that globalisation has the potential to destabilise the field more in the immediate future than it has ever been destabilised in the past by external variables. It is not, as they and others suggest, a harmonious contribution from scholars in parts of the world other than the USA that will lead to positive engagement. An emerging contribution from scholars in China, the Middle East, and South America with linguistic, cultural, legal, and political differences will form independent pools of theory and practice, forcing an end to US hegemony (for a discussion of this and other aspects of the future for media and public relations, see chapter 13).

3

Media Relations Campaigns: Defining Campaign Strategies and Models

- To see how media relations campaigns are designed and constructed.
- To gain an understanding of how campaigns begin with research and take shape through the establishment of measurable objectives.
- To learn how to develop a campaign strategy from our research.

Creating campaign strategies

In media relations, we need to develop a strategy because everyone else is competing for the same space in the public sphere. A strategy is more than a plan. It requires us to think *competitively* and to gain some *advantage*. We can gain an advantage from a successful strategy by the *actions* we take. Strategy was first described more than 300 years ago as being part of a military campaign. It has its basis in the art of projecting and directing military campaign operations. In military terms, it usually combines itself with what is known as the art of a commander-in-chief. The characteristics usually associated with the terms 'strategy' and 'strategic decisions' are as follows:

1 Strategic decisions are likely to be concerned with or affect the long-term direction of a campaign.
2 Strategic decisions are normally about trying to achieve some advantage, for example, over competition.
3 Strategic decisions are likely to be concerned with the scope of campaign activities: should it concentrate on one area of activity or should it have many?
4 Strategy can be seen as the matching of campaign activities to the environment in which it operates. This is sometimes known as the search for strategic fit.
5 Strategy can be seen as building on or stretching campaign resources and competences to create opportunities or capitalise on them.
6 A strategy may require major resource changes.
7 Strategic decisions are likely to affect operational decisions.
8 The strategy of a campaign will be effected not only by the environmental forces and resource availability, but also by the values and expectations of those who have power in and around the organisation.

Strategy exists at all levels within all organisations. It is also something that is used by individuals. An person may say they have a strategy to further a career. This is more than a plan because it requires the individual to act competitively. A plan is not always strategic. A plan can be as simple as making a decision to go to the movies and acting out the sequence: gather friends together, find the money for the tickets, get to the theatre, buy tickets and refreshments, watch the movie. Such a plan only becomes strategic when circumstances become competitive. The plan to go to the movies becomes strategic if the movie theatre decides to give free tickets to the first twenty people who arrive for the session, an offer that is widely known, so getting some tickets becomes strategic because your plan now has to compete against others if the free tickets are to be secured. This is a simple example, but it is important to understand that all media relations plans become strategies because they are in competition with others who have similar plans. In media terms, a campaign proposal is strategic because our client is competing with everyone else's clients for finite media space. A newspaper, for example, does not add extra pages to its daily run because it finds an important news story that needs publishing. Newspapers increase their page numbers when more advertising is sold. News is not considered important enough to increase page numbers. So the important news story replaces a less important story that gets pushed back in the hierarchy. News, as we will see shortly, is ranked according to its worthiness,

news schedule

the timing and placement of news within a media organisation such as a newspaper or broadcaster.

dialogic relationship

a relationship based on the importance of dialogue, or conversation; the idea that conversation or dialogue can act as a constructive communication between two parties at all levels of interest.

so if there are insufficient pages on a given day, some news items may get dropped from the **news schedule**. A client's newsworthy story may be newsworthy for the client, but it may not make it into the news pages because it was outranked by more important news. So developing and designing a client's media campaign strategy requires us to keep in mind that we are always competing for limited news or feature space in newspapers, on radio, and on television. How other media spaces can be used as effectively as what is known as mainstream media will be discussed in more detail below. In media relations terms, a strategy statement describes how, in concept, an objective is to be achieved by providing guidelines and themes for the overall campaign.

The dialogic starting point

All media relations activity begins was a **dialogic relationship** between two interested parties: the media relations counsellor (agent) and the primary stakeholder (client). If an initial dialogue proceeds past a point of agreement where the client perceives the need to engage the agent, it will be incumbent upon the agent to demonstrate to the client the most appropriate course of action to achieve media goals and objectives. This is most often done by the agent preparing a proposal, or campaign strategy. A media campaign may be successfully completed by the relatively simple act of writing a letter to a newspaper editor, or sending a one-off news statement. In these cases the strategy is simple and the tactical objective cost-effectively achievable. In theoretical terms, a dialogic position can be described as a system rather than monologic policies (Botan 1997). A dialogic relationship, instead of being *two-way asymmetrical*, builds trust and reputation (symbolic capital; see Bourdieu) between a client and stakeholders. Media relations campaigns that begin from this premise have a much greater success rate than those that do not. Part of the reason concerns the informed nature of stakeholders. In historical terms, there was less information available to stakeholders who were asked to accept on faith the policies of governments, corporations, and other organisations that then frequently went about doing harm. The invention of the internet assisted the information process and its wider dissemination to disenfranchised stakeholders, with the result that those organisations with poor policy goals had to change their ways.

Defining campaigns

A campaign is defined as an organised course of action that has *boundaries* or specific objectives. It can be any type of activity that is designed to arouse support for any cause. For media relations, campaigns are the central activity around which issues and events revolve. Campaigns are made up of particular elements that form to present an image of an issue or event to media stakeholders so that they will act in some way towards the issue or event that will assist in reaching a desired result. For media relations, the campaign is always pitched at the media as the primary stakeholder. (The desired result for most media relations campaigns is the publication or broadcast of the relevant material.) Generally speaking, campaigns are designed so that they have a successful outcome for all stakeholders. But they are not always successful, despite the best intentions of the campaign designer or producer. Campaigns may not always be successful but they are always strategic. Campaigns are built around an agglomeration of discrete elements. They are designed by media relations experts for submission to a client with the goal of being accepted so they can be acted upon. They should be presented to clients in such a way that they will agree to the funding and enactment of the campaign. The written campaign strategy must be flexible. It must be presented in a form that will be easily recognisable by the client and thus supported. There are a number of ways to present a campaign strategy. It might be a simple narrative, a summary of specific points, or a budget (for a discussion of budget and campaign timing, see chapter 10).

To present a campaign proposal to a client, we first need to understand a bit about the client. This is important for the initial dialogic relationship building. If the agent does not know anything about the client's business, then that agent is not going to be seen by the client as someone who can build other relationships on their behalf. The agent may be an expert in media relations, but a client must feel comfortable that the agent can represent and communicate the issue or event in an optimum way. If the client is in the business of government, that client may be receptive to a longish document with a number of headings and subheadings, all divided into sections and labelled according to the Dewey Decimal System. For government, the most important elements of the campaign proposal document may not be the budget or the proposed time scale, but the detail of the tactics and the method of achieving them. Or it may be that it is interested in the creative aspects of the campaign, such as the events being constructed. This proposal might be produced as a narrative with report overtones. An example might be the campaign to educate the wider Australian electorate about the virtues of changes to its industrial relations legislation. This is known as a *public information campaign*, which requires for its success the building of strong dialogic relationships between the federal government (client) and a large number of stakeholder groups, including unions, industry associations, and provincial governments, as well as the primary stakeholder, the media.

For a small business, for which time and finances are the most important considerations, a proposal might be a four-page summary outlining the main elements with one page for timing, another for budget, and two earlier pages describing the strategy and tactics as briefly as possible in a language that can be easily digested. Campaign documents will also take into consideration the cost to the agent. But how do we get to a point where we are ready to present a campaign proposal to a client?

Models for campaign development

Campaign proposals in media relations, like campaign planning in war or any other field of action, require details that can be assembled in a specific and rational order so that they reflect what is proposed in a linear fashion from beginning to end. They can be difficult to construct because they require a balance between meaning ascribed by an agent, meaning ascribed by a client, and the transference of the agreed meaning to stakeholders so that goals and objectives can be reached within mutually acceptable frames. While a client may have a limited knowledge of the technical skills required to run a campaign, nonetheless, from a narrow perspective, the client will have a definite understanding of the required outcomes. The campaign proposal reflects both the client's desires and the agents capabilities. (The client will also have a preconceived opinion about the media, which is not always a positive thing.)

Practitioners and theorists generally agree that the most frequently employed campaign models are those described by Marston (*RACE*) and Hendrix (*ROPE*). Both models describe a four step process leading off with *research* (R), but then differ before coming together at the fourth stage. Marston (1979) suggests the second step is to circumscribe the *actions* (A) that will take place within the campaign while Hendrix (1998) says the second step is to set *objectives* (O). The third step for Marston is *communication* (C), execution of the actions. Hendrix describes this step as *performance* (P). They don't differ on the fourth step, which is to *evaluate* (E) the campaign at various stages throughout its life. Both the second and third steps in each model are really the same. Objectives, as we will see below, must have their basis in measurable or quantifiable values, so they will, for media relations purposes, always be the same as action. Similarly, performing actions and communicating actions may be conflated. The communicative action and the performative action are one and the same in media relations because they are directed at a goal, or measurable outcome (see Habermas's *Theory of Communicative Action*, 1987, for a wide ranging discussion about communicative and performative action). Let us examine the first step—research—more closely to see how it shapes our campaign and provides us with a preliminary idea of how our objectives and strategy will unfold.

In chapters 4 and 10 we will examine specific campaign details, such as tactics, budgets, and time scales, while in chapter 12 we will examine more closely the types of evaluation and research we can apply to all types of media relations campaigns.

Campaign design

The success of the campaign proposal relies to a vast extent on its content, as well as on its presentation and layout. A client is more receptive to a proposal that appears to have been polished and that demonstrates the professionalism that the agent expects to be attached to the content. A well-presented proposal will use an easily readable typeface such as Times New Roman, Garamond, or Palatino. It is best to avoid *san serif* faces (except in headings) such as Helvetica and Arial as they are hard to read over long measures such as an A4 page. Type and font selection, though, is a matter of individual taste. The clue to the right selection is to use not only what is elegant, but also what is readable.

A campaign proposal should be designed so that a client can access sections quickly. Most likely the proposed budget will be the first thing the client turns to, but it does not need to be at the front of the proposal. It is better towards the back so that clients can be taken through the *emotional* sections and built up to the rational.

A campaign proposal might include the following sections in this order:

- Contents
- Introduction
- Issue identification
- Stakeholder identification
- Strategy (Goals and Objectives)
- Tactics
- Timeframe
- Budget
- Evaluation.

Each section of the campaign proposal will link to the next. The campaign *proposal*, when it is approved, will become the *campaign brief*. It will be the document the client refers to at subsequent meetings. Each section of the proposal should be written in clear and unambiguous terms. This proposal is both a pitch document and the subsequent brief. As a pitch document—something that will make you stand out from the competition—it must include some information about you as the agent. This may take the form of a background section that describes the work the agent has done in the past. All media relations agents begin from nothing so it may be that this proposal is a first step, in which case it will have no past to reflect upon. It is the potential that the client will be investing in. Spell out the potential. Clients get just as enthusiastic about a proposal that reflects newness because there is the added attraction of a smaller investment for possibly the same result. The most important thing about this section is to not exaggerate or embellish. Like all emotional individuals, media relations counsellors sometimes get carried away when pitching to a new client. There is a tendency to think at the last moment that the proposal, the campaign document, is not strong enough. The author has been in meetings where an agent has increased the stakes without any persuasion from the client. All this succeeds in doing is making the agent look unprofessional. Worse still, if a client decides the increased stakes are worth it, then the agent has the added responsibility of making them happen. This is most often a reflection of an agent being underconfident rather than incompetent. The best example is the agent who proposes a campaign to secure modest media coverage, then, when confronted by the client, attempts to ratchet up the stakes to guarantee national or international coverage. Such a strategy is doomed to failure.

The number of charts and tables and the amount of colour used in selecting a campaign proposal design should reflect the complexity of the campaign issue or event. A small client with an issue that might take a day or two to resolve will be terrified of, say, a five page, full colour, glossy photographs and graphics proposal and the cost of such a campaign. A government or corporate campaign worth millions of dollars, on the other hand, will require a large investment in the campaign pitch document. As a rule of thumb, the campaign pitch document should reflect the value of the campaign. The agent has, after all, made some initial investigation of the cost of the campaign, so is not putting something to the client that is likely to cause a heart attack. A discussion of budgeting and getting the figures to add up so the client smiles at them will be discussed in chapter 9.

Campaign content

It is equally important that the content of the campaign proposal reflect the reality of the issue or event for both the client and the agent. Understandable content for one client might be gobbledygook to another.

Let's say a client with an engineering business has invented a device to measure air pollution in tunnels. The client has sold the idea to the consortium building road tunnels around Sydney. The client has asked three medium-sized media relations consultancies to pitch for the business of publicising the issue of tunnel air pollution. One agent has previous experience with engineering and construction companies and writes the pitch document so that the engineers who will evaluate it feel comfortable with the language used. The other two, who have worked in different areas, beat up the language to reflect an academic, theoretical knowledge of the industry.

Another example. A client with an international stakeholder network is keen to contact some of the stakeholders who appear to be less than enthusiastic about a new idea the client is proposing. This client also asks three agents to pitch. Two have had international exposure with former clients in the field and with international media.

The third has billed itself as an international network but its media work has been circumscribed by local issues and events in Auckland, New Zealand.

In both examples, the way the content of the proposal is written will reveal the extent of the agents' capabilities. Which raises an important question. How much material from one proposal can an agent use when designing and writing future proposals? In the case of the inhouse agent, the answer is simple. The nature of the business will reflect a continuity of the theme of the issue or event forming the campaign. For a consultancy that relies for its future on new business, the time spent working up a campaign proposal is important. Campaign proposals are usually unpaid. In other words, a client expects to get a proposal, make a decision, and not pay. This can be time-consuming and costly for an independent agent so there is a tendency to remodel existing proposals for different clients in different fields. Such action can be fraught. Under threat of deadline, many is the agent who has slipped and left some confidential item about another client in a rejigged proposal, the result of which should be obvious. The solution is to create a template from which parts that suit a particular client in a particular area can be extracted. But each new client should be the subject of extensive research, particularly when an agent is confronted by a new area.

This is the same as constructing a media database from which an agent can extract and create a particular media profile for an issue or event. In Australia and New Zealand in the last decade, media relations consultants have shifted away from generalist offerings to the supply of narrower and narrower specialisations. This is partly to do with the cost of research. It is much more cost-effective to keep working one area as a specialist than to explore a new area every few weeks or months. The only problem with this is when other experts move in to the area and offer similar specialisations.

Content also depends on what the client is used to reading for its style. An engineering client is more likely to engage with a report style proposal in which there are short, one-paragraph sentences, dot points, and numbered points, whereas a fashion or cosmetics client may prefer a well-written narrative, similar in style to a feature story. These variations demonstrate the agent's writing capabilities, if in a limited way—it lets the client know the agent is on their frequency.

Presenting a campaign proposal to a client

A campaign proposal has design and content that must be presented in such a way that the client acknowledges its capabilities. The proposal could be posted, emailed, or hand delivered. Each way has its own response. The best way to present a campaign proposal is in person at a time that suits the client. This may appear to give the client an unintended advantage but it must be remembered that in any agent–client relationship, the power is tilted in favour of the client until such time as the proposal is enacted. An agent should go through a proposal in as much detail as is necessary for the client to be satisfied that the campaign can be successful. Each person in the meeting should have a full copy of the campaign document. The discussion should be led by the agent. At the conclusion of the meeting, it is important for the agent to have a sense that the work is to begin. If the campaign proposal has been well prepared and the dialogue with the client has proceeded well in the lead-up to the formal pitch meeting, then the agent will be able to agree to begin work on the campaign.

One of the most important elements of the face-to-face meeting with the client is for the agent to obtain an agreement on the budget and the timing of the campaign. The budget (see chapter 10) is the financial investment made by the client in the campaign. It is seen by the client the same way that other expenses are seen and must be justified accordingly. The timeline, or deadline, for each element of the campaign is the responsibility of the agent. If the client is interested in the investment, then they will be more interested in how the investment is going to be measured as being successful.

THE CHRONICLE: LOCAL GOVERNMENT ELECTIONS

How to develop a campaign structure

In Australia, a candidate for election to local government must have a campaign strategy. The strategy may be as simple as placing an advertisement in a local newspaper, it may be the design and distribution of a small mono flyer in letterboxes around the district, or it may be the candidate walking around the neighbourhood knocking on doors talking to citizens. Whatever the level of commitment, it has a strategic intent because the candidate is competing with all the other candidates. Some candidates make big investments in their campaigns. Candidates at local level have been known to spend $25 000 in advertising and controlled media to gain a seat on a council. One candidate, Pete, was elected to a local council partly because of the application of a strong campaign and partly because the campaign was evaluated frequently during its three month life. In June 1999, Pete began his campaign. His decision to stand for election had its basis in a land development approval adjoining his home. He considered the local council decision to be problematical and set out to 'get elected so I can stop this type of thing happening'.

It was necessary for Pete to frame a public relations policy campaign, but in order for that campaign to generate public interest, a parallel media campaign was required. Pete was not a member of any community organisations; nor were he and his wife well known in the city, conditions that meant there were no preconceived opinions formed by potential voters. In this Pete was an *ideal candidate* because any opinions had to be informed by what he did in the future rather than what he had already undertaken. His decision to nominate was based on an empirically developed belief that the existing council was not looking after a number of interests of the wider community adequately. It created the possibility that an independent, not connected to party machine politics, and thus to financial assistance and ideological motivation, could carry through a professional campaign using orthodox media relations tactics.

Prior to his nomination as a candidate, Pete was a good citizen. He voted conscientiously and thought about city issues and policies. He had very little political experience and no clear idea of how to develop a campaign that highlighted his proposed policies other than to use his sales skills in the street, meeting people at every opportunity, presenting what he believed was a genuinely honest package of intentions. He required professional assistance to understand the three elements of campaigning: the political motivation of his competitors, how to gain the greatest advantage from publicity, and an understanding of the importance of a strategy.

Although Pete had been employed as a salesman with one of the city's television stations, he was naïve and uneducated about news reporting processes and how to generate publicity. He presented himself as a an independent candidate outside the sphere of influence of established political groupings and other independent candidates, a position he maintained throughout the campaign, despite powerful persuasive arguments in favour of joining an existing ticket. Within the framework of the Australian Electoral Act, any candidate who chooses to run individually—without a running partner or the support of a political party—is automatically ungrouped, below the line, at the far right of the ballot paper, which is where Pete's strategy placed him.

As part of his campaign, Pete developed a policy platform designed to present specific information to citizens through traditional media channels. His objective was to obtain media coverage of his policies in at least one news medium at least once a week. The objective was tightly focused on the tactic of explaining the complex issue of voting preferences within the proportional system. While the issue was complex, Pete developed a simple method of presenting information, explaining in non-political terms the workings of above-the-line and below-the-line groupings on the ballot paper. His adoption of an educative mechanism (see Mayhew 1997) demonstrated his objectivity and assisted his pursuit of legitimacy.

Through the news media he also attempted, unsuccessfully, to provide the electorate with a ten-point policy platform focusing on what he considered to be the most important issues and goals for the city. To achieve this he distributed, at reasonable intervals, one- or two-page news releases headed *Media News*. All media except the public broadcaster rejected most of his policy statements during the three month campaign. Ironically, his election to council was considered newsworthy because of his outsider status.

He campaigned busily around the streets, doorknocking in the near freezing July and August conditions, including an occasional snowfall, attempting to educate citizens about the complex system of voting, as a result of which he was perceived as being sincerely interested in citizen wellbeing.

To reinforce this message he published a four-page campaign newsletter, the *Independent*, which was distributed free at strategically located news agencies. The newsletter, which gave the impression of objectivity, achieved an instant communication success.

Throughout the three month lead-up to polling day, Pete maintained a constant physical presence. On polling day, his most valuable tactic was to present himself personally to as many voters as possible at as many polling stations as possible. This meant being at the closest station to his home when polls opened at 8 a.m., and being at the furthest station at 7 p.m. when polls closed.

Pete had a reasonable level of personal and contributed funding, but took no advertising space in the local newspaper, believing it was more beneficial to remain outside the traditional media. Interestingly, one candidate believed the public had an 'inability to see the person as distinct from the actor some candidates bec[o]me for the period of the campaign'.

In response to his true independence presentation, Pete was frequently told by electors that they thought every candidate was independent. Alternatively, citizens saw the election more cynically as a contest between the two major parties, believing that there was no such thing as independence.

Figure 3.1 Orange City Council candidate, Peter Hetherington's newsletter, the *Independent*

An explanation of the RACE and ROPE models

Campaign research

Research can be defined as the study or investigation of something to identify new facts that will help draw inferences or conclusions about that thing. As we might expect, research requires investigation, which, by its nature, must be systematic. It requires care and specificity. It must also relate to what we already know. Research in media relations can take a variety of forms, but generally speaking, it is circumscribed by the financial investment that is made in it. Thus it relies heavily on case material or existing data as a base so that at each invention of a campaign strategy it will not be necessary to start from scratch.

When a global organisation, such as the United Nations, prepares for a media or public relations campaign, it starts by investigating what it is that it is campaigning for and about. In the case of the UN, as have many large international and national organisations, it has a stockpile of material that it can draw from: previous campaigns as case material and qualified researchers who know where to begin investigating the material that will form the basis of the campaign. The UN refers to some of its campaigns as communication campaigns or public information campaigns, but the process and delivery are the same as they are for media relations campaigns. Small local special interest groups and organisations begin campaigns in the same way.

Taxonomies of campaign research

Campaign research can be achieved in a number of ways so we need to determine the taxonomies (categories) in which we might be operating. Three of the categories that interest us are:

- exploratory research
- descriptive research
- confirming research.

Exploratory research is the most common form of investigation. It could include:

- gathering information about media ownership
- finding out if an editor of one trade magazine also edits other publications in the same house
- gathering material written by a specific reporter
- gathering background on the history of the client wanting you to write media material
- gathering wider material on a specific issue that relates to a client.

Descriptive research does what its name implies: it describes things. It is important because it moves facts beyond the gathering stage to turn them into information. Information is valuable, whereas facts alone are less valuable. Descriptive research might include:

- searching for cross linkages to media ownership that show certain patterns in reporting news (John Malone's Liberty Media stake in News Corp, for example)
- analysing the material written by one editor of a trade publication against material written by the same editor for another publication in the same stable

- analysing material written by a specific reporter
- analysing a client history
- analysing material that might relate indirectly to the issue or event under discussion.

Confirming research, the third category of research, is that which confirms assumptions about the facts that have been gathered and turned into information. We use it frequently to test the relationships that exist between pieces of information to determine their validity. Confirming research might include:

- confirmation that Liberty Media stock ownership plays a role in the news policy of News Corp
- confirmation that an editor of one trade publication uses material from that publication to generate stories and news angles in a sister publication
- confirmation that a specific reporter displays subjectivity toward a certain issue or event
- confirmation that a client's history is ethically disposed to the issue or event being developed.

Surrounding these elementary taxonomies are two important research types that require a more detailed explanation. For the purposes of media relations and, indeed, all other social and political sciences, research is either *qualitative* or *quantitative*. When we talk about qualitative research, we are talking about information and assumptions that are derived from intuitive sources. When we talk about quantitative research our information and assumptions are derived from specific, or countable, sources. Both work equally well in the subfield of media relations (see chapter 12 for more detail).

A focus group is an example of qualitative research. A focus group might be used to see which of the two Sydney newspapers, the *Daily Telegraph* and the *Sydney Morning Herald*, people like reading. The results provide us with quality information that we can use to assist us in preparing a campaign strategy for a client.

An opinion poll is an example of quantitative research. An opinion poll might be conducted to see if people actually read the *Sydney Morning Herald* and the *Daily Telegraph*. The results provide us with quantity information that will assist in the campaign strategy preparation.

If we know which bits the focus group members enjoy reading and why, we can frame our campaign to suit. The same research techniques apply to other aspects of a campaign proposal. We might run a focus group to find out whether a government policy is popular or, more importantly, whether it is understood by a particular *universe* that has some relationship to our client.

Campaign actions and objectives

The *actions* taken in a media relations campaign are known as *tactics*. Chapter 4 provides a full description of tactics, as well as a range of available tactics and how they can be executed. In the meantime we need to understand the fundamental reason for applying a specific tactic and its relationship to goals and objectives.

Objective is a slippery term that is used widely to describe all types of activities. It is used synonymously with goals and confused with aims. It frustrates and irritates almost everyone who comes into contact with it. Yet once it is understood, it appears obvious in its simplicity. Part of the reason that Marston used *actions* rather than *objectives* as his second stage in the campaign development process may have something to do with the difficulty in defining objectives. Actions are those things that are done to reach goals. So, too, are objectives. In grammatical terms, which we will turn to again in chapter 5, an objective is described as expressing, designating, or referring to the object of an action (*Oxford English Dictionary*). So action and objective can be used concurrently. Objective is also used synonymously with aims and goals, further creating a difficulty in definition. When combined with action, objective becomes clearer in that it is something to be *aimed* for. Thus it is also a *goal*. When aiming to reach some point or some defined goal it is necessary to travel along a path or planned route. When boarding an aeroplane, arriving at the *destination* becomes the *goal*. It is what is aimed for as the aeroplane travels along a planned route. The objective of the first officer is to read the plane's instruments and pilot the plane along the route without incident. The *goal* of a basketball team is to *win* the game, but this can only be achieved if the team meets its *objectives* and *aims*, which might include using all the team's interchange players.

Objectives and goals work within an overall campaign strategy. But a strategy usually takes a longer-term vision for an issue or event while objectives and goals fulfil the short-term requirements within the strategy. For media relations purposes, objectives are either **informational** or **motivational**. The difference is that **motivational objectives**, constructed to change attitudes and behaviour, are more easily measured than **informational objectives**, which are designed to create awareness.

> **motivational objective**
> the injection of enthusiasm into an individual or organisation through the exercise of persuasion and influence so an objective can be achieved.

Objectives (actions) rely on tactics to reach a goal. An objective is a stated aim but it must be combined with the right tactics to be measurably successful. Selecting tactics to fit the actions of a campaign is one objective of the media relations practitioner, but equally, the selection must fit the wider goals and objectives of the client. An objective or action must have a stated aim so that both the agent and the client can see how it will be achieved. Informational actions and motivational

informational objective

the communication of facts or information to individuals or organisations as an act in itself; the provision of information.

actions are different in their stated aims. Informational actions seek to create awareness of issues or events so they are stated in general terms. An example might be a government health initiative to make people aware of the dangers of obesity. It would be difficult to measure the short-term success of such an initiative. Even in the longer-term evidence might be difficult to gather as populations shift. Motivational objectives, on the other hand, are easier to measure but difficult to achieve.

A corporation might have an informational objective to make stakeholders aware of a new technology that it is using in its products. Measuring the awareness factor would be difficult and it may not translate into greater product use. A motivational objective for the same corporation might be to use the technology to increase its share of the market in which it operates. A problem for the media relations practitioner arises when attempting to differentiate between informational objectives and motivational objectives and whether there is some inbuilt overlap between the two that can be useful in campaign building.

Campaign building requires an understanding of what it is that is being aimed at and which objectives will allow a campaign to successfully reach a goal. Research will identify the strategic direction for a campaign in the same way that the media investigate a story, and then choose an angle that will give it a **strategic advantage**. The objective for a journalist is to write a story that will inform, hence the use of the word to mean balance. Just as the journalist undertakes research into the material in order to write a balanced story, the media relations practitioner must also look

strategic advantage

the ability to move ahead of or to outflank competitors.

for research to underpin the objective nature of a campaign. When a number of objectives or actions are bundled together, they form a strategy. A strategy is simply the way the bundle of objectives is to be described in the campaign proposal. A media relations practitioner may bundle together a number of objectives in a single campaign, all of which will be described

as part of the strategy section of the document and will relate to the tactics that are to be developed to achieve the objectives. So it becomes clearer that objectives or actions cannot be stated in a campaign document in isolation. They relate to each other and have a direct impact on the goals of the campaign. A campaign proposal will include all the objectives required to reach a successful goal for a client, but it may not necessarily spell out all the details of how the tactics will be employed to carry out the objectives or actions. A proposal that includes tactical details might be used indiscriminately by an unethical client. The need to understand objectives and to be able to explain them coherently to a client obviates the need to spell out the tactical approach of the campaign. The expert understanding and technical competency of the media relations practitioner in being able to carry out the proposed actions, such as that of the lawyer or medical practitioner, is what delineates the field from other fields, such as advertising and marketing.

THE CHRONICLE: FORMULATING OBJECTIVES

How to choose the right frame

The client is an organisation concerned with dangerous levels of debt among 18–25 year olds. The client would like a story in a mainstream medium outlining the problem and showing some extreme examples of how high levels of debt can lead to tragic events. The agent targets the *Sydney Morning Herald*'s 'Radar' section as a good place for the story. (Research shows this is what 18–25 year olds read in this newspaper.) But, the *Herald* has another section called 'Money', which is sponsored by bank advertising and is designed to get people to borrow larger sums. So the agent will need to frame the issue in such a way that it gets a run in 'Radar', but might also be seen to be useful for the 'Money' section. The objectives need to be measurable, so they need to be realistic. Should the agent get coverage of the youth debt issue in the *Herald*? Or should there be a change of tactics to consider local suburban newspapers? How realistic is it to pitch at the *Herald*?

Campaign communication and performance

The development of a research profile and the establishment of objectives or actions circumscribe a campaign's strategy. The communication of the strategy, or how it is performed, requires the actions be put in place. The first two components might be analogous to a person wishing to take up scuba diving. Before suiting up and getting wet, there is a long theoretical discussion about how to dive and all the things that can go wrong. Then there is another session to discuss the practicalities of what to do when diving to depths that require timing and recompression. The first stage is the theory or research stage in which a future diver finds out all there is to know about the subject. The next stage is more serious because it requires an understanding of what could happen if goals are not met. The goal for the diver at a depth of 30 metres is to reach the surface without sustaining an embolism. The objectives, then, are not to stay below longer than a prescribed time and to surface slowly so that an embolism cannot manifest itself in the bloodstream. But all this is an acknowledgment of the theoretical. When it comes time to dive, the theoretical becomes real; only with practice does the diver learn to do things that make scuba diving enjoyable rather than a life-threatening experience. While there is no suggestion that the third stage of a media relations campaign might be life threatening, it is now time to put into practice all those things that have been gathered together to form objectives, and to head for the goal.

On this basis, the performance stage of the campaign is all about how we judge ourselves rather than how we are going to be judged after the event. Like the scuba diver, we need to ask a few questions at this stage:

- Are we competent to put into action all those things we have proposed in the campaign document?
- Have we misrepresented some objectives so that the campaign appeared to be slicker and more polished than we are capable of delivering?
- Can we build the stakeholder relationships that we claim we can build?
- Is our own level of symbolic capital high enough so that we are seen by stakeholders to be an agent with whom they can deal?

Media relations counsellors answer these questions in the way they act. In this the presentation of the campaign document to a client in an ethical and transparent manner must be paramount. Many professions overstate the capabilities of the products and services they offer to the extent that the dictum *caveat emptor* must now be applied to almost all activities in both the public and private sectors. Public relations institutes in most Western countries, including the Public Relations Institute of Australia and the Public Relations Institute of New Zealand have codes of ethics that reinforce the duty of the practitioner and counsellor to act in a clear and transparent manner when dealing with all stakeholders.

Planning the third stage

In this section we see the importance of how the third stage of the campaign is run; how the objectives fit into a strategy, become tactics, and get acted out.

The best way to align strategy with tactics is to refer to case studies or to experience. A media relations practitioner is likely to re-use a tactic in a campaign strategy when it has been successful in the past. A hierarchy of tactics will cascade from most successful to least successful. Failed tactics can be recycled but they should be assessed for damage before being sent back out. The communication or performance stage sets out for the client exactly how the objectives of the campaign will be met. It is here that the theoretical concepts of framing and relationship building through dialogue are transferred into practice. In chapter 6 the methods of building relationships with the media are discussed in detail, but for now we are interested in how those details are put into play for the benefit of the client.

A campaign proposal sets out to reveal the steps that will be taken to reach a goal and how many steps there are on the path from the starting point to the goal. It shows how the steps can be taken to avoid falling over cliffs, landslides, and washaways. If the path leads up a mountain, the campaign proposal shows where the crevasses lie, where the rock is unstable, and from which side the weather is likely to descend. It is a map, based on research and empirical evidence, of former journeys into the same territory. What is does not provide is the skills to enable a non-practitioner to journey far.

The campaign proposal is the starting point for relationship building between the agent and the client. As equal partner stakeholders, the agent and the client have the same goal expectations. They must also agree on the meaning of the issue or event that is the subject of the campaign. Shared meaning is one of the goals of the campaign and extends from the agent and the client to all relevant stakeholders. Before an agent constructs a campaign proposal, it is important to arrange a briefing session with the client. At the briefing a number of things will be discussed, including the meaning of the issue or event under discussion. They are these:

- the frame that can be constructed to support the issue or event
- the style the proposal should be delivered in
- the aims, goals, and objectives of the campaign.

It is important to draw up a list of items for discussion prior to the meeting and for the agent to provide leadership and direction. The client is an expert in their field, the agent the expert in media relations. (In this context, 'agent' includes inhouse managers providing expert services to senior executives. The inhouse practitioner or manager is the agent, the senior executives the client.)

An initial meeting between an agent and a client should be planned to last around one hour. Within that time a good agent will be capable of framing the issue or event in such a way that it reflects their expertise and imbues the client with the confidence that the delivery of the proposal is already an acknowledgment that the work will go ahead. So an agent should use the initial meeting to gauge various reactions and behaviours emanating for the client. At the conclusion of the meeting, the agent should have enough information to construct a campaign proposal. At this point a number of things can happen.

1 An agent can supply a proposal to a client in which there is substantial detail, enough for the client to undertake the campaign without the agent.
2 There is insufficient detail for a client to feel confident that it can be enacted successfully.
3 The agent presents a balanced campaign proposal from which a client can acknowledge the expertise of the agent and agree in principle to fund the campaign.

Campaign evaluation

Measuring the success of a media relations campaign is the sharp end of the business. It is an essential component of any campaign but a relatively recent addition and one that is still not done satisfactorily by a large number of practitioners. The traditional measure of success used to be the number of column inches or centimetres that appeared in a print medium. A client expected to pay a certain amount based on the number of mentions and where they appeared in the medium. A front page story attracted a premium loading, much the same as an advertisement near the front cost more than one at the back. This form of measurement locked media relations practitioners into the idea that publicity was the most important aspect of their work because it was the only one they had any real success in measuring (for a full discussion of evaluation, refer to chapter 12).

Measuring or evaluating what goes on before and during a campaign improves the probability of achieving success. Evaluating a campaign on completion assists a media relations expert in learning what to avoid in the next campaign. Evaluation can be described as a systematic application of research procedures to help in understanding the conceptualisation, design, implementation, and utility of a campaign. Evaluation determines effectiveness, achievement of goals and objectives, and efficiency of goals and objectives.

THE CHRONICLE: OSAMA BIN LADEN AND GEORGE W BUSH

How to differentiate campaign objectives

As commanders in chief of two very different organisations, Osama bin Laden and George W Bush have developed strategies and campaigns for influencing and persuading their primary and secondary audiences of the importance and validity of their goals. Both campaigns are goal and objective related and use media relations tactics to achieve them. While Osama bin Laden uses press and television releases to describe the campaign of Al Qaeda, a terrorist network, George W Bush, as president of the world's oldest continuing democracy, uses the same tactics to renounce the campaign of the terrorist network. Media organisations throughout the world receive news releases from all types of organisations, though they are not obliged to use them as the basis of news or feature reports.

Part 2

Elements of Media Relations

4

Tactical Approaches for Successful Media Relations

CHAPTER OBJECTIVES

- To understand how to add value to a strategic campaign by including actions (tactics).
- To understand how tactics make a campaign a success.

Tactics can best be described as those actions that have to happen to make a strategy successful. They are the components that we bundle together to inform and drive a campaign. Or, put another way, we can say that they are the individual components of a strategy that combine at any particular time to give us some competitive advantage. A motor vehicle requires a number of complex components to work in harmony before it will move. By removing important individual components, the vehicle will be unable to function to its imagined capacity. If we do not fill the fuel tank, the car won't go. If we do not have spark plugs, the car won't go. If we remove the steering wheel and tyres, we can't drive it. Even so, if some other parts were not present, we can still start the car and drive it—carpets on the floor, say, and, in an emergency, without a windscreen, maybe even without doors or seatbelts. Like the motor vehicle, a media relations strategy requires a complex number of components to work in harmony with each other for it to be effective and successful. Without certain components, or tactics, it will still work but, like the motor car, if we fail to develop some of the more important tactics, we will not get where we want to go—or maybe not even get started. For any given strategic campaign we can select from a variety of tactics that will gain a competitive advantage within an acceptable operating budget. The tactic that is central to most media relations campaigns is the news statement. It is also referred to as a **press release** or **media release**.[1] The news release in a media relations campaign is the closest thing to the fuel component in the motor vehicle. We can fill our car with different grades of fuel to make it go better and in the same way we can fill our campaign with different grades of news release. As when we fill a car, the campaign will go better with a higher-grade fuel.

> **press release**
> see media release.

> **media release**
> the supply of information on issues and events to the media usually in written form.

Tactics should be described in sequence as the specific activities that put the strategies into operation and help to achieve the stated objectives. A more elaborate way to describe tactics is to say they involve using the components of communication to reach stakeholders with key messages.

Building tactics into a campaign

When a campaign is being constructed there are decisions to be made about what to put in and what to leave out. A media relations campaign differs little in this regard from a newspaper editorial meeting at which editors and reporters make decisions about what to include in tomorrow's newspaper, and what can safely be left out, either for holdover or to **spike**.

> **spike**
> the act of placing filed copy on a sharp metallic spike.

Campaign tactics

While the news release is the cornerstone of a media relations campaign, it relies on additional important tactics to complete the frame. We can separate tactics into manageable sections. How and when we employ them will be discussed below.

All campaign tactics must have an objective that is directly related to the provision of meaning to stakeholders. A tactic, if it is unable to be comprehended by those it is aimed at, is of no value to a campaign. It is also important to consider the method of

---

1   The word *release* is problematic for us, though. It implies withholding, or holding back, and that in itself implies it is not *new*. We need to think about this in relation to how we work with issues and events that we frame as *news*.

delivery of these tactics to the media. If we are sending a news release and a **backstory**, plus a copy of an annual report, we might consider bundling them together in a folder or jacket so it is clear that they have some relationship to each other. We might then post the package or, if there is some urgency attached to the material and we have discussed it with the journalist, we might courier it. Mail and courier delivery are used less today because of the immediacy of email and email attachments, but an email is not always the best mode of delivery. (Most media won't accept email attachments because they have the potential to corrupt an entire editorial technology system.)

Written tactics

News release, backstory, feature story, letter to the editor, newsletters, flyers, pamphlets, brochures, handbooks, annual reports, books.

Spoken tactics

Face to face, speeches, interviews, word of mouth, radio community service announcements.

Acted tactics

Press conference, television community service announcement, community meetings, demonstrations (direct action), factory tours, trade displays, street theatre.

Imagined tactics

Interventions pictures, videos, music, drama.

Written tactics

Written tactics form the basis of a campaign's meaning. They must be able to be linked and overlap so that they present a single frame for an issue or event that can be easily and quickly comprehended by those to whom they are pitched. Written tactics include backstories, feature stories, and letters to the editor (known as uncontrolled tactics), newsletters, flyers and pamphlets, brochures, handbooks, and annual reports (known as **controlled tactics**).

> **controlled tactic**
> an action that does not rely on an agent or other force for its success.

The news release

In any campaign a news release stands as a **ritual tactic** (one that has a historical position in the subfield of media relations). Shortly, we will look at tactics that embrace new media as well as other technological dimensions of the twenty-first century, but it the news release that remains, throughout the world, as the single most important tactic for all media relations campaigns. A news release is not just something to be

ritual tactic
a tactic that has become embedded through convention or long-time use; a tactic that is habitually embedded in a campaign; for example, a candidate mug shot in a newspaper advertisement.

sent to the media. It is used in campaigns that have no media component to inform all types of stakeholders of the issues and events that an organisation considers important. A small computer company preparing to list on a stock exchange, for example, may not have anything to tell the media due to the sensitivity of its technology, but it will use a one- or two-page statement to disseminate news to shareholders and others directly interested in its future (see chapter 5 for a detailed account of how to design and write a news release).

Editors, reporters, and journalists are inundated with news releases. Organisations and individuals send news releases in hard copy and by email to thousands of media organisations, twenty-four hours a day, seven days a week. It is no exaggeration to say that during any shift, a reporter can expect to receive a couple of hundred unsolicited news releases as emails. In any given day the innovation reporter for the *Australian Financial Review*, Peter Roberts, for example, can receive up to 150 news releases on new products, services, issues, and events that media relations practitioners consider important. So the question for media relations practitioners is how to present the news release on their client's issue or event in a more favourable way than those with which they are competing. In the case of the space in the *Australian Financial Review* devoted to innovation, the story will need to be pretty good to get a run. This is the point at which designing and writing a news release becomes strategically linked to the actions of framing and media relationship building.

Backstories (backgrounders)

The **backstory** should have a direct relationship to the news release. It can highlight some of the most important points from the news release, and it must provide evidence that it is factually accurate. If a news release is framed by the action that is taking place in the foreground of an issue or event, then the backstory frames the support cast. The backstory can be framed around the support cast of the action in much the same way that a backstory is framed in television drama such as *Angel*, *Buffy*, *Last Man Standing*, or *Home and Away*. Newspapers, radio, and television news and current affairs programs frequently employ backstories to support their news frames. These backstories are also known as **personality profiles**. So it is important to understand how a media organisation might use a backstory before submitting one.

The *Australian Financial Review* is a great example of a high-quality newspaper into which a huge number of media relations practitioners want to get their clients. The *AFR* might use a news release as a news story then rework the backgrounder as a longer feature piece. It does this because the available number of news pages is limited

Media News

July 26, 1999

True independent seeks consensus on jobs program

True independent Peter Hetherington has promised to establish a clear and unambiguous 'pathways program' for local Koori community employment if elected to Orange City Council on September 11.

Hetherington met recently with leaders of the local Koori community to discuss ways in which local government and general employment could become more accessible.

At present there are limited avenues available to the Koori community, despite extensive developments in vocational education and training.

"It is vital the whole community benefits from opportunities in employment when they become available.

"It is my intention, if elected on September 11, to see that Orange City Council and indeed, all local government in the central west of New South Wales creates a 'pathways program' which allows equal opportunity of employment.

"Such a program must also apply the principles of industrial democracy and occupational health and safety at the highest levels, which means every candidate for a position is offered the same opportunity," he said.

Hetherington added he was preparing a detailed investment policy, in co-operation with local investment advisers and stockbrokers, including an examination of the present tendering system for council contracts.

Ends
For further information contact:
Peter Hetherington
Telephone 6361 6888
Facsimile 6362 3791
Mobile 0419 637004

Figure 4.1 Media release

by the amount of advertising space. Generally, the longer backstory will become the property of a reporter or journalist who will investigate the material further, but the initial idea springs from the backgrounder and news copy. An additional asset is that sometimes a reporter will hold a backstory over and use it later as a feature to support an initial news story. This is not exclusive to the *AFR*. Most metropolitan newspapers in Australia and New Zealand publish glossy weekend magazines in which they devote much space to expanding news stories into features. These features are frequently imagined and drawn from backstories provided by media relations experts.

A good backstory should be thought of by the media relations practitioner as four or five pages of information that:

- supports the news story
- substantially reduces the reader's or viewer's knowledge gap on the topic
- provides evidence of thorough research.

A backstory is frequently more interesting to write than a straight news piece because there is more room in it for creative licence. A backstory is not a product description or a list of client activities. Rather, it should be thought of as something that can be used by the media and other stakeholders to comprehend an issue or event in a more detailed way. In this respect the frame for the backstory will be the same as for the news release but it will have the added dimension of additional material that may have been superfluous to the shorter, punchier news story. A backstory must be framed in such a way that it will resonate more with the media person or other stakeholder to whom it has been pitched.

Feature stories

Feature stories are different to news releases and news stories. A feature story is one that occupies more space in a medium such as a newspaper or current affairs program. It may be built around a backstory or around a profile of an individual or group of people.

A feature is differentiated by a number of elements:

- It has a narrative style in which a central actor or actors form the basis of an issue or event.
- It has a passive voice in which emotional values can be explicated.
- It links issues and events into some historical or chronological sequence.

Features are sometimes commissioned. Trade magazines and other types of media that have limited resources will request feature-type material from public relations sources. When this occurs there is little to distinguish between the role of the public relations media writer and the freelance journalist. A public relations source must be prepared to produce a feature story that reflects the importance of a client as well as a balance that enables a publisher or broadcaster to act objectively. The importance of the focus on the client is the primary reason for writing the material, but there are numerous ways that this can be accomplished along with the provision of objectivity. This is where the feature story comes into its own for media relations sources.

The feature story angle

Let's say a public relations agent has a client with interests in agribusiness. Agribusiness is the economies of scale that enables agriculture to be practised in a larger than normal fashion. While the client may be peripheral to the main policy issues of the day, the client is nonetheless interested in being involved. Let's say that, up until this point, the client has been all but invisible in the wider agribusiness policy scheme. The job of the media relations source is to increase the *visibility* of the client and thus the *awareness* of its activity and valid contribution to the agribusiness sector in Australia and New Zealand. The first thing the media relations counsellor must do is investigate which media is covering the issues of agribusiness policy. The investigation leads to a number of trade magazines. Specialist agribusiness magazines cover all aspects of policy, as do specialist newspapers, such as *Land*. But in the investigation the media relations counsellor discovers there are peripheral magazines that have covered some policy issues less deeply, yet are widely read and respected within the part of the agribusiness sector that the client is interested in reaching. The next step in building a relationship with one or more of these magazines is to frame the client's story in such a way that it will be of interest to them. There are a number of ways to do this. In discussing the potential for supplying a story, a discussion with the magazine editor might:

- suggest an angle that has not been covered by the specialist magazines
- play down the client
- play up the wider field of agribusiness
- draw on an important but as yet uninvestigated area of research.

For these tactics to be successful a media relations practitioner will need to understand the nature of the feature story within the magazine. This understanding includes the length of a normal feature story and the writing style of the magazine.

When contacting the editor or feature editor of the magazine for the first time, the media relations practitioner will need to be cogniscent of a number of things, which include the magazine's subscription base and how many features have already appeared on the issue or topic.

After the initial discussion and negotiation, the media relations practitioner must then write the story so that the client is seen to be an important part, but not so important that the feature becomes a puff piece that will be spiked by the editor (see chapter 5 for details of writing a feature story, for an example of an investigative feature story see the *Chronicle: IMC* in chapter 9, and for an example of a think-piece feature story, see the *Chronicle: Watching black comedy after 9/11* in chapter 5).

Letter to the editor

The letter to the editor is the last of four written tactics that can be considered uncontrolled. By uncontrolled we mean that, unlike newsletters and flyers, which can be sent directly to the stakeholders for whom we are intending our message, news releases, backstories, features, and letters to the editor are *mediated* by reporters and editors between the client and the intended stakeholder recipient. The media in these cases control the outcome, whereas newsletters, flyers, annual reports, and other direct-to-the-stakeholder material are controlled by the media relations practitioners.

Letters to the editor are an underrated but highly valuable tactic in the strategic campaign. A letter has the capacity to introduce an issue or event to stakeholders or to keep alive an issue that begins to fall away before it is supposed to. Letters present issues and events in a similar way to a news release, but they have the added dimension of expressing the opinion of the writer. Research into a publication or a television program that takes letters, or a radio talk-back program in which emails and faxes are featured, will show where the opinions that suit the issue or event are best displayed. Letters should be written over the signature of the client.

But letters compete in a difficult environment. It might be harder to get a letter to the editor published in the *Age*, for example, than to get a business news story published in the business section of the paper. The *Age* letters editor receives upward of 250 letters each day by email and hard copy. A letter to the editor thus competes not only for space in the newspaper—if it makes it that far—but also with all the other letters that must be read so that a selection can be made for the next day's edition.

The importance of style and length is paramount. The issue being written about must also be timely and bear a strong relationship to whatever is happening with high-profile current issues and events.

Newsletters, flyers, and pamphlets

Newsletters are most often standard-sized sheets numbering between one and sixty-four pages. Anything over sixty-four pages and the newsletter becomes a magazine. There are post office-preferred sizes for all types of publications and guidelines that make it easy for a newsletter publisher to conform to a standard size. Standard sizing is also a more cost-effective production method.

Newsletters are a controlled medium in which a client's issues or events can be widely or narrowly circulated dependent upon the profile of the stakeholders whom the client is interested in reaching. They are used to disseminate information by all types of organisations and individuals, from stockbrokers and banks to local tree preservation and bush regeneration environmental groups. No matter who or what organisation produces a newsletter, their purpose is the same worldwide: to disseminate information to stakeholders in a controlled fashion. This means the information can be written in a different way to that pitched to the news media (for a description of newsletter writing, see chapter 5). While it is always good to use correct grammar and syntax and conform to some guidelines when writing, the newsletter does not need to be as formal in its construction as the material sent to news media. Newsletters also have the happy advantage of being able to employ more jargon and technical language in their pages than material written for media. The *New Zealand Alpine Club*, for example, may send a sixteen-page monthly newsletter to its members describing in vivid detail new climbs that have been made in the Southern Alps. It might include technical details about the type of equipment used on the climbs—karabiners, pitons, bugaboos—and describe the types of terrain that have been traversed—arêtes, cols, gendarmes—all jargon that is impenetrable to the uninitiated, but for which the newsletter can be a vehicle. It was this type of publication that led Habermas to contemplate and investigate eighteenth-century English pamphlets as a source of information dissemination by the merchant classes. As I have mentioned earlier, Habermas used a specific time and place to investigate the importance of communication to what he termed 'the public sphere'. Newsletters, flyers, and pamphlets perform the same function within a similar public sphere two and a half centuries later. Stockbrokers, for example, mail hardcopy editions of newsletters to clients and prospective clients. Prospective clients' names and addresses are purchased from mailing lists. The stockbroker also has a website from which potential clients can obtain information, but at the beginning of the twenty-first century there is a still a strong belief, even among such elite groups, that not all potential clients will access this technology. Older, less technologically attuned citizens are more likely to have disposable investment potential than younger, more computer literate citizens.

To be effective, newsletters must sparkle. This means that the content and the design must be easily accessible to stakeholders. The award-winning American writer Tom Wolfe once said that reading a newspaper was as enjoyable as stepping into a warm bath. For a stakeholder recipient of a newsletter, the same or a similar sentiment must apply. It must have a strong emotional appeal as well as providing rational content. People are receptive to all types of information but they are more receptive to something with which they have some familiarity. If they are becoming interested in the stock market, a newsletter arriving in their letterbox could provide the motivation they needed to start investing. If they have noticed the bush regeneration work that has been going on along the path beside the sluggish river that they drive past every day and they get a newsletter in their letterbox showing happy volunteers, enthusiastic and fulfilled by a weekend's hard slog pulling out weeds, they may be motivated to join in the fun. Newsletters are, therefore, a cost-effective way to reach specific or diffuse stakeholders.

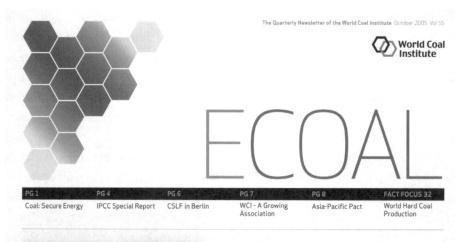

The Quarterly Newsletter of the World Coal Institute October 2005 Vol 55

World Coal Institute

ECOAL

PG 1	PG 4	PG 6	PG 7	PG 8	FACT FOCUS 32
Coal: Secure Energy	IPCC Special Report	CSLF in Berlin	WCI - A Growing Association	Asia-Pacific Pact	World Hard Coal Production

North American blackout 2003 - before and after

WORLD COAL INSTITUTE REPORT

COAL: SECURE ENERGY

>> While discussions on energy were for many years dominated by issues surrounding environmental performance, energy security has rapidly risen up the global agenda. >>

Energy security is a global concern. Its importance and influence is not limited to energy policies – energy security has implications across a range of national and international policies.

The World Coal Institute (WCI) has examined the role of coal in enhancing energy security worldwide in its new report *Cool: Secure Energy*. The report – published later this month – is the latest in a series of reports by WCI on the contribution of coal to global sustainable development.

The Need for Secure Energy

The need for affordable, reliable and dependable power to provide the essential needs of lighting, heating, cooking, mobility and communications – as well as driving industrial growth – is without question. Modern technologies, requiring high quality power supplies, underpin today's societies and facilitate economic growth in many underdeveloped countries.

Interruption of energy supplies can cause major financial losses and create

"Secure, reliable and affordable energy sources are fundamental to economic stability and development. Rising energy demand poses a challenge to energy security given increased reliance on global energy markets."

G8 Communiqué 2005

havoc in economic centres, as well as potential damage to the health and wellbeing of the population.

Global economic growth, the primary driver of energy demand, is conservatively forecast to average 3.2% per annum between 2002 and 2030, with China, India and other Asian countries expected to grow most quickly. Population growth will continue, with the World population expected to reach over 8 billion by 2030, from its current level of 6.4 billion.

As a result, and if governments continue with their current policies, global energy demand is projected to grow almost 60% by 2030. Fossil fuels will account for the bulk of this increase and will continue to dominate the total demand for energy for the foreseeable future.

As global demand for energy continues to rise - especially in rapidly industrialising and developing economies – energy security concerns become ever more important. To provide solid economic growth, and to maintain levels of economic performance, energy must

be readily available, affordable and able to provide a reliable source of power without vulnerability to long-term or short-term disruptions.

Providing a secure supply of energy comprises two distinct, yet related issues:

i) long-term security or resource availability; and

ii) short-term security – associated with supply disruptions of the primary fuel or of the electricity generated.

Resource availability is the actual physical amount of the resource, e.g. oil, gas, coal or uranium, present around the world. In the case of renewable energies, this could be considered as the amount of time the wind blows at the right speed, or the number of 'sun hours' at a particular location.

System reliability refers to the continuous supply of energy, particularly electricity, to meet consumer demand at any given time.

The forecast growth in energy demand means that we will need many sources of energy in future. A diverse mix of energy sources, each with different advantages, provides security to an energy system by allowing flexibility in meeting each country's needs.

Figure 4.2 Front page of *ECOAL*, newsletter of the World Coal Institute

Handbooks

A handbook, or guide, is a vital part of a campaign's tactical armoury. A handbook is a reference tool that has the capacity for a longer life cycle than some other written tactics. It could even outlast an annual report as a reference tool. Like an annual report, a handbook is updated regularly to provide new or additional information. A university handbook, for example, showing undergraduate courses, regulations, and faculties, changes part of its content every year. It may make minor amendments to its regulations or it may make major amendments to its courses. Similarly, a handbook such as *Margaret Gee's Media Guide* lists all media, and all people, contacts, and publishing details for all media in Australia. Its publisher, Crown Content, amends the print edition three times a year and has a version available online that is amended each day. This type of handbook is an invaluable reference tool. On behalf of clients, media relations practitioners compile handbooks for all types of stakeholders with different requirements. The Australian Taxation Office compiles and publishes a number of handbooks for its different stakeholders: one for corporations, one for small businesses, and one for sole traders. All government departments at national, state, and local level publish handbooks and guides. Handbooks and guides differ from marketing tools such as product disclosure statements (PDS) in that they are information sources to assist stakeholders. PDSs and other marketing materials are generally published as a requirement of law with the responsibility on the purchaser to investigate as thoroughly as possible before committing. This type of marketing material is published in a format that is designed to influence and persuade without the additional requirement of factual integrity. Handbooks and guides, on the other hand, are published to provide factual information for the express purpose of providing benefit to stakeholders.

Handbooks vary in style and design, as well as in shape and size. They usually contain lists of information that have been thoroughly researched and judiciously gathered. Like the telephone book, the train or bus timetable, or a travel guide to the world, they are an invaluable source.

Annual reports

The annual report is one of the most important written tactics available to organisations, particularly those required by law to publish financial and corporate details. In Australia and New Zealand, as in most Western countries, government regulations require public companies to divulge their financial activities each year. This information, usually published in printed form, could also appear in electronic form on the website of the organisation. The writing of the annual report and its associated design, printing, and distribution, and the conducting of the organisation's annual general meeting are the responsibility of media relations practitioners.

Annual reports form the basis of the relationship between a public company and its stakeholders, but many other organisations, without legal obligation to do so, choose to report issues and events annually as part of their **corporate social responsibility**.

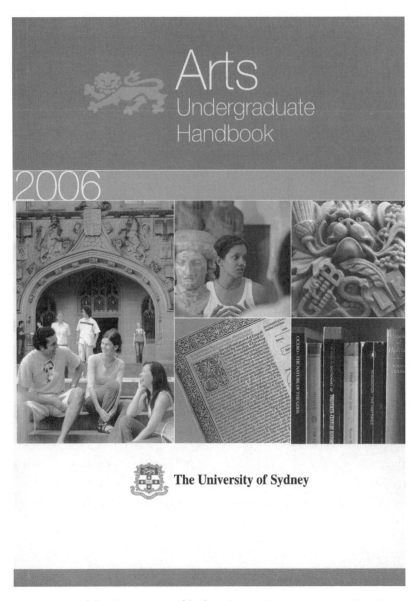

Figure 4.3 Cover of the University of Sydney's *Arts Undergraduate Handbook*

An annual report is a progress report, a process as much as a publication because it provides a comprehensive review of issues and activities. In this regard it is different to other written tactics because it is not information about what is happening in the present or what is going to happen in the future. It is a summary of what has already happened. It might include projections by senior management of what it thinks may happen in the future, given certain business, social, and political conditions, but, in general, the body of the report is historical.

An annual report provides a historic record of the highlights and challenges that faced the organisation during the preceding year. As the public profile of an organisation, an annual report can be presented in a number of ways. It may contain the financial data that a company or organisation is required by law to publish, or it may be presented as a glossy magazine-style publication in full colour. A glossy magazine-style report, perfectly bound, using high-quality stock and high-resolution images, is the most expensive single written contact that an organisation is likely to have with stakeholders. Included in this list of stakeholders are financial analysts and financial media. By creating and publishing wider information, an organisation demonstrates to its stakeholders that it is serious about its business or activities. As a tactic, this influences stakeholders, particularly investor stakeholders, to remain loyal to the organisation. It also helps to attract new **investors** who see themselves in the image of the organisation. The importance of the quality of the publication should not, therefore, be underestimated.

corporate social responsibility
the awareness of organisations that there is more to their bottom line than profits and that to be sustainable in the long term they need to consider their social and environmental interests as well as their economic interests.

investor
one who supplies financial or other capital to the interests of an individual.

Figure 4.4 Fairfax 2005 *Annual Report* cover

Books

Books are designed and written with persuasion and influence in mind. Fiction and non-fiction play a part in shaping sociopolitical ideas and behaviour. A book can act as a very important tactic in a strategic campaign. The difficulty with it is the lead time required for production and publication. A media relations campaign can use a book as a tactic, but it is usually part of a long-term campaign.

A book is most often effective as a strategic tactic when used in conjunction with other campaign tactics. It has the capacity to generate ideas and discussion because it is seen as a respectable product. The ubiquitous cookbook or do-it-yourself book used as a tactic is good for the sale of cooking utensils and handyman tools. It may not encourage the sale of particular products, but it reinforces the field in which it is embedded.

Figure 4.5 Books generate ideas and discussion

Spoken tactics

Speeches, interviews, face to face, word of mouth, and radio community service announcements can all be considered to be spoken tactics.

Speeches

Books have been written about speeches and their capacity to influence and persuade. Just as the news release is the underpinning of written tactics, a good speech, well crafted and delivered, is the most important spoken tactic. A speech begins life as a piece of writing but it must be balanced with delivery to have the desired effect. A speech is a controlled tactic. It must be reported as it is spoken and so is best used on television and radio, or live before an audience. A media relations practitioner writes speeches for clients and arranges events for their delivery. When the secretary-general of the United Nations, Kofi Annan, makes a speech in the media room at UN headquarters in New York, it has been drafted and edited by his media relations secretary. When the prime minister of Australia makes a televised speech to the nation about the need for changes to the Industrial Relations Act, it has been crafted and edited by his media relations adviser. At a different, but no less important level, when the managing director of a medium-sized organisation is invited to act as guest of honour at an industry breakfast, a media writing expert is employed to draft a speech. Speeches must captivate and leave a lasting impression. A breakfast, lunch, or dinner speaker competes with a variety of other elements in a room—waitstaff moving between tables, people eating nice food and drinking copious quantities of alcohol. Global speeches, those events that capture the attention of thousands of individuals who turned out to hear a politician or a famous person in a public place, have become the province of television, but the speech also has enormous value in other places. The speech is still a vital part of the public sphere, despite its shift to television in the last half of the twentieth century. A speech made by a senior government minister over a private lunch at a media corporation such as John Fairfax, for example, can have a lasting effect on how *Sydney Morning Herald* and *Australian Financial Review* journalists and editors frame a government issue. A speech by the chief executive officer of a public corporation to a lunch for 300 analysts and brokers at a posh Melbourne hotel is reported in the media, but its impact on those present will be heightened by their attendance. If it were not, the advice from the media relations expert would be to simply draft a news statement about the particular issue or event. Public companies have the added bonus of the chief executive officer making a speech at the annual general meeting of the company.

There are a number of important venues for speeches and speechmakers. A country's national press club is one. But there are other equally important venues that are more accessible to a broader stakeholder base. They include chambers of commerce events, university graduation ceremonies, and other institutional functions such as the monthly lecture series run by the PRIA.

A good speech is not restricted to elites and elite activities and issues, but it is most often the sphere in which the media relations expert plays a significant role. Good speeches can also be made at primary school prize-giving ceremonies and at engagement parties, but they rarely germinate in the mind of the media relations practitioner.

Figure 4.6 Chris de Bono, UN Department of Public Information, preparing to write speeches.

Interviews

As a spoken tactic, an interview contributes strongly to all types of media relations strategies. An interview can best be imagined as a layered structure with the base being the elementary dialogue between a media person and a member of the public from which might come a reported news story. At the top of the hierarchy lies the sophisticated pugilistic interview, a dialogic exchange with strategic intent in which the adversaries look to defeat each other on points. There are any number of layers underneath, depending upon circumstances, including the glossy magazine-type television show interview, the eyewitness at the crime scene, and the Oprah Winfrey guest who has lost 500 kilograms. An interview has the potential to cut a client out from the herd and to present an issue or event in an important emotional way. But there is a risk. A media relations practitioner must prepare a client to expect rigorous and intelligent questioning from the media. An unprepared interviewee will experience the full wrath of the media at the time of the interview and later in public.

A number of theories attach to the interview, from both the journalistic and the public relations perspectives. The most important are framing theory, dialogic theory

(Botan & Taylor 2005), and conversational analysis theory (Clayman & Heritage 2002). As a tactic, preparation for the interview is the same whether a client is being interviewed for a spot on *Australian Idol* or is the subject of investigation as the chairman of one of the largest corporations in Australia. The single most important factor is to consider an interview to be as important as if a client were acting as an expert witness in a court of law: preparation and research provide the underpinning of a successful result. As well as being informative, a successful result also requires direction (the issue or event frame for the dialogue) and the ability to make sense quickly to stakeholder publics. An interview between a journalist and a client in the casual atmosphere of a lunch meeting that becomes a newspaper or magazine story, may also inspire radio and television spots. The face-to-face newspaper interview over lunch can be more relaxed than the broadcast interview, but it is important to recognise that the direction of the dialogue is always *on the record*. This means that the client should understand that any engagement with a journalist is expected to be publishable or broadcastable; nothing remains as background.

A media interviewee should never be put in a position where they may not know the answer to a question. The importance of such a statement relies on the establishment of a frame for the issue or event in which the interview is simply seen as a mechanism for engagement in a power struggle between elites. Another argument against the value of the interview as a tactic is that it is seen to be non-dialogic (Botan 1997) and, at worst, a primed ritual that fails to allow stakeholders other than elites to find meaning in the engagement. It is the responsibility of the media relations counsel to implore a client interviewee to act within an ethical frame, to discuss all that the client is capable of discussing without resort to the revelation of economic or politically sensitive information. The situational nature of the interview can, however, be dangerous territory for those who have not been adequately prepared. It is the responsibility of the journalist to investigate and probe using questions designed to shift an interviewee from an established frame and into an area that is less well known. So it is incumbent upon the media relations counsel to make sure an interviewee is entirely confident and capable in both the information being divulged and the method of presentation. There will be times when an interviewee is treated to Dorothy Dix questions, that is, questions that have been pre-arranged between the interviewee and the journalist in order to enable the interviewee to give a particular answer, but generally, journalists and reporters are duty bound to investigate and dig deeply into an issue or event. If an interview can elicit a shred of information that is not in accordance with the journalist's perception, then the journalist will pursue it with rigour.

Journalists and reporters often seek interviews to provide background information for feature stories or to provide a profile that might act as a sidebar to a main feature. But it is the role of the media relations counsel to advise a client on the efficacy of agreeing to the interview. In other words, it may be inappropriate timing for an interview. An environmental group, for example, that is preparing a campaign against a multinational logging operation in Tasmania may not be ready to contribute to a newspaper profile because it has not yet elected its spokesperson.

The spokesperson for an organisation is often the media relations counsellor. In other situations, the spokesperson may be an elected or nominated representative but in all circumstances the spokesperson must be briefed on or understand everything there is to know about a specific issue or event. Whoever it is, they must have *credibility*.

A different type of interview is one in which a journalist seeks to ask a bystander or eyewitness about the issue or event in question. In this situation the media relations counsel is not controlling the flow of information.

Australian and New Zealand media are similar to their European counterparts when it comes to interview techniques. They tend to investigate deeply and to make every attempt to expose information that could be relevant to their story. US journalism, on the other hand, while it is rigorous in its pursuit of investigative material, is less intrusive, less forthright in its pursuit. It is important to understand the difference when dealing with multinational clients.

In some cases an interview situation can lead to consequences that were unintended by the journalist. The author, as a magazine editor, once interviewed a senior federal politician who appeared to be less than knowledgeable about the area of technology over which he presided. It was not the intention of the interview to expose the lack of knowledge: the minister did that himself by pursuing a line of discussion that had been outside the frame intended by the author. The published story began with its intended angle but added information that clearly made the minister appear inadequate. It was used by the federal Opposition in parliament, along with other media material, to discredit the minister, who was removed from the portfolio soon after.

Community service announcements

Community service announcements (CSAs), whether in print, on radio, television, or the internet, begin life as a written tactic. They become spoken tactics when they are produced for radio, and acted tactics when produced for television. A CSA is really an unpaid advertisement that crosses the boundary between media relations and advertising, but it has a place within the tactical armoury of media relations. A CSA is something the media provides when space allows, so it is uncontrolled. It may appear on television in the middle of the night, in a suburban newspaper among the deadline notice and late classifieds, in no man's land after the sports pages, or on radio at 4 a.m. Some charitable organisations, because they have tax exempt status and limited budgets, are provided with prime-time space during their annual collection appeals, but generally, CSAs fill spaces that media find hard to sell. Nonetheless, a CSA should be produced in a professional manner so that it reflects an overall theme.

Press conferences

The press conference, or media conference, is a prime opportunity to gather together all media and make a single announcement about an important issue or event. It is itself an event but it must be used judiciously, otherwise any level of trust—symbolic capital—will be diminished. Press conferences as ritual are held within the spaces of parliaments, but they are also used by non-government organisations (NGOs) to make announcements. Care needs to be taken in deciding when to arrange a press conference for a number of reasons, including budget, timing, and the importance of the announcement.

As a media relations counsel to a large international information technology corporation, the author once arranged a press conference at the behest of the company's marketing department. At the conference, it was planned to launch a new piece of technology that would lead to a change in computer use. A problem arose when the invitation to the conference was issued and accepted by national television media. The managing director of the organisation refused at the last minute to divulge sensitive details and would not speak to journalists representing nightly news broadcasts.

Press conferences range in size from a local gathering for suburban editors and trade magazines, to international settings within global organisations, such as the UN and the International Monetary Fund. United Nations headquarters in New York, for example, provides a large dedicated space to the media for its daily news conferences. Parliaments throughout Australia and New Zealand provide similar, if smaller, spaces to house reporters and to provide a venue for news conferences. In the USA the president holds press conferences in the Rose Garden, part of the grounds surrounding the White House and fronting Pennsylvania Avenue in Washington, DC. In Australia, the prime minister holds news conferences in various parts of the country, depending upon where he is, but most often, while in Canberra, he holds them in a small garden within the confines of Parliament House. The setting for a press conference assists an issue or event to carry a sense of occasion. The Rose Garden has become a moment of symbolic capital within American press politics, having been used continuously by presidents since John Kennedy. The ritual attachment of a venue to an announcement means all other media conferences are expected to achieve some level of occasion through a venue as well as having the media extract value from the issue or event at hand.

A press conference on a level somewhere between the local gathering and the international occasion can be an effective means of disseminating information in a timely and cost-effective manner. The importance of the venue is realised when an issue or event is complex and cannot be distilled into a simple frame. Then, it becomes important to provide a visual means of interpretation for the media. When, however, there is a possibility of a reporter meeting stakeholders who are not in agreement with the proposed announcement, or when there is some sensitivity attached to the issue or event, this is not always welcomed by a client. It may not be wise, for example, to hold a press conference in an abattoir where the throats of animals are being cut, their skins are being mechanically drawn from their bodies, and their body parts are being boned, cut, and packaged for distribution to butcher shops. The media may get to see all the action, but the nature of the business may suffer due to too many links being made between what is killed and what is eaten. Similarly, an announcement at a state hospital about a lack of beds may allow a reporter to roam freely, talk with hospital staff, and obtain sensitive background information. Like most public servants working in special environments, hospital staff must sign confidentiality agreements, but that does not stop them providing damaging background information. It is important, therefore, to select a venue that will provide a relevant setting for an announcement and a secure space in which to make it. Press conferences in public spaces require an additional investment in security given the threat posed by terrorists, although the nature of the media conference is such that it is announced privately. It only becomes public after the event so the threat is less than it might be at a public gathering.

A press conference is a good way to present an issue or event to a diffuse media, but it must be organised well in advance of the proposed announcement time and decisions must be made about who to invite and who to omit. It is just as important to make the correct decision about the type of invitation to issue. Some media relations counsellors advise sending glossy, four-colour invitations, while others choose novelty acts to accompany the written invitation—products that can be linked to the announcement. The important things for the media are the timing, the relevance of the issue or event, and the accessibility of the venue. When IBM announced its decision in Australia in the 1980s to cease production of typewriters at its Victorian manufacturing plant and to begin production of computers, it did so by shipping planeloads of journalists and editors to its Wangaratta factory and showing them exactly what it had planned. This took the better part of a day, during which IBM graciously hosted a lunch before returning the journalists and editors home. A press conference that takes a day out of a journalist's busy schedule not only requires detailed designing and planning so that it will have the maximum effect, but it must also make the media feel satisfied that the material presented has been worth the time taken. A simple rule for arranging media conferences is that the scale of the conference is equal to the value of the issue or event in question.

While press conferences are universally recognised as an important tactic, they vary in style and content from country to country. In Australia and New Zealand, as in Europe and the USA, they are circumscribed by the value of the issue or event being announced and the time available to attend the announcement. Media will attend a high-profile press conference because they do not want to miss something that might be picked up by their competitors. At lower-profile conferences, such as a weekly 'beat' at which a local police commander or government official briefs suburban newspaper reporters, there is less likelihood of a reporter showing up each week because the reporter knows a telephone call can be made later to get the information. They are less worried about deadlines. In some countries, particularly in Eastern Europe and South America, press conferences can last for half a day, after which the main drawcard is a free meal. A similar situation existed in Western countries up until the mid 1980s. At this time media proprietors began reducing editorial staff numbers so that reporters were unable to be away from their desks for an afternoon of drinking and eating when they had more pressing deadlines and work levels. In parts of South-East Asia and in Indonesia, there is an expectation that a press conference will be attended by a large number of special guests who usually have only a passing attachment to the issue or event. High-profile, powerful guests add a dimension to Asian press conferences, which changes the dynamics of the announcements and level of questioning from the media.

Figure 4.7 Press conference at the UN Security Council

Press tours

The media inspection tour poses an ethical question for both the client and the media. From the media perspective, a decision must be made concerning how much payment can be made before the balance of information obtained is seen to be compromised.

From the viewpoint of the client, the decision involves how much of an operation can be shown to stakeholders other than those directly involved in the operation before it will be compromised. Once these barriers are overcome, a media inspection tour can be a valuable tactic for all types of stakeholders. There are different types of press inspection tours: the most common is a trip somewhere to see something that is paid for by the client. Usually, it involves a free meal, transport, and the presentation of a gift as a vote of thanks for turning up. In extreme cases, the media are provided with luxury travel, accommodation, meals, and expenses. The author was the object of such a trip while working as a senior editor for a national business magazine. The ten-day trip included business-class travel to Europe, meals and accommodation in first-class hotels, and the opportunity to drive a new luxury European motor car, culminating in all-area access to the European Touring Car Championship in Monza, Italy. This is not unusual. Such trips are undertaken with regular frequency by motoring journalists for newspapers and business to business (B2B) magazines.

The ethics of this situation is not in question for the motor vehicle manufacturer. What is in question is the ethical obligations of the journalists. At this level, there is an expectation that the media will absorb as many trips as clients offer. They are part of the big end of town market, where corporations and governments need to expose their issues and events under conditions that may not be available in their home markets. Again, anecdotal evidence from the author was a trip to the UK, sponsored by the UK government, during which the author travelled business-class from Australia to London for ten days to undertake tours of manufacturing plants around England in the lead-up to a world exposition. The tour was designed and planned by the UK government to attract advance publicity for its World Construction Expo. The organisation of such a large tour, which was attended by more than thirty journalist from Europe, Canada, the USA, and Australia, was undertaken by an independent media relations firm based in the UK. The principal of the firm accompanied the media on the eight-day bus tour.

Most media tours are less attractive to the journalist and to the media relations counsellor. They involve complicated planning and there is no guarantee the media will turn up. Like the press conference, invitations must be realistic in framing the tour around an issue or event that will resonate with the media, but equally, it must allow time for media deadlines.

Another type of tour or visit is that which familiarises the media with a particular environment. Tourism, transport, and information technology rely on this type of familiarisation tour to give the media a sense of what is being presented. It is not uncommon for media relations practitioners with tourism clients—airlines, resorts, hotels, restaurants—to provide all-expenses-paid tours of their businesses with the expectation that the media will write about them. A slightly different approach to the tactic of taking a media group to a destination is that used by computer and information technology organisations. These organisations tend to take their senior management on roadshow tours, which means they go to the media. They might travel between Brisbane, Sydney, Melbourne, Adelaide, Perth, Auckland, and Wellington, setting up in central hotels and inviting the media to examine new computer technology in a working environment. Other organisations also use this tactic but it has its limitations, based on the type of thing being demonstrated.

Figure 4.8 Press tour

Demonstrations and direct action

A demonstration, the act of gathering large groups of people in public spaces to protest or validate an issue or event, is a tactic that is sometimes called into question for its ethical basis. A demonstration can have a broad, convincing effect on an issue or event and it can lead to actions beyond the control of the media relations practitioner. But when it is properly planned, a demonstration, like a community or town meeting, can be one of the most important tactics available to a client with limited resources. Town meetings have been the subject of academic investigation (see, for example, Wild 1974; Schudson 1999; Stanton 2006) and provide evidence that peaceful dialogue is part of the relationship building process between stakeholders. There is also evidence that town meetings in the eighteenth and nineteenth centuries have transformed into the peaceful demonstration of the twentieth and twenty-first centuries. Like a media tour or conference, a demonstration will attract a lot of media attention, more so than a community meeting because of its perceived potential for non-peaceful action. Trade unions, student groups, and environmental groups are seen to be the most prominent in organising demonstrations. The role of the media relations practitioner may not always be visible in the planning of a demonstration as part of a campaign strategy, but it exists. Unlike media tours and conferences, in which the media relations counsellor is directly involved in planning, writing, and distributing material to the media and building relationships directly, those involved in planning a demonstration tend to be less visible, as the demonstration is not first and foremost a media-driven tactic. Like the community meeting, the demonstration is used to engage with a number of stakeholders. It may be that one objective is media coverage of the demonstration as an event, and additional coverage of the issue that caused the event, but it is foremost to show solidarity where there appears to be fragmentation. In some countries, demonstrations are an extension of street theatre. In most Western countries, a demonstration or rally requires a permit of some kind before it is allowed. University students demonstrating against the imposition of higher fees, or some other government-imposed legislation, appear at first sight to be a threat to the stable order and to have the potential to grow and get out of control. But this is not part of the planning for a demonstration. It is usually the addition of street theatre or other activities that surround the planned demonstration. There are, of course, unplanned demonstrations and rallies that occur frequently that sometimes lead to violence and other unacceptable activities, but they are not usually part of a campaign strategy.

Community meetings

As a tactic, a community meeting usually starts without the input of a media relations counsellor. It is spontaneous and occurs most often because an individual or group is opposed to or dislikes something that is happening in its neighbourhood. It does not always attract the professional assistance of the media relations expert because community meetings do not have large financial resource bases. In the event that they are funded, they seek assistance with their campaign after it has begun. A community meeting is a strong relationship building tactic as it can demonstrate to larger stakeholders, such as governments and corporations, that an issue or event is being taken seriously. A community meeting in a small town, for example, like demonstrations and rallies, has been part of the sociopolitical scene in Australia and New Zealand since the eighteenth century. Community meetings today tend to be better organised in that they develop clear objectives, understand the role of the media in securing their objectives, and nominate a specific person to represent them in the media.

As a tactic, a community meeting might also be organised by a media relations counsellor on behalf of a client. An issue or event may not have resonated as strongly with a community as anticipated, so the planned meeting provides a sense of cohesion and meaning. This type of meeting may be arranged by the media relations counsellor on behalf of the client where the client provides information to the community about an issue or event, or it may be arranged on behalf of the client where the client is less visible and the community leads the issue. An example of a client-sponsored meeting might be when a sensitive development is before a local government body—a marina, a sanitation plant, a high-rise building—and the client wishes to provide the surrounding neighbours with as much information as possible about the development. A community meeting might also be established because neighbours, although they already have plenty of information about a development, remain opposed to its approval by government. Where development of anything is concerned in Australia and New Zealand, the most frequent role for the media relations practitioner is on the side of the developer. As a primary stakeholder, the developer is in a better financial and strategic position to hire a skilled practitioner to undertake a campaign. How the developer approaches the relationship building between it and stakeholder communities is the same as the approach taken to building media relationships.

Street theatre

As a tactic, street theatre is more highly visible in countries where emotion plays a major part in the development of issues and events. In the West, street theatre is becoming a more acceptable campaign tactic, but it is nowhere near as valuable as it could be. Street theatre is a pacific tactic, a celebration in which the actors ritualise issues and events and inject meaning into stakeholder relationship building. Sydney's Gay and Lesbian Mardi Gras is probably the best example of street theatre as a campaign tactic. It is a celebration of a subculture that receives benign or positive media attention and it provides meaning about the subculture to diffuse stakeholder groups who watch it live or on television (see the *Chronicle*, chapter 9, for a discussion of street theatre in Australia).

Imagined tactics

I define imagined tactics as those that have no basis in reality but require planning and development in real time.

Interventions

An intervention is the capacity of a primary stakeholder (client) to inject an issue or event into a medium where there was previously no basis for it to be part of the original. It is the embedding of an issue or event somewhere it was not previously considered and, when observed, appears to be part of the original structure. It is the placement of an issue or event in a strategic position so that it provides meaning to stakeholders who may not have previously considered its implications or extent.

Product placement in television drama is an example of intervention, but it lies outside the definition of media relations tactics because, like traditional advertising, it relies for its existence on a contractual monetary exchange (payment). Other interventions in television drama, however, are vital to some issues reaching stakeholders where there is a low recognition but a need for high recognition. Teenage pregnancy, for example, is an issue that, when built into the dialogue of television dramas such as *Neighbours* and *Home and Away*, has a subliminal impact on viewers in the age group most affected. To get an issue placed in such media, though, is not an easy task. It requires relationship building of the highest order. According to Ray Kolle, a former scriptwriter for *Neighbours* and *Home and Away*, producers and writers are approached by a large number of organisations each year with plans on how their issues or events can fit in with the theme of the drama. All types of issues can be categorised as relevant to drama placement: health, finance, insurance, travel, employment, and obeying the law are some. Each has a champion. It may be the Cancer Council of Australia wishing to highlight the difficulties encountered by teenage leukaemia sufferers and the importance of family and friends in the recovery process. It may be an insurance company wishing to highlight the risk Generation Ys run when they go overseas with no travel insurance. An intervention may resonate where traditional advertising, seen as a sales pitch, is unsuccessful. Health issues are among the most important interventions in reaching stakeholders who take little notice of traditional advertising campaigns, even when the campaigns are designed to improve their wellbeing. An intervention tactic requires the media relations expert to build relationships with a variety of stakeholders, including producers, writers, and financiers, and to understand the complex task of script-writing. It is not for the faint-hearted.

Pictures

If the old expression 'A picture is worth a thousand words' were true, most media relations practitioners would be looking for some other way to occupy their time. Images—computer-generated, photographed, painted, graffiti—all have a place in the strategic campaign. But they need to be used well. A picture accompanying a news release adds meaning, but is wasted if the picture does not link to the written tactic. Media relations counsellors go to great lengths to spend client funds on photos that are sometimes as useful as a pocket in a singlet. Media owners employ highly skilled professionals to frame and shoot images and footage for publication and broadcast. With this in mind, media relations counsellors should think about images as background the same way they think about a backstory.

Figure 4.9 Manufacturing and printing CD sleeves

Videos and compact disks

The advent of email attachments and the speed of delivery of the internet for high-resolution compressed images has almost concluded the need for media relations practitioners to send video and compact disks as part of a media package. Really, the only time that they become important is for clients in the music business. If there is a requirement to attach a digital video disk (DVD), compact disk (CD), or videotape to a press kit, then it should be professionally produced. The only other time it may add value is as a demonstration disk for a new piece of computer software or other product.

Music and drama

Concerts and other musical and dramatic events are important imagined tactics. They may not always be rational in the same way that a news release or factory tour are, but they add a dimension to a campaign that is unsurpassed for emotional appeal.

Music as a tactic can be as globally embracing as a fundraising concert for those living in poverty, or it can be as local as a side event attached to the issue of compulsory student unionism. Music, with all its hidden symbolism and ambiguous messages, is an ideal tactic for reaching stakeholders who may not respond to more traditional tactics. Political messages have long been framed around music and drama. Witness William Shakespeare and Ben Johnson, Leonard Cohen, Vanessa Carlton, and Jack Johnson. Music and drama also bear a strong relationship to street theatre as a tactic.

Figure 4.10 Making music

5

Writing Client Prose

CHAPTER OBJECTIVES

- To understand why grammar and syntax are important to media relations campaigns.
- To develop an understanding of the different expectations of media.
- To understand strategic and creative media material.

Why do we have to bother with grammar? Why do we care about syntax? Because there will be a reporter waiting somewhere who will get hold of a media relations practitioners' news release and who will be one of those people who studied Latin all the way through high school and knows all about adverbial accusatives, dative of the remoter object, third, fourth and fifth declensions, perfects, and supines.

Media relations practitioners spend a lot of time writing prose, which is the underpinning of the field. Prose defines media relations and separates from advertising, marketing, and events management and links it directly to the profession of journalism.

Prose can be described as a form of written discourse based on the sentence and without the stylised patterning of verse. A negative perception of prose is that it lacks strong features and creative vigour—thus 'prosaic', meaning dull, commonplace, and unimaginative.

The most interesting thing about prose for the purposes of the media relations practitioner is that it is similar in many ways to speech and is frequently thought of as speech transferred to paper. Normal speech is less tightly structured than prose, although we can pick up pretty much any newspaper today and find lead paragraphs that are looser than any speech we might make in private.

Prose is used to:

- write technical instructions
- write legal reports
- write fiction and drama
- write journalism
- write media and news releases.

More prose writing was published in the twentieth century than in all past centuries combined. The invention of the internet in the late twentieth century means that there is the possibility that more prose will be published in the first twenty years of the twenty-first century than all other centuries combined.

So how do we write sparkling prose that will catch the attention of the media person or people that it is pitched to (the reporter, editor, or producer), for example? What do we do to make our prose—which is what we spend a lot of time constructing, so we want it to be worth something—more strategic than others?

For media relations purposes, correct use of grammar becomes important because we are required to present our message in a highly readable, clearly understandable fashion. A basic understanding of grammar is crucial to our ability to make our prose sparkle. In this, grammar is synonymous with syntax and excludes morphology. What we are interested in here is the syntactical process—phrases, clauses, and sentences. As in the structure of a news story, a news release requires that we convey meaning clearly and with structure. So the well-constructed sentence becomes our best friend.

Writing a news release

The same structure as a news story—the inverted pyramid—is a good place to start thinking about our prose. We can argue later about the relative merits of the alternatives, but for now let's use it as a basis for discussion and investigation of a few examples of news releases that have become news stories.

In the days before computers, news reporters and journalists used typewriters. A ten par (paragraph) piece of copy was typed onto separate *takes*—half an A4 sheet. A subeditor could then shuffle the takes if they thought the lead or angle needed to be changed. The same happens today in cut and paste mode on a computer, which is a follow-on from journalism practice when an editor might flick a news release to a reporter and say 'This is a cut and paste', which generally means the story is good enough to run without the reporter taking any additional time to source or rewrite.

As we know, it is all about deadlines. If a news release gets passed on by an editor because its prose sparkles, then the reporter will simply cut and paste. So, let's have a look at a news release and see if it will get to a reporter as a cut and paste. Copy arrives from media relations practitioners as hard or electronic. Do not send both.

The first paragraph should—like news copy—contain all the elements of the story. Don't make a reporter or editor work hard to find the angle. They do not have time. They are not interested in a follow-up phone call as a way to explain a buried lead.

Here's a lead par from the front page of a suburban weekly:

> Serving in the Women's Auxiliary Australian Air Force during the Second World War taught … how to manoeuvre around life's obstacles.

This has been written by a reporter, not from a news release but from a lead supplied by a different source. (Leads from news releases make up the majority of material used in suburban weeklies that are not covered by reporting on local councils.) In this copy there are three problems with the lead par that media relations practitioners must avoid.

1   It is written in the passive voice—media copy, especially front page news copy, should be in the active voice. Otherwise, it is considered a feature story.
2   It does not state its purpose, nor does it provide the reader with an idea of what the story is about, which is, in fact, about an elderly woman attempting to get money from the federal government.
3   It begins with a present participle which is one of the biggest sins in journalistic prose writing.

Here is a slightly better example from the keyboard of the same reporter:

> The … community remains split after a people-power victory to stop a proposed mobile phone tower.

Aside from the hideous clichés—'people power', 'the community remains split'—at least the structure is a bit better and we can have a better idea of what the actual story is about.

Here is one that is clearly identifiable as a news release:

> One of the world's largest land transport operators is the new part-owner of the Westbus Group.

A lead news par should have around seventeen to twenty words, be in the active voice, and in the present tense. The par above runs close to this requirement. Here's another, this time from the *Sydney Morning Herald*:

> The Egyptian biochemist suspected of building the bombs used in the
> London terrorism attacks has been arrested in Cairo.

No clichés, no present participle opener, active voice. Here's another, which is good except for its length:

> Early trials of a vaccine to protect women against cervical cancer show
> it could virtually wipe out precancerous disease, as long as girls take it
> before they become sexually active.

This was a page three lead in the *SMH*, the source of which was the Children's Hospital at Westmead. The reporter balanced the story with additional source material from the head of public health at a leading university. So it was effectively a news release that became a strong news story. The reporter provided balance by sourcing additional comment from an objective observer.

Here is a business story from the *Australian*—randomly chosen (business news is frequently written in the past tense):

> Shares hit another record yesterday but the dollar fell after the US
> Federal Reserve lifted US borrowing costs for the tenth time to guard
> against inflationary pressure.

At twenty-seven words it is a bit long but a good angle, and all the relevant information is available.

And another, but this time a simple cut and paste supplied by the company:

> Income tax cuts and the scrapping of the New South Wales vendor duty
> on investment properties will help lift a weak retail sector, according to
> furniture retailer Nick Scali.

Horrible cliché 'lift a weak retail sector', and again, too many words at twenty-seven but the information is good.

The point here is that we want to provide a reader with sufficient information in the first paragraph to make a decision—a decision to keep reading. We do not want a reader to stop reading the story after the first sentence, but the very act of putting all the relevant information in it might become the cause of them moving on.

One final example, then we can move on.

> Origin Energy has found a new gas field in the Perth Basin near Dongara
> which could hold as much as 50 billion cubic feet of gas.

At twenty-six words it, too, is a little long, but the syntax is perfect. And joy for the client and the media relations source because the name of the company is right at the top.

Rules for writing news releases

There are specific ways to write news material. Here are some of the things to do and others that must not be done. In writing a news release a media relations practitioner must ask the same questions that will be asked by the journalist receiving it. Is it news or newsworthy?

- Find an angle that localises the issue or event. International corporations, governments, and other high-level organisations write news releases about their issue or event as if the whole world is interested. This may be true for a global organisation such as the UN or the World Health Organisation, but for a multinational food manufacturer, for example, a news release about a new French cheese will have little interest in New Zealand unless there is a local angle. If the French cheese maker is set to obtain government subsidies for export to New Zealand, this, then, is the local angle. Otherwise, it's just cheese.
- Write a lead paragraph that contains all the elements of the story. This is the same as it is for the journalist. It contains the who, when, where, why, what, and how of the issue or event. The lead paragraph, like each subsequent paragraph, should be a self-contained sentence.
- Write in the active voice, present tense. The journalist will alter the tense if appropriate.
- After the lead paragraph, write four or five paragraphs that focus on the details of the issue or event.
- Contain the news release to a maximum of fifteen paragraphs. Any more and it risks becoming boring or overcompensating.
- Use the last three or four paragraphs for quotes. Make the quotes relevant and related to the issue or event. Do not include quotes from a senior official talking up the organisation.
- Avoid advertising the name of the company or organisation. An issue or event must stand on its merits without the perceived backing of a company name or product.
- Avoid long, drawn-out material that fails to state the issue or event in clear and unambiguous terms. The main reason this rule is difficult is that issues or events are not always newsworthy.
- Avoid clichés, jargon and pompousness. An issue or event, while it may be special for someone, is not 'unique'. Unique means literally one only. It is one of the most despised words in journalism. Use it at your peril. If the media wishes to use clichés to describe issues and events, let them. Don't set up the clichés for them. An event is not a 'spectacular success', and it is not 'riding on a tide of opinion'. A government does not 'come clean' before it 'suffers at the hands of the electorate'.

- Remove technical jargon so that the news release can be easily understood by a journalist who is not familiar with the issue or event. Don't assume that everyone knows all about an issue or event just because you and the client know about it.
- Avoid personification and anthropomorphism. Inanimate objects don't need human qualifications (a living, breathing corporation) and animals don't need human qualifications (a horse with the intelligence of a man).
- Write clearly, concisely, correctly, and completely (see Hunt & Grunig 1994).

LAUNCH OF GREEN POWER POSTER DESIGN COMPETITION

A shared concern about the impacts of climate change has resulted in a combined State Government and Local Council Green Power educational campaign to encourage steps to reduce greenhouse gas emissions.

Green Power is a national government accreditation program that sets stringent environmental and reporting standards for renewable energy products offered by electricity suppliers to households and businesses across Australia.

The community-based Green Power educational campaign aims to encourage consumers to switch to accredited renewable energy—reducing the impacts of climate change.

Commenting on the launch for the North Sydney Council, the Director-General for the Department of Energy, Utilities and Sustainability, David Nemtzow, said one of the potential consequences of climate change is an increase in the frequency and intensity of severe weather events such as droughts. 'Regions in New South Wales are already experiencing the worst drought in a century and the Bathurst region has witnessed a dramatic change with the drought,' said the Minister. 'Coal-fuelled electricity creates 36 per cent of New South Wales's greenhouse gas emissions. Everyone can make a difference and do their bit to reduce greenhouse gas emissions by signing up to a Green Power accredited product. They can do this to help reduce greenhouse gas emissions by contacting their local electricity supplier Country Energy or calling 1300 852 688 for details of other Green Power accredited retailers.'

North Sydney Council plays an important role towards sustaining the North Sydney local community's environment. The council will launch a poster design competition as part of the Green Power educational campaign.

'We are inviting primary and secondary school students to come up with a fabulous poster that we'll use on our website, in our newsletter and on our community noticeboards to encourage people to make the switch to Green Power,' says North Sydney Mayor Genia McCaffery.

'I'm sure the creativity and artistic talent of our young people will come to the fore.'

Cr McCaffery said North Sydney Council did a lot of great work with schools on sustainability education. 'So we're expecting lots of fabulous entries from our schools.'

The Green Power educational campaign will cover New South Wales over a six month period from September 2005 to March 2006.

Figure 5.1 Green Power draft media release

Setting out a news release

A news release must be set out so that it can be read quickly and clearly. It must be apparent that time and care have been taken in its final design. It is much like a gift: a modest birthday present appears more attractive if it is well wrapped. The same rules apply to news releases distributed by electronic means as to those delivered by hard copy.

- Set page margins for 3 centimetres left, 2 centimetres right, and at least 3 centimetres top and bottom.
- Include a catchline (slug) such as *Dog, Cat, Rat* in the top right-hand corner and title the release *News Release* or *Media Release*. As a last resort, you could use *Press Release*, but remember you may also be sending it to the electronic media, so press release is a misnomer because it refers only to print media. The title of the release should be on the top left or at the top, centred on the page.
- Include a dateline but don't put it within the body of the release. Very few media use datelines in copy, and anyway, it will be obsolete by the time it arrives.
- Write a headline but don't expect it to be used if the material is published. The head should be only a few words that describe exactly the issue or event.
- If the material spills over one page, in the bottom right-hand corner include an ellipsis, followed by a backslash and the word *more*. (.../more) to indicate to the journalist that more copy is extant, especially if it appears that at the end of the first page the story has ended (which should not be the case if it has been properly written).
- At the top of the second page, repeat the catchline (Dog, Cat, Rat).
- Conclude the material with the word 'ends' to provide clear evidence of an ending.
- At the end of the material, include all contact details. These should be prefaced with the words 'For more information, contact ...', then telephone numbers (including home and mobile phone numbers if there is an expectation that a late edition might take up the issue or event), and email.

Writing a backstory

So far we have been dealing with strategic material—stuff we want to be considered serious enough for the news pages, news broadcasts, and leads on websites. What about the creative stuff, for example, backstories, letters to the editor, and community service announcements?

A good backgrounder should be thought of by the media relations practitioner as four or five pages of information that:

- supports the news story
- substantially reduces the reader's or viewer's knowledge gap on the topic
- provides evidence of thorough research.

A backstory is frequently more interesting to write than a straight news piece because you have more creative licence. By this I don't mean you can tell fibs; I mean you can frame the backstory in such a way that it might resonate more with the media person to whom it has been pitched.

Let's think about framing a backstory. We might have written our news piece as a straight-up story—blood, guts, death, romance—framed around the action that took place. The backstory can be framed around the support cast of the action, in much the same way that a backstory is framed in *Angel*, *Buffy*, *Last Man Standing*, or *Home and Away*. In prose terms, the backstory, or backgrounder, lives by the same rules as the news story but it can have a more creative punch.

Framing a backstory to reflect an issue in a different way

Let's look at the construction of a Telstra tower in a northern Melbourne suburb as our issue (or anywhere the telecommunications company is constructing towers). The story has been framed by the local newspaper reporter from a local council business paper source. It has three stakeholder groups—Telstra, the local bowling club, on whose premises the tower is being constructed, and unidentified residents who attended the council meeting. The local council voted against the tower construction. The bowling club wants the tower to be constructed because it will get income from leasing the airspace above the club—it is an identifiable stakeholder around which the story has been framed. The bowling club frame provides the reporter with an unusual angle—most often the community appears to be unanimous in its rejection of anything corporate, the not-in-my-backyard syndrome. Telstra has an opportunity here to keep the issue alive by:

- providing information to the newspaper about other community groups around the country that support the towers
- promoting a letter campaign by the 400 club members who support the construction
- investigating the residents who influenced council in its decision to reject the application.

Writing a letter to the editor

A letter to the editor can continue to keep a story alive. It can be written under the client's name or, what occurs more frequently today, a third person writes in support of the action or issue. This has ethical drawbacks. In 2005 a letter in a regional newspaper was identified as fraudulent. The name of the writer was 'Dustin Lane'. The person the writer was defaming in public could find no reference to the writer in the local telephone book or on the electoral roll.

A letter to the editor can have a powerful influence on an issue. The more letters a media organisation receives on an issue, the more likely it is to take notice. Letters should be written in the exact way prescribed by the media organisation to which they are being sent. In the Telstra tower case, 400 letters from 400 club members would provide a strong case for the local newspaper to continue to run its story.

Correspondents to suburban newspapers will be told:

> Letters should be kept brief. Name, address and telephone numbers must be supplied. Letters are submitted on condition that the publisher may edit and has the right to reproduce in electronic form and communicate these letters.

Correspondents to metropolitan newspapers will be told:

> All letters and email (no attachments) must carry the sender's home address and day and evening phone numbers for verification. Letter writers who would like receipt of their letters acknowledged should send a stamped, self-addressed envelope. Ideally, letters will be a maximum 200 words. By submitting your letter for publication, you agree that we may edit the letter for legal, space or other reasonable reasons and may, after publication in the newspaper, republish it on the internet or in other media.

Correspondents to a business magazine will be told:

> Please keep letters to a maximum of 250 words, and include all contact details. By submitting your letter for publication, you agree that we may edit the letter for legal, space or other reasonable reasons and may, after publication, republish it on the internet or in other media.

Here is an example of a letter written to an Australian business magazine as a follow-up to a story that appeared a few weeks earlier. The author wanted to make comment on the story and to amplify the issue in question. The letter received a reply from the magazine editor.

THE CHRONICLE: MANAGED INNOVATION

How to write a letter that will receive a reply

From: Allan Ryan [mailto:allan@managedinnovation.com]
Sent: Wednesday, 5 October 2005 2:03 PM
To: Tony Featherstone
Subject: Innovation Officer, BRW, 26 Sept

Tony,

It is too obvious to say that everyone is responsible for innovation in an organisation. The question is how does the organisation define innovation? What are the goals and roles?

I agree that HR is the last place that should provide the innovation initiative. HR is not customer facing, has no direct bottom line responsibility and usually has tight budgets. (Innovation is expensive).

The engineers are responsible for new product development and currently the pre eminent methodology is STAGE-GATE developed over twenty years ago. Over 70 per cent of manufacturers in the USA and presumably in Australia use STAGE-GATE. Recent research from the inventor of STAGE-GATE reveals that new to world innovation and new to company innovation is actually falling as a percentage of new product development. So engineers should not be responsible for innovation initiatives.

I agree that marketing is closer to the customer and a likely place for innovation. The problem is that markets and customers change. The Marketing Manager of the Horse and Buggy company was probably as close to the customer as the Marketing Manager for the Petrol driven vehicle is now. Should they be responsible for innovation initiative? Not completely.

The key to successful innovation is in the design of the innovation process itself. This is something you can not get from a book. Best practice just does not work. Best practice means that everyone becomes the same, innovation means you become different. Hence a different approach.

I operate a consultancy that has assisted some of Australia's leading companies and several global organisations. (Over 200 companies have participated at various times in our programs) My research has led to the development of the GATE ZERO method that develops unique approaches to innovation for organisations. This may make an interesting story for your readers. Some clients that may be interested in participating would be George Weston Technology, Roche Pharma, Selleys and Chevron.

My answer is that everyone is responsible for innovation however there are very different roles under the one title. The roles can be summarised as seeing, thinking and doing. When an organisation gets these roles correct and the systems to back them up then innovation flourishes.

I hope my thoughts are of interest.
Best regards
Allan Ryan
Managed Innovation International Pty Ltd

The correspondent (client), unlike the journalist or media relations agent, has the luxury of commenting upon an issue or event from a singular perspective. As we can see from the above letter, the correspondent is keen to add substantially to the issue of innovation. But at the same time he has been prudent in his choice of language. He has not said the writer of the original article was wrong, nor has he implied that there is some problem with the story. For most letter writers to newspapers, the issue or event being written about is seen as being provocative and requiring a response. Business publications require rational rather than emotional engagement, as we can see from the response to the letter from the editor.

From: Tony Featherstone [mailto:TFeatherstone@brw.fairfax.com.au]
Sent: Wednesday, 5 October 2005 2:40 PM
To: Allan Ryan
Subject: RE: Innovation Officer, BRW, 26 Sept

Hi Allan
Thanks for your excellent letter. It's a conundrum isn't it, finding the right person for a CIO role? You raise many interesting points. I agree with you on engineers and on the marketers (although I think one of their shortcomings is that they don't think about future customers needs, when that should be their main function).
  I'll point out your company to our Innovation Editor, Simon Lloyd. That might make a story for him.
  Keep the comments coming!
Kind regards
Tony Featherstone
Managing Editor
BRW

Writing a community service announcement

Community service announcements are generally free advertisements placed in unusual timeslots on radio and television by organisations that can't afford to pay commercial costs to buy space. They appear by convention—there is no legal requirement of media organisations to accept them but they can have a powerful reinforcing role in message consumption. An example of a CSA might be a 15-second spot on late-night radio supporting the work of a charity or a government-sponsored initiative. It should be constructed in the same way as a backstory—creative, but to the point. The frame should take into account the relationship of the client to the issue.

Writing an annual report

Annual reports, as described in chapter 4, must be written clearly, concisely, and informatively, but, unlike news releases, they may be constructed as a narrative.

The rules for news release writing also apply to annual reports. The importance of the accuracy of the annual report, for public companies especially, is that they are scrutinised by more than one stakeholder group. Annual reports are subdivided into sections to convey specific information. Subdivisions include:

- a chairman's report
- key result areas
- key performance indicators
- strategic direction
- divisional operational lines
- management presentation
- corporate direction and performance.

The subdivisions on financial performance require no understanding of prose. They are usually arithmetical. The prose subdivision of the report appears towards the front. It includes information on the organisation's:

- corporate social responsibility
- environmental responsibility
- corporate governance
- promotion of equal opportunity.

Corporate goals and objectives are embedded in the prose. When reading an annual report, a stakeholder will identify and link the reading to known strategy. The clue to writing successful prose for an annual report is to write as if you are the stakeholder most interested in the material.

The section on corporate social responsibility should begin with a description of what it is to be socially responsible. In this the writer must avoid jargon but present the material so that it has veracity. The question to ask at this point is: What is corporate social responsibility? Once that has been defined as the first part of the section, the middle section should reflect what socially responsible objectives the organisation has achieved and what it is intending to achieve. This section will be a lot easier than the environmental responsibility section. Writing about environmental responsibility tends to illuminate a conflict rather than show that the objectives are embodied in the organisation. To write this section well requires thought about the actual objectives and whether they are framed inside or outside the organisation. For this section to be effective and to have resonance with stakeholders, it must be written as if the environmental issues are part of the organisation rather than outside the organisation. This is very different to how the section on corporate governance might be written. Corporate or organisational governance require a writer to present images as the language of leadership, whereas environmental responsibility and social responsibility both require the language of inclusion.

The language of leadership in a corporate governance section might also invoke inclusion:

> The organisation is committed to attaining the highest level of corporate governance to ensure the future sustainability of the organisation and to create value for shareholders. To achieve this, the organisation promotes a culture that rewards transparency, honesty, meritocracy, teamwork, and social responsibility.

The language here is undeniable. It shows direction as well as inclusion. It values its employees.

Another example is an organisation that might elect to describe corporate governance before revealing its own philosophy.

> The term 'corporate governance' refers to the promotion of fairness, transparency, and accountability in a company's conduct and principles. A corporate governance policy specifies the rights and responsibilities of different participants in a company, such as its board members, managers, staff, shareholders, and other stakeholders. It also sets the rules and procedures for making decisions on matters such as the appointment of directors, voting practices, auditing arrangements, and disclosure.

The organisation might then describe its own position.

> We strive to enhance our risk management framework while also creating long-term value for you, our members.

Again, this type of language shows both leadership and inclusion by referring to stakeholders more directly in the second person. This style presents stakeholders with a written communication that is balanced and easily understandable. It is also an acknowledgment that the organisation will do everything possible, within a legislative and ethical framework, to achieve the success required by its stakeholders.

Writing a feature story

Feature stories are part of a media relations practitioners' capabilities, whether for submission as uncontrolled material to journalists and editors or as controlled material for inclusion in annual reports, brochures, flyers, or on the internet.

A feature story should be thought of as a long news release with the added benefit of creativity. It is something that can be shaped and written in a more creative style than the news release so that it brings out those *features* of issues or events that are unable to be expressed in detail in the shorter news release format. The internet is a valuable medium for the placement of features. Here is one written by the author for placement in an online journal of opinion. It is written in a more informal style than the news release and can find a home in more unlikely places. Like annual reports, feature stories are also governed by the rules for news release writing. The feature provides the *emotive expression* that is needed to support the *rational expression* of an issue or event as a news release.

THE CHRONICLE: WATCHING BLACK COMEDY AFTER 9/11

How to frame an issue around a feature story

Two darkly witty plays with similar themes of masculinity bound up in anti-Semitism, racism and child abuse, provide audiences in vastly different cities with similar high levels of irritation and offence. Richard Stanton questions audience reactions and why we pay big bucks for something we don't want.

Theatre is no longer a popular form of entertainment. Fewer people attended plays in the whole of the Western world than attended the cinematic opening night of *Star Wars, Episode Three*. Cinema has changed the nature of entertainment to the extent that we pay to become a movie audience so that we can avoid reality. We go to the theatre also to be entertained, but less frequently (ticket price differentials aside) and with additional personal requirements. Cinema provides us with a distraction. Theatre provides us with a connection.

Going to a play is, today, all about the play, rather than both the play and the audience as it was in Marlowe's England. So I was surprised to find myself observing the audiences of plays in Sydney and New York recently as keenly as I observed the content. During a performance of Hannie Rayson's *Two Brothers* in Sydney, I was surprised by the reaction of a couple of thirtysomething women sitting next to me who loudly claimed shock and disbelief that the actors, Gary McDonald and Nick Eadie, were 'demeaning' Muslims. They were offended by the political incorrectness of it all (but not the frequent use of the f-word) and failed to return for the second act and its perfectly clever ending. A week later I attended a performance of Martin McDonagh's *Pillowman* in New York, when two fortysomething women sitting in the row in front of me mouthed disgust at each other as actors Zeljko Ivanek and Jeff Goldblum offended them with vividly politically incorrect f- and c-word descriptions of Jews and Catholics.

The intersection of audience reactions was thought provoking. What was the expectation of these members of the audience? Have they been glazed by their unattached relationship with cinema? Have they never experienced the reality of actors on stage, close by? A Jewish friend who lives in the Bronx provided part of the answer. Audiences since 9/11, she said, no longer seek stimulation through 'trauma entertainment'. Life is now perceived as being too difficult for us to want to engage with reality theatre because there is the ever present possibility that trauma will one day visit each one of us. Audiences have grown comfortable with the distance between them and the medium of cinema. The closeness of a play's content is publicly more confronting.

And it is in the public space of the theatre, connected directly to a traumatic event or issue through the actors in front of us, that we are forced to confront reality. Public discourse shapes opinion and action but public plays about trauma that have their origins in real events appear to be unpalatable, even in cities such as New York and Sydney where the shock of the new is ho hum.

One of Australia's greatest writers, David Foster, once told me he believed now is not the time (historically) for humour in writing, nor for irony. He made this prescient statement well before 9/11. So a brief look at both plays is valuable to see if there is an underlying reason for their audiences to exhibit irritation rather than to laugh out loud at the irony.

Hannie Rayson's *Two Brothers* follows her equally ironic but less confronting *Life After George* (after all, everyone is usually happy to laugh at academics), providing a sketch of political masculinity in all its naked truthfulness. The play is all about two brothers (naturally) one of whom is a neoconservative politician intent upon higher duties, while his younger brother is portrayed as a sociohumanist intent upon finding the best in his fellow beings and working (at relatively low pay) on behalf of refugees. The politician brother appears to be capable of living by the Richardson manifesto 'whatever it takes' as he reveals himself to be capable of pragmatism that embraces all possibilities from adultery to murder. The overarching frame is the international issue of refugee status narrowed down to an Australian perspective and a revisiting of the Australian government's 2002 policy on 'asylum seekers'. There is nothing in the play (beyond the notion of covering up senior ministerial murder) that one could not read in a national newspaper, nor, indeed, in numerous books on the topic.

Martin McDonagh's *Pillowman*, a play that also focuses on two brothers in a similar relationship to Rayson's characters, is about one brother (the ingenious Billy Crudup) defending the other (Michael Stuhlbarg) against a totalitarian police state in which a number of murders have been committed. Crudup plays a writer named Katurian Katurian Katurian (thank you Joseph Heller) who writes about murdered and tortured children, and who, upon discovering that his brother has been acting out his fictional writing, does what he can to protect him from the police, played by Jeff Goldblum and Zeljko Ivanek.

In *Two Brothers* the politician is both the centre of attention and the character requiring protection and support from his brother. It is also he who provides the greatest level of 'offence' to the audience. In *Pillowman* the offending characters are the policemen but they are not the centre of attention.

Both plays take contemporary politically incorrect images—anti-Semitism, racism, child abuse—and fling them at their audiences in the hope that they will hit home and that, as stakeholders, audiences will take a hard look at what is really going on around them. There is an expectation that they will break with their self absorption and begin to make sense of the reality of political and cultural existence. Our self-absorption decreased marginally in the aftermath of 9/11 but we are again moving to higher levels the further we travel in time from that date. This provides part of the answer to the question of why audiences are shocked and offended by these plays. As individual citizens we are moving quietly away from the trauma of 9/11, the trauma of having to be confronted by asylum seekers and the possibility that totalitarian states in which freedom of speech through novel writing could be grounds for persecution. Both plays bring us back to the reality of events that we would rather leave in the past. The cinema does this too, but with less connection; witness the reactions to two recent films, *The Passion of the Christ* and *Downfall*. But characters in movies are on big screens presented as images that are larger than life; we are confronted but in a disconnected way. Theatre is personal; actors are real rather than imagined so we engage with them in real time. Both Rayson and McDonagh have found a way past the barrier that Foster alludes to. They have written provocative works brimming with cleavage rather than consensus, the latter being the position of choice in a politically correct Western world. Or maybe the members of the audiences who were disappointed by the contents, thought they were buying a completely different commodity.

In feature stories we can frame opinions and make statements that are outside the boundaries of the news release or the news story. As we can see from the above example, a feature story can also act as a response to an issue or event that can bring a client directly into the sphere of discussion without appearing to be overtly compromising of the issue or event (for an example of an investigative feature story, see the *Chronicle*: *Inland Marketing Corporation*, chapter 9).

Writing online

The internet is a place for all types of media relations material and most of it appears in some form of disguise. It is difficult for stakeholders to distinguish between material that has been placed as part of a media relations campaign or in its own right unless it appears on a site that is clearly owned by an organisation that uses the same style for its printed material. For the purposes of writing material for online publication, the same rules that govern news releases apply. The differences lie in the embedding within the medium. A feature story about an issue or event, such as that shown above, appears in a serious format in a well-respected journal. The same material appearing in a blog might have a different level of acceptance by stakeholders. Differentiating the levels of acceptability is reflected in the writing style. A large amount of online writing appears in the first person. A site such as US journalist Matt Drudge's *The Drudge Report* provides links to serious news writing as well as providing material written in a skilfully irreverent style that reflects the publisher's personal viewpoint on all types of sociopolitical issues and events. The UN's website, on the other hand, is written in the same style as its printed material. The style for the UN is the style of the organisation no matter where it is placing the material. The style for *The Drudge Report* might not translate into print, just as the UN style has difficulty with the transition to the virtual.

Writing brochure material

A brochure, or flyer, is a short story—a very short story. It must be written in a style that captures all the elements of an issue or event in the same way that a television advertisement captures a story in images lasting thirty seconds. It can be a very effective media relations tactic but only when the text and images are aligned and when the text can transfer meaning quickly and accurately. Brochures are most valuable as political communication tactics but they are frequently written by politicians who have a tenuous link with stakeholder communication. They require the same level of writing skills and professionalism as all other media material.

The writing style for a brochure must be the same as a news release, that is, it must present all relevant information in the first paragraph. A brochure that waffles and floats about looking for a suitable angle somewhere in the body is not effective. Write the lead paragraph for a brochure much the same as you would for a news release. A brochure will usually be limited to between fifteen and twenty paragraphs so it must present all its information succinctly and accurately, with the objective of getting a stakeholder to act on it. It must be written in the first person active voice and present the issue or event in positive language. It will not include quotes. It's denouement will be as strong as its introduction.

A brochure will use short sentences to make its point quickly and concisely:

> Energy security is a global concern. Its importance and influence is not limited to energy policies. Energy security has implications across a range of national and international policies. The need for affordable, reliable and dependable power to provide the essential needs of lighting, cooking, mobility and communications is without question.

This is a good example of a lead item in an eight-page brochure where the essence of the material is distilled into words that should resonate with the wider community as well as being directed at specific energy stakeholders. The idea that energy is used for everyday activities such as cooking but also powers vital global business requirements such as communications stands out as an example of the writer combining emotive and rational images.

Writing a personality profile

Using a profile is a **historicist** tactic. While it can be argued that a news release is a structuralist tactic, in that it relies on its textual message rather than any association with a writer, the profile is rooted in **historicism** and thus modernity. It provides a personal linkage between a stakeholder and an issue or event by interposing information about someone

historicist
an adherent of historicism.

or something that appears to add value to the issue or event in question. In this it is easier to write than the rational news release because it relies for its veracity on emotive style and colour. The personality profile has an additional advantage: it is a personal link that humanises the difficult issue or event and places it within the individual's conceptual grasp. It provides a direct relationship to the emotional links individuals can develop with all types of organisations. It is the human face of media relations and it is used extensively in the Western world's media. Glossy lifestyle magazines, television current affairs programs, even corporate annual reports draw on the personality profile to create attached meaning for diffuse stakeholders.

One of the first media tactics used by the Australian Red Cross on the appointment of former politician Robert Tickner as its managing director was to arrange a personality profile in the magazine supplement of a leading Sunday newspaper. The profile favoured Tickner and focused on his personality and life, an elementary tactic in a media relations strategy designed to reposition a mature organisation.

A personality profile can be written in almost any style. It can be serious, flippant, aspirational, or exotic. It can throw out snippets of information about a person that may not have come to light before. It can be written in the active or passive voice, present or past tense, and does not need a beginning, middle, and end in the conventional sense of the narrative.

6

Developing Media Relationships Around News

- To identify the actors in media relations campaigns.
- To define the characteristics displayed by various actors.
- To understand what is meant by news.

Media relations is a two-way process. Media need sources and sources need media. Media relationships are built strategically around trust and reliability, usually over a long period of time. Media relations practitioners spend a lot of time thinking about how they can get the media interested in their client's issues and events. But on the other side of the wall, the media are thinking about how it can get information about issues and events from clients, or, if clients have them, their media relations people.

THE CHRONICLE: RADIO 2GB AND THE NEW SOUTH WALES PREMIER

The two-way panic

An interesting example of the media seeking information but getting publicly frustrated and more irritated by its unavailability occurred in Sydney in late 2005. The event was the partial subsidence of land above a road tunnel being constructed under the suburb of Lane Cove. The collapse caused a block of apartments directly above the tunnel to break up, and for part of them to fall into the hole that had been created by the subsidence. Heavy peak-hour morning traffic on the adjoining Epping Road was being diverted around the site, as Epping Road remained closed.

A leading Sydney radio broadcaster, Mr Alan Jones, claimed on his early morning program that he had arranged for the New South Wales state premier, Mr Morris Iemma, to contact the program at 7.10 that morning to discuss the issue of roads and their associated tunnel problems around Sydney (this was at a time when Sydney motorists refused to pay a toll to use a newly opened underground road known as the Cross Sydney Tunnel). At 7.15 a.m. when Mr Iemma had not contacted Mr Jones, he began to question why the premier was unavailable and why he had not contacted the station as promised. Mr Jones continued for some minutes during the course of the program to ask where the premier was and to state that he had 'disappeared'. A few moments later he announced that the premier was attending a Ramadan breakfast in Lakemba (a Sydney suburb with a large Middle Eastern population). He went on to say that it was probably lucky the premier was there and not on the radio because he would get a better reception in Lakemba than he would have had he come on air to talk about tunnels collapsing and the generally poor state of the roads in Sydney.

There are a number of things that are important about this anecdote that are related to framing and relationship building. Mr Jones is one of Sydney's leading broadcasters, with a large audience share between Monday and Friday. His radio station 2GB has a talk-show format and a strong relationship with listeners through the provision of talk-back access. Mr Jones is not a supporter of the state Labor government in New South Wales, but had respect for Mr Bob Carr before he resigned from office as the state's longest-serving premier some months before the collapse of the road tunnel. Mr Jones showed less respect for Mr Iemma. Over a long period of time, through his program, Mr Jones demonstrated a dislike for some ethnic groups who showed their lack of respect for the multicultural policy of the New South Wales government. So on one level, there is a pointed attack being made on the premier for paying attention to the issues that concern Middle Eastern groups—terrorism and new security legislation—while ignoring what Mr Jones considers to be more important issues, 'real' problems that affect motorists and the commuting public.

On a second level—the media information-seeking level—this example provides evidence of the two-way panic relationship that exists between the media and those from whom it seeks information. While Mr Jones was content to have built a relationship with former premier Bob Carr, which saw Mr Carr talking regularly on air and thereby keeping Mr Jones's listeners directly informed, the same had not been established with

Mr Carr's successor. Mr Carr's media strategy was very different to Mr Iemma's media strategy. Mr Carr was open and accessible, and he was willing to talk to most metropolitan media every day of the week, including Saturdays and Sundays. For Mr Iemma, other stakeholders—community groups, organisations, and schools, for example—are of equal importance to media stakeholders. Where government business is concerned, Mr Iemma was inclined to give the media information after he had provided it to the other, equally important, stakeholders.

The problem for Mr Iemma is that the media functions well only when supplied with information about issues and events. In the case of the collapsed road tunnel, there was sufficient information for listeners to make immediate decisions about travel arrangements, but Mr Jones was inclined to politicise the issue, thus seeking to get the premier to take some responsibility for the event. For the purposes of acting as a source of information, Mr Jones did not need to seek a discourse with the premier. The relevant spokesman for roads or transport could have supplied all the information that was needed. But for Mr Jones and other high-profile media people, the issue was also one of responsibility and leadership; it was also one of urgency. By failing to speak to Mr Jones that morning, Mr Iemma allowed him to play on the prejudices of his listeners relating to the poor record of infrastructure development undertaken by the state government during its tenure.

The question is one of how best to balance a relationship so that it will not lead a media commentator to imply that there is some urgency or panic attached to an issue or event. In the example, Mr Jones also suggested Mr Iemma's media minders should have contacted him. The general implication or tone of Mr Jones's on-air statements was that the state government of New South Wales is taking no responsibility for actions nor showing any real leadership. Mr Jones was able to frame the road tunnel issue in these political terms because he had developed a specific perception of the premier. We cannot draw an assumption about the relationship that existed between the premier and the broadcaster. We can, however, conclude that, while there may be some relationship building strategy in place within the premier's office, at the time of the road tunnel collapse it was not evident that it was working.

Building a media relationship requires two things: information in which the media are interested, and the ability of a media relations practitioner to supply it. From the perspective of the practitioner, the supply of information that has the potential to become news is part of every campaign that involves the media. A practitioner, or agent, must investigate the angles on the issue or event to build a story that has news potential. But this raises some interesting questions that will be discussed in the following sections:

- What is news and how is it perceived by different media?
- Is news the only element in a media relationship building process that interests a practitioner?

- Is news something that exists between the media and those issues or events from which it emanates?
- How is news imagined by the media? How is news imagined by practitioners?

News as it is imagined by the media

Analysis of the media generally focuses on a linear argument leading off with the media being controlled by markets, markets presenting an image of what they want reported as news, media shaping news in the image of markets with the result that citizens receive and accept unquestioningly the resultant reportage, isolated as consumers rather than intelligent, if stratified, human beings. Supporting this argument is the notion that state power provides the means for news media manipulation through the dissolution of regulation in favour of a liberal global media market in which mergers and acquisitions lead inexorably to a global oligopoly, unfettered and rampant, motivated by profit and intent on subsuming all cultures under a consumer rubric in which sales of goods and services produced by affiliate corporations will forever sustain a global consumer market. Unfortunately for this view, it chooses to conveniently ignore a number of crucial factors in the news process that make such an accusation unsustainable. One is the position of the individual in the process of news gathering, construction, and dissemination: the journalist, reporter, editor, or producer. Another more ridiculously obvious factor, but one that is consistently overlooked in the rush to demonise news media, is the intelligence of the citizen consumer, the person at the end of the line who is inculcating the news.

The news media investigate, analyse, and report to stakeholder publics on issues and events that occur around the globe on a twenty-four-hour, 365-day news cycle. News is a highly valued commodity, particularly for its capacity to assist the process of trade, and specifically for its ability to provide a reference point or a mirror for society to reflect its own actions, behaviours, and attitudes. News has always been crucial to the balance of trade: early on as a localised commodity travelling between villages and towns in a small geographical area, then later developing a life of its own to become a highly valued element in the global trade between nations and other unified actors in the twenty-first century. Unlike gold or other high-value commodities, the financial value of news has remained consistent and unchanged for the past 500 years. Its ownership value, however, has changed markedly between the establishment of the two most important related inventions during that time, the printing press and the personal computer.

News is a product of technology and trade, yet most global news is received by its publics after it has been localised. Terrorist acts in North America, Indonesia, and Spain, earthquakes in Japan, and floods in South America become news in other parts of the world when the event or issue has been *imagined* in terms of its local actors. Media localises news so that it can be easily digested and rendered practical. Harmonisation of tariffs or the issue of codification of standards remain theoretical until they are grounded in the *local*. Codification of standards for the manufacture and distribution of a particular good—a computer component—is a non-newsworthy issue until it is grounded in the local, for example, Hungarian manufacturing standards being maintained at a particular level if Hungary is to continue trading with its EU partners.

Figure 6.1 Working to meet a deadline

Imagining news ownership

What do I mean by 'imagination'? The eighteenth-century English writer Samuel Taylor Coleridge suggested that imagination is either primary or secondary. Primary, he argued, was the living power of all human perception. It is no coincidence that Coleridge, like many Western writers, moved freely between literary and journalistic pursuits, and thus applied imagination equally to the literary task as to the journalistic.

Reporters and journalists produce news on behalf of client stakeholders in the same way that coal is produced and generated as energy on behalf of clients. Coal is extracted from the Powder River Basin in the USA and generated as energy in steel mills in Japan and Korea. It is extracted from the Hunter Valley in Australia and generated as energy in power stations to provide electricity to the states of New South Wales and Victoria. Clients of the commodity owners in the Powder River Basin are Japanese car manufacturers and Korean shipbuilders. There is no citizen involvement in the trade. Clients of the commodity owners in Australia are the governments of New South Wales and Victoria. Clients of commodity owners can be involved in private or state enterprise, or can be dual organisations with interests in both private and public sector activities. Clients of commodity owners of news are the same manufacturers, the same shipbuilders, and the same traders, all of whom have an interest in the validity of the trade taking place in the competitive market in which they operate.

Thus, journalists and reporters are producing news for the benefit of those with the capacity to act upon or to verify something in response. The citizen is not part of the action or verification in any important way. Citizens may act or verify in some marginal way—acquiring end products or services generated by the initial activity—but involvement is restricted to a peripheral role as observer of the main game. The mere act of consumption of news does not place a citizen in the main game other than in a minor role. There is no avenue for that citizen to become an important actor in either a political or economic sense. In this, business journalists and reporters are of special interest as they work in an environment where the citizen is even more marginalised. The news gathering and producing activity revolves around generation of interest by commodity owners for commodity owners in much the same way as economist David Ricardo outlined the operations of earlier mercantilists in a competitive market in his *Principles of Political Economy and Taxation*. Business journalists and reporters gather and produce news specifically for business clients. Most citizens have little or no interest in it. Business news is thus imagined in such a way as to fit the frame of business activity. Whether it is global or local is irrelevant; it is the news of business that creates actions or verifications in the competitive market.

In seeing how the news media imagine issues and events in political and economic terms, we can begin to understand how these imaginings are translated into a twenty-first-century society and how news might shape all types of communities.

Media news frames

Media conferences about issues and events are not accessible to citizens. United Nations, presidential, and indeed, corporate press briefings are all held in private. They are contractual arrangements between the members of the media and the news generator. At the UN, news media are issued with green and white identity cards that allow them to attend closed briefings with the secretary-general. UN delegates with full rights to all other spaces in UN headquarters, including the Security Council chamber, are not allowed into the news media briefing room. The news media briefing reinforces the notion of exclusion by imagining the requirement of engagement to be between equals.

The media imagine and then frame issues and events in parts of the world that are accessible. Closed economies, such as those of North Korea and Cuba, provide no engagement for imagining, so they are excluded from the news cycle. Media imagine events and issues on the margins of their own experience. They report when there is a direct connection from the event or issue to their own experience. In terms of engagement all others are considered alien.

Aspects of the reporter's work have been described as the interpretative moment, the interrogative moment, and the adversarial moment (see, for example, McNair 2000). A typology of reporting is, therefore, required to relate the three aspects to news generation, news gathering, and news reporting. But it is the adversarial moment, the actual interview between a reporter (actor) and a performer, that is of interest here, as is the other defining element of the typology, news reception when viewed as normative. An important aspect of the typology of the adversarial moment is the reporter interview in which information from the performer is accepted without qualification, transcribed as fact, and published as opinion.

A typology of reporter relationships highlights some of the problems confronting those gathering and interpreting news. Reporters can be proactive or reactive in sourcing material and assessing its newsworthiness. Proactive reporters are those who develop and maintain a strong book of contacts, regardless of political affiliation. In this group, contacts would be those not outwardly motivated by political partisanship or commercial gain—clergy, school principals, police commanding officers, senior government officials, business owners, senior health administrators—those able and willing to provide background information on issues and events. In the event that a reporter does not maintain a strong contact list there must be a reliance either on the reporter's own knowledge or in the veracity of the information supplied by the source.

As the motivation for supply of information from a source is frequently self-interest, it must always be verified. Reactive reporters rely on politically motivated sources for most, if not all, their information. This is a dangerous position to be in, as reporters are already vulnerable to disinformation, the reporting of untruths, and sophisticated information and propaganda machinery.

The power of newspaper reporters lies in the decisions they make regarding what to report, which is a process of informed decision-making rather than luck. While the reporter must make a decision about inclusion or exclusion as a primary motive there are numerous other factors that assist in the decision process.

News as commodity

News is a commodity that is traded at elite levels between producers and consumers. There is no space for the public to engage in the trade other than as observers. Observation status is accorded to the public to validate news as a tradable yet scarce commodity. Receipt of the commodity by a buyer provides no validation on its own; there must be a third party, one that is unable to purchase or use the commodity for it to have value. The public, for example, is unable to purchase coal directly from the producer because the public has observer status in the production and generation of energy from coal. The whole process of extraction, production, and generation of electricity from coal bypasses the citizen in a complicated relationship between producers and generators, in much the same way as the complicated process of news production and generation bypasses the citizen, whose only recourse is to engage with the process as an end user. There is no coincidence in the fact that producer and generator act in the same way for coal as they do for news.

Reporters and journalists, when acting as producers on behalf of generators, set aside the act of being a citizen—end use—and move into a position of power with a direct relationship to commodity owners. By removing themselves from the act of being a citizen, reporters and journalists are able to act as producers on behalf of generators in much the same way as theatre actors take on a stage role that is different to their normal lives. Reporters and journalists must work with a degree of separation from normalcy to act as producers. Otherwise, the vagaries, the dross of everyday existence, would come into play as part of the process of news production. It is difficult enough for reporters and journalists to imagine news in terms other than those proscribed by wealth and power without the addition of the burden of citizenship.

As good citizens we actively seek information for a variety of reasons but it is rarely information that has a bearing on our behaviour and attitudes. We cannot always act on the information in relation to our own selves or to others. News of local weather may help us decide what to wear each day but news of global weather has no bearing on our behaviour, unless we are planning to travel, although we will need additional information by the time we arrive.

News as it is imagined by the media relations practitioner

For the reporter, there are two important stakeholders: the media owner and the news source. Audiences, readers, viewers—stakeholders who absorb news as a commodity—are secondary to the ritual of news gathering and production.

Figure 6.2 A media relations strategy meeting—working on a soft-drink campaign in Europe

For the practitioner or agent, there are also two primary stakeholders: the client and the media themselves—reporters, journalists, editors, and producers. In the case of the agent, the relationships are more complex. The client, like the media owner, is the primary stakeholder with financial control of the commodity. But it is also the source. While the reporter is building two relationships that run parallel, the agent is building two separate and discrete relationships within one entity: the client as owner and source. For the agent, a third stakeholder relationship—the media—is equally important. In this the relationship between agent and reporter is sometimes unbalanced. A reporter may use an agent as a source but is free to use other sources and to produce news that is unsourced—issues and events that are observed and reported without interpretation. The agent, however, is usually obliged to interpret and find an angle from material sourced directly from the client. This has been the traditional method of building media relationships. The agent investigates client source material, interprets it, finds a suitable angle, then directs it to the media. The strategic intent is to find a suitable angle that reflects a particular medium, and then, find an alternative angle for another medium. A tactic that is in wider use is to find partnerships in the angle. This enables the agent to split the source and the client and, in doing so, to create a more objective frame for the story, the same way a journalist seeks an alternative viewpoint for story balance.

This tactic requires the client's agreement to include an additional stakeholder in the frame and to have an understanding that the additional stakeholder may end up getting more media coverage than the client.

THE CHRONICLE: THE CAR DESIGNER USING COMPUTER TECHNOLOGY

How to present an issue to a business magazine

Examples of third-person stakeholders becoming part of the primary campaign frame are everywhere. One that the author was involved in establishing concerned a client who was a manufacturer of sophisticated three-dimensional computer-design technology, a nice thing to make, but as such, holding little interest for media other than computer publications. The media campaign objective was to find a way to interest the business press in the technology, that is, business magazines such as *BRW*, which are highly influential. Organisations use such media to support strategic acquisition decisions. If a corporation is preparing to purchase new information technology, then management, as well as reading about operational specifications in specialist trade publications, also wants to know what the company's competitors are using and thinking. For this they turn to business magazines and television business programs such as Nine Network's *Business Sunday*.

The client with the design technology was a large North American organisation with a relatively new presence in the Australian, New Zealand, and Asian markets. Having a feature story in a business magazine had the potential to introduce the company as an organisation with strong overseas credentials, but not much else. There was not much chance of it being accepted by the editor as a straight reporting piece on the arrival of yet another big American company, but what the organisation did have was a relatively new relationship with a Victorian industrial design firm that had secured a contract to design and model a new version of a well-known family sedan. The client had supplied the designer with computers and the design technology that was needed to secure the motor vehicle contract. While the designer was relatively well known in the Victorian market, it was not nationally or internationally recognised as a leading motor vehicle modeller. So the strategy had a twofold impact: it would link the client to a local user of its technology—a user that had secured a major deal with an international car maker—and it would provide the design firm with much-needed publicity, an endorsement for the car maker that it had selected the right modeller. In this the media are complicit, especially the specialist media. For specialist media to be successful they must find feature stories and images that reflect a high standard of professional journalism, but as they are working in a limited market, they must look more creatively for their source material.

The issue for the agent was to form an agreement between the client and the third person—the design firm—to invite a business journalist from a highly influential magazine to tour the design plant in order to see in operation the highly sophisticated technology and, crucially, to see how a motor car is modelled from its early design phase. But this was a sensitive area. The car maker did not want its design revealed before the company was ready; a confidentiality agreement with the designer for just such a contingency had been signed. The compromise was to show the reporter as much as possible without revealing the final design. The issue for the agent was to frame the story in such a way that it reflected a possible interest for the journalist in how business partnerships are formed. A second frame represented the small design firm securing an important modelling contract through business growth and development with support from an information technology manufacturer.

The agent's job was complex. As well as estimating a budget for the campaign and establishing a timeframe that fitted three stakeholders—the magazine deadline, the designer's availability, and the client having the technology in operation—the agent was responsible for writing the initial background material, organising and scheduling the travel and accommodation arrangements for the reporter and the client, and keeping an open dialogue between the client and the designer in the weeks leading up to the event (the event, in this case, being the tour of the design plant, interviews, and lunch with the client and the designer, and arranging the whole schedule so the journalist could use free time in Melbourne to attend to other magazine business).

The result was a three-page feature spread in the magazine that highlighted the design company and the car company contract. The success of the campaign, for the client, was measured by the number of enquiries that were made about the technology immediately after publication. The name of the client was mentioned three times.

This example shows the value of using a third person to provide balance to a story and to build a media relationship that indicates to a reporter that a client is not using deception when presenting information. The additional source acts in the same way as the reporter's additional source. Not only does it provide legitimacy, but it also offers the reporter the potential to build a relationship with the third person for future information gathering.

The use of the term 'third person' in this context differs from that explored by W Phillips Davidson (1983) and developed by Hyun Soon Park and Charles Salmon (2005) where the third-person effect is defined as occurring when one believes media content has a greater effect on others than on oneself. But it does have some resonance in that a reporter will behave in a way that is proposed by an agent when there is a belief that there is objectivity attached to the issue or event in question. It could be distilled to something like: if you don't believe the stuff works really well, come and talk to the bloke down the road. He uses it and he swears by it.

Building a media relationship

As described above, a media relationship with specialist print or electronic media can be built through inclusive mechanisms such as the introduction of a third person. It also requires the establishment of trust. A reporter receiving material expects it to be accurate and factual. If at some stage it emerges that it is not accurate or factual, any level of trust that has been established will disintegrate and the reporter will never use the source again. For agents, the prospect of a reporter refusing to deal with them should be catastrophic. Many media relations practitioners believe, however, that there is an infinite supply of reporters waiting for them to pitch client material to. There is a tendency in some agencies and among some inhouse practitioners to treat the media as a disposable commodity. Frequent telephone calls and emails asking if a news release is going to *get a run* are the irritating tactics used by agents to attempt to influence the media. As every media person knows, the build-up of irritation and annoyance that accumulates from this daily routine is mostly responsible for poor relationships. The main culprits are the inexperienced and those who have very little to say about a client's issue or event. Despite this, they persist in sending reporters and journalists news releases every time a client breathes. The solution lies in building a stronger relationship with the client and in not overemphasising the importance of the media relationship. Part of the problem for media relations practitioners begins when they make promises they know they are unable to deliver on. To promise to obtain coverage in a major national or metropolitan newspaper for some minor client or event is asking for trouble. The agent is locked into a position from where there is no retreat. Yet the promise has been made in the knowledge that it would be almost impossible to find an angle on a minor piece of information that would give it news value. Another part of the problem lies in the fact that public relations practitioners are sometimes not as familiar as they should be with news values and news gathering. It is one thing to be competent to write a news release. It is another altogether to be able to create a strong angle that might have news value or to know when and where to offer it to a medium.

A good media relationship can be built by anyone, just the same as a good personal relationship can be built. The difficulty for media relations practitioners is twofold. It begins when they believe they have a stronger claim to the relationship than non-PR experts. In this the media will sometimes appear to have stronger relationships with citizens whom they perceive to have no active involvement in attempting to gain from influence and persuasion. The media sometimes view clients in this way; they do not view clients in the same way that they view practitioners. And they do not view all practitioners through the same lens. If they did, there would be no space within the public or private spheres for relationship building or dialogic communication.

Building client–media relationships

Media relations practitioners make decisions about whether to introduce clients to reporters and journalists, just as the media make decisions about whether to accept the invitation. Inhouse agents appear to be more forthright in making introductions on the understanding that they will continue to develop the relationship as a whole-of-organisation strategy. The image of the managing director of a corporation, for example, is the image of the company, so a media relationship built around the managing director is also being built around the company. Freelance agents, on the other hand, tend to be more cautious in their introductions. There is a residual concern that once the relationship has been established, the agent will no longer be required. In some cases, the media use this to distance themselves from an agent while maintaining communication with the client. From an ethical perspective there are arguments for and against such behaviour.

It can be argued that it is always in the best interests of the client to expose them to media practices and that, in doing so, the agent will strengthen their own relationships with both the client and the media. Exposure enables the issue or event in question to be enunciated by the client and the agent. The agent can interpret the issue or event into a media frame, and the client can maintain it in a technical sense to add value to its meaning.

Before setting out to establish a relationship, an agent must decide who in the media is most important to a client and to an issue. This is achieved by creating a research program that builds profiles of media people. There are a number of proprietary programs that provide information about media people but any proprietary program will benefit from the addition of individual research by an agent.

Some agents choose to pitch all their clients at one or two media people. Clients in the financial services sector, for example, can be introduced to journalists at the *Australian Financial Review*, banking trade publications, or to television producers on programs such as *Good Morning Australia*. Full service agents have a more difficult task. Their clients range across industries and sectors so they need to keep track of and contact with a range of media people. This makes client introductions riskier (for a discussion of risk, see chapter 11). It takes some time to develop and maintain relationships with journalists, and so agents with a broad range of clients tend to control the relationship, or at least try to control them. An agent might invite a reporter on the *Australian Financial Review* to lunch with a client, while actively engaging in the promotion of other clients.

THE CHRONICLE: CLIENT OVERLAP

How to successfully link client issues

One example in which the author was involved concerned the issue of apartment construction in Sydney's central business district. The city council was in the process of changing legislation to allow highrise apartment development, which affected the client organisation in question. The organisation's managing director was advised to establish a dialogue with the property section of the *Australian Financial Review* so that information about certain technical elements of the policy change could be set out. The agent suggested inviting the property editor of the newspaper to lunch.

At the same time, the agent had as a client a major international hotel that wished to publicise its involvement in an event that would not normally be considered by a newspaper such as the *AFR*. The agent set up the lunch in the hotel's first-class restaurant and arranged for the hotel's marketing manager to drop by the table towards the end of the lunch. The hotel marketing manager dropped by the table, then went off to find the hotel manager and, as a matter of courtesy, introduce him to the client and the editor. The hotel manager offered the party complimentary dessert and coffee and, in passing, mentioned the event that was to occur the following week. The editor was interested in establishing a relationship with the agent's construction client as a source of valuable information but at the same time was pleased to have been introduced to the manager of an international hotel group without having to do any leg work. The agent was pleased because the construction client became a source for the *AFR* editor on an important issue. The hotel client was pleased, too, because its event was publicised in a newspaper with a strong circulation among the hotel's stakeholders.

The profile of the *AFR* property editor that had been built by the agent included background on previous employment and writing style. It also included the direction or theme that the editor had taken in the past on issues such as government policy change. This allowed the agent to build a profile which showed the editor was sympathetic to the idea of highrise apartment construction and was receptive to the arrival of international hotels as spaces for business discussion.

Building a profile of a journalist is something that must be circumscribed by the ethical standards of the profession. It is not acceptable to investigate a journalist's personal or family history, or to seek information from colleagues and friends. The ethics of the action of profile building is not codified by governing bodies in public relations, yet its continuous use and importance is undeniably part of the structure of relationship building.

Profile building in public relations terms is the same as in media terms. The media investigate issues and events and the individuals and organisations with which they are associated within the boundaries of a code of ethics. But at the same time they build profiles of individuals and organisations from which they frame and write stories. The advantage for the media lies in their capacity to publish and broadcast, whereas the media relations practitioner investigates and gathers information for the express purpose of understanding a journalist's motivation and behaviour in order to frame a client's issue or event for the journalist.

Setting media and client priorities

In building a media relationship, a campaign issue or event is the central focus. The client and the media are attached to the campaign at either end. The campaign is the dog, the media the tail, the client the head (body + head + tail). Development of a campaign strategy requires an agent to think about how the dog's body is going to relate to the head and the tail. An agent must put together three elements:

- a coherent issue
- an informed client
- a receptive media.

It is the agent's responsibility to shape the client's informed-ness just as much as it is to shape the receptiveness of the media. So the agent must be totally informed and receptive to the issue or event.

When framing an issue in a certain way, an agent must think about the type of people it is being framed for. The agent must think about the type of event or activity that might support the issue and assist to frame it in a favourable way. Sending a picture of an event such as the launch of a new car to a radio program is not a good way to develop a relationship with a radio journalist. Similarly, sending a ten-page detailed backstory about the technical specifications of the car to a morning television entertainment program would be equally silly.

So, how do we develop relationships with various elements of mass media— journalists, reporters, editors, producers, bloggers, or with specific newspapers, magazines, trade journals, radio stations, television stations, internet sites?

In the process of working out how best to capture an image of journalists and why it is not a good idea to inundate them with press material that bears no relationship to their medium we need to keep in mind the image of reporters, looking thoroughly bored and irritated, sitting at their computer terminals and surrounded by large stacks of news releases.

An agent has a number of things to deal with besides getting copy to sparkle. Once upon a time an agent could make a telephone call and invite a journalist to lunch, a tactic that would stop the journalist from being irritated and cranky for a short time and get them to focus on a client's issue or event. Now there are far fewer journalists to deal with the same amount of work. But there is more to this than the demise of the long lunch. Reporters are not always cranky and irritated and they think very seriously about why they accept material that could have an angle and become copy for their publication or broadcast. The angle is the most important element.

While a reporter must find a good copy angle, so a media relations practitioner must find an angle that will interest a reporter and at the same time satisfy a client. It is not enough to satisfy the client. Most times, if a client is happy with an angle, it won't reflect a strong news or feature angle for a reporter. An agent must try to balance the media interest with client satisfaction. This is the most difficult part of building a media relationship.

Sometimes it is not a good idea to put a client in the same room as a reporter. At other times it is the best thing to do. For this to be successful a client must be well informed and educated about media practice.

Here we need to ask ourselves a number of questions about our client:

- Is the client capable of handling a general press conference?
- Is the client capable of handling a radio interview?
- Is the client capable of presenting a positive image in a television interview?

How to trade on the relationship

The best relationship between a client and the media occurs at B2B publication level (but don't confuse *best* with *ethical*). Trade publications (B2B) are industry and specialist magazines in which advertising plays a central role in profitability. All media relies on advertising for its profitability and sustainability, but trade publications have a convention whereby buying an advertisement will almost guarantee editorial space. Ads don't usually appear on the same page as the editorial, which enables the publisher to claim objectivity. Advertising sales people on these publications generally offer an editorial placement as a sweetener as part of the ad package if a client is a bit reluctant. This places the editor or reporter on the magazine in an interesting position. But many of these publications are subscription-based (a large part of the revenue). Subscribers want to know everything about the specific product or service offered by the publication to their industry, so they are usually quite happy to receive additional information in an editorial form. Most of the time client material is run as is by trade magazine editors and reporters. But is this enough to sustain a media relations professional? Does the practitioner have a fistful of clients who are interested only in trade publications? Most media relations practitioners have a regular group of clients in selected industry sectors. On top of this, they have clients who come and go, depending upon what is required. An agency might be very good at building relationships with health industry reporters and might have two clients for whom they regularly place material. They might then call themselves 'specialist health public relations' and pitch for more clients in that sector, or they might be more generalist and work across, say, health, fashion, the environment, and energy. But the environment and energy don't fit very well together, so they might not have too many environment clients if they work for a uranium miner, for example, or a petroleum explorer.

Media relations practitioners tend to specialise in complementary areas, for example:

- energy = mining + electricity + building products
- fashion = clothing + footwear + textiles
- health = aged care + nurses + private hospitals
- environment = fishing + forests + national parks

Natural synergies tend to form around specific areas of industry. Other examples might be:

- information technology = mobile telephone + software + games
- banking = products + services + technology
- finance = investors + insurance + leasing
- retail = products + service + textiles
- education = universities + high schools + tafe
- sport = netball + hockey + softball
- aviation = airlines + insurance + fuel
- motor vehicles = cars + trucks + motorbikes.

From this we can see that trade and specialist publications are relatively simple to build relationships with. To build these relationships an agent must:

- provide crisp, clean copy
- provide plenty of potential copy
- have clients in a related industry
- have a client advertising budget
- link a client and an editor together.

But the question is whether this strategy will work for other media. Can the agent apply it to:

- regional newspapers
- regional radio and television
- metropolitan newspapers
- national television
- metropolitan radio
- international news magazines
- other country media?

Some of the tactics will be the same—crisp, clean copy, for example. But the strategy will be different. The first principle in developing a strategy is to understand with whom the relationship is being built. Therefore, an agent must build a profile of the person or people they are seeking to influence and persuade.

We all think we know a bit about Rupert Murdoch and Kerry Stokes because they are high-profile media owners. We think we know a bit about their politics and which political parties they support. But can we translate this to all Stokes and Murdoch editors, reporters, journalists, and producers? Can we stereotype them because they work for the same media organisation? Does Paul Sheehan fit the same stereotype as David Marr, both of whom write opinion pieces for the *Sydney Morning Herald*? As writers for the education section of the *Australian Financial Review* do Peter Roberts and Tim Dodd have the same ideology and thinking on issues? Does Julie Robotham, the health editor for the *Herald*, have the same ideas and thinking as Margot Saville, a business writer for the *Herald*? The answer to all these is, of course, no. To begin to get a feel for how each individual reporter or editor or journalist or producer thinks and feels, we can research and investigate the material they have already had published. What we will find is that Paul Sheehan is a bit right of centre, but David Marr is left of centre, that Paul Sheehan takes a macro view of the economy while David Marr takes a micro view of the economy. This is the start of profiles on both these opinion writers based on a simple investigation of material. An agent could go back further and discover that Sheehan turned right sometime during the early 1990s but that Marr has always veered left. This information would help to understand how to frame an issue relative to the opinion writers the agent might like to get to write an opinion about a client's issue.

Not all media relationships are equal

The media itself is big business, so there is a natural inclination for media proprietors to develop business and government relationships at high levels. By any measure, the relationships that develop between the media as big business and other big business, such as banking and finance, mining and construction, or textiles and clothing, to name a few, are persuasive and influential. And they are all the subject of strategic intent that flows from public relations, public affairs, and public diplomacy.

The UN, for example, with 191 countries as principle stakeholders, is a powerful global organisation that is continuously maintaining and building relationships with a huge number of other stakeholders, among them the media. The UN has a department of public information with a full-time undersecretary devoted to developing and maintaining relationships with global media organisations, while at the same time the secretary-general is constantly developing and building relationships with media owners and proprietors as part of the organisation's public relations, public affairs, and public diplomacy strategies. High-level relationship building from a powerful organisation is sometimes easier to construct than that proposed by a local media relations agent interested in local media. But the principle is the same. Just as media proprietors use certain strategies to attempt to persuade and influence governments, corporations, and communities, so, too, does the media relations agent use the same strategies to persuade and influence the media.

In the case of the UN, Secretary-General Kofi Annan can ask for a meeting with high-level media owners such as Sumner Redstone (Viacom), Rupert Murdoch (News Corporation), or John Malone (Liberty Media) without fear of rejection and with every likelihood that any discussion will be guaranteed to form part of the day's news. The relationship is already established between powerful elites. A local agent attempting to establish a meeting for a client with a journalist, editor, or producer, while the same in principle, has no established link that presents the client's credentials in the same manner. The relationship must begin with a strategy that positions the client at a level that is perceived to be acceptable to the journalist in question.

Building relationship equality

Corporations, governments, and media in Western democracies function at a level above all other groups and organisations. In a vertical public sphere, corporations, media, and governments have staked the high ground, while others, such as NGOs, not-for-profit groups, and special interest or grassroots groups attempt to climb from the lower levels of the hierarchy so that they can be seen to be operating at the same level as corporations, the media, and governments with the concomitant resources and wealth attached to such position.

Within the conservative framework of existing Western democracies this is a difficult—almost impossible—task as these outsiders do not share the ideologies of corporations, media, and governments in that they are less focused on profit. The outsider groups, however, continue to seek funding from governments and publicity from media, but frequently fail in their endeavours because they do not present themselves as equal in stature to the triumvirate.

This implies that hegemonic structures preclude these stakeseekers from being part of the game, thus rendering them unable to develop or build relationships with media. There is, however, an alternative path to recognition, a cleverly concealed path that does not require an organisation to demonstrate its credentials within the triangular frame on the corporate, government, and media plateau at the top of the hierarchy. A level can be attained that can exploit the triumvirate if an organisation (a stakeseeker) has the capacity to represent itself in a non-threatening manner.

I call this a *mezzanine level*. Mezzanine level groups or organisations claim space between NGOs and the power elite (corporations and governments). In this regard they lie outside an acknowledged frame that requires corporations and governments dealing with grassroots groups to act confrontationally. Mezzanine groups are capable of influence and persuasion at a high level, outside established conventions of confrontation that occur between governments and grassroots groups, without allowing their various publics to redeem what Mayhew has referred to as **rhetorical tokens** (Mayhew 1997). Grassroots groups are viewed as confrontational by institutionalised power, as provoking conflict rather than consensus. Mezzanine status, because it lies outside this framework and is difficult to label, confers a degree of consensus, thereby removing conflict and confrontation, and enabling an organisation to present harmonious proposals and strategies. Examples of organisations that have claimed mezzanine status are Greenpeace and the World Energy Council. Australian examples are the Lowy Institute and the Sydney Institute. A clue to mezzanine success is the capacity of the organisation to present its strategies to media and government in such a way that it will appear to exist at the same level as the institutions it is attempting to influence and persuade. Grassroots community groups, on the other hand, most often fail to influence and persuade the institutions of media and government because they fail to understand their complexity and their relationship to each other. (For a discussion and further detailed example of a mezzanine success strategy, see the *Chronicle: Inland Marketing Corporation*, chapter 9.)

rhetorical tokens
political promises.

Part 3

Organisations and the Basis of Practice

7

Framing the Story in a Corporate Campaign

CHAPTER OBJECTIVES

■ To develop an understanding of the position of the corporation in media relations.

■ To understand how framing and relationship building are used in the corporate and business world.

The hegemonic position of the corporation in the field of media relations is axiomatic. Corporations exercise power over all types of stakeholders in the pursuit of profit. They are enormously influential by virtue of their ability to fund issues and events at high levels. Corporate funding of media relations rivals presidential election campaign spending. A motor vehicle manufacturer has a budget for an event such as the launch of a new car that includes flying hundreds of motoring journalists around the world first class, providing five-star accommodation and meals, and access to the new cars. A computer company might have a similar travel and accommodation budget, but it might also include the cost of providing thousands of reporters worldwide with the software or hardware that is the reason behind the issue or event. As *Vogue* magazine says, the goodies bags or the gifting of products to media and others in the fashion world has become an industry in itself (*Vogue Australia* December 2005). It is not unusual for a fashion reporter to walk away from an industry event with a goodies bag worth more than $3000.

This opening paragraph is an acknowledgment that power emanates from a strong financial position. For media relations, the capacity to ignite and sustain successful campaigns has its basis in strong financial investment. But the financial investment in relationship building made by a corporation must have its basis in the efficacy of the product or service on which an issue or event is hung. The result is three-cornered. This position is also known in literature as a *tricolon* or, in philosophy, as a *triple tau* and is not unusual. Stability for a media relations tricolon occurs when three requirements are met: an optimum injection of funds, a well-planned and ethical issue or event, and an acceptable product or service. The corporation, or its products and services, must be seen to be part of a milieu, by which I mean they must actively engage at a local level with those at whom they are pitched. A media relationship will fail if the corporation is perceived to be above or beyond its stakeholders. A car maker, for example, operates a complex multibillion-dollar manufacturing plant in which it assembles the world's most expensive consumer products. In building a media relationship, the car maker will take journalists on factory tours to show how the car is built, but even the most technically fastidious among them will omit such detail from filed copy. They might write about the robotic technology, or the level of finish quality, but overall the frame will reflect the image of the vehicle as something that relates directly to the individual stakeholder purchaser at the end of the production process, and it will all be planned as part of the media relationship building process. Similarly, in the world of high fashion, which trickles downwards from elite access to designer clothes, bags, and shoes worth hundreds of thousands of dollars, to the same designs mass-produced for general consumption, the tricolon must be established. When the fashion house Louis Vuitton opened its new headquarters in Paris in late 2005, its presence was an issue and event on its own. The corporation had commissioned the design of a new building in a prominent position in Paris's most spectacular thoroughfare, the Champs Élysées. The unveiling of the building, the associated event, and guests who included actresses Uma Thurman, Catherine Deneuve, and Sharon Stone, was a media spectacular. It generated worldwide media interest on a scale normally associated with natural disasters or stock-market collapses. The entire purpose—the multimillion-dollar building, the multimillion-dollar party, the multimillion-dollar media coverage—was all about selling expensive products.

Building corporate content through media relationships

The media are not merely important to the image of a corporation, they are also its lifeblood. Advertising plays a seriously important role in building a corporate image, but news has the capacity to cause all relationship building to collapse in on itself.

A corporate image that takes years to build through advertising and the generation of good products and services can be destroyed overnight with bad news reporting. Media relations plays a vital role in building a corporate image or corporate identity, but it is the policy or actions of corporations that generate news and stakeholder interest. Image and identity flow from actions and policies. A corporation or business going about its day-to-day routine is not news. It makes and creates products and services. It is when its products or services alter the shape of the public sphere that they and their owners become newsworthy. The job of the media relations counsel in the corporate world is twofold: to keep some issues and events away from the media and to put others forward.

British public relations scholar Kevin Moloney (2005) suggests that public relations (and thus media relations) has been unduly demonised as being responsible for the power exercised by corporations and businesses when, in reality, public relations is communicative actions and methods employed within a market economy. While its skills set neither favours nor denies business, it has historically been instrumental in assisting businesses and corporations to exert their powers. But, as I have shown in other chapters, it also plays a role with governments, interest groups, community groups, and global non-government organisations such as the UN in exerting influence and persuasion as power. The fact that all types of organisations at the beginning of the twenty-first century use media relations strategies and tactics at all levels of experience is a clear endorsement of their relevance and efficacy.

Part of the problem for the media when attempting to report corporate and other business activities is access, which is why television footage of a corporate issue or event is confined to the outside of buildings, occasionally to a foyer or lobby, and to corporate logos.

Corporate practice

As I have mentioned elsewhere, the nature of the corporation is to produce profitable goods and services. Profit is the motivating force and thus *positive*, so the exercise of persuasion and influence is *strategic*. During the last quarter of the twentieth century Grunig (1984) defined the subfield of corporate relations around four models which he himself had apprehended from the work of Thayer (1968) on **synchronic** and **diachronic communication**. As mentioned above, the models were called press agentry or publicity, public information, **two-way asymmetrical**, and **two-way symmetrical**. The two-way asymmetrical and two-way symmetrical models both received sustained attention from critical scholars, with the result that the two-way asymmetrical model was demonised as part of a positive theory that explained how corporations used

synchronic communication

communication that occurs at a particular time in history; in particular with reference to language and culture.

diachronic communication

any type of communication that can be tracked through time; especially with regard to language or culture.

two-way asymmetrical

the third of James Grunig's models defined by the ability of a stakeholder to extract information from another stakeholder and to use it to some advantage without a concomitant advantage for the other stakeholder.

two-way symmetrical

the fourth of James Grunig's models defined by the ability of stakeholders to share extracted information to their mutual advantage.

persuasion and influence to their advantage, while the two-way symmetrical model was viewed as a normative theory that only explained how corporate relations should be practised: it was not in reality a workable model. Grunig developed his models and published widely, resulting in further negative engagement with the ideal of two-way symmetrical communication.

A great deal of scholarly work has investigated the relationship of corporations to their stakeholders and has concluded that the two-way asymmetrical model, or at least exemplifications of it, serves to sustain the goals and objectives of corporate communication strategies. This assumes corporations are uninterested in dialogue with oppositional stakeholders and uninterested in relationship building with other stakeholders such as media.

Corporations, however, are not the bad guys, unless one is opposed to a market economy. In today's global political economy, as Grunig himself acknowledges (Heath 2001), the exercise of persuasion and influence on and from a variety of stakeholders, including activists opposed ideologically to corporate existence, has created a shift towards the two-way symmetrical model, not as a utopian theory, but as a dialogic relationship-building model. The shift may not yet have been satisfactorily measured. It may remain normative, but if the emergence and diffuse adoption of one important element known as corporate social responsibility (CSR) at the beginning of this century is a guide, then there is some degree of intuitive change occurring in corporate communication in the direction of a dialogic relationship building model based on Grunig's two-way symmetrical model.

Strategy selection in corporate communication

This book is about media relationship building. Its central theoretical model is framing, but to present framing in a clear contextual way the book must also describe some of the other relevant models and theories. One of the most important theoretical developments, especially in the corporate communication sphere, has been the work of US communications expert Vincent Hazleton. Hazleton argues that Grunig's models associated with the excellence theory are flawed because they do not adhere to the situational requirement inherent in the term *strategy*. Hazleton built on Grunig's work to develop empirical taxonomies of corporate relations strategies which include message and receiver variables in describing the corporate relations behaviour of organisations. They should be seriously considered when looking for an alternative to Grunig's normative theory (for a full discussion of Hazleton's work, see Botan & Hazleton 2006). Hazleton argues that corporate communication strategies selected by organisations are dependent upon a number of variables connected to different stakeholders. Corporations, he says, will not use the same strategy in any two similar situations if the variables alter. His work is based on a large survey in the USA.

Hazleton's seven strategies are these:

1 *Informative*—based on the presentation of unbiased facts. A presumption that a stakeholder public will infer conclusions from accurate data.
2 *Facilitative*—making resources available to a stakeholder public that enable it to act in ways in which it is already disposed to act. Best used when a stakeholder public recognises a problem exists and agrees remedial action is necessary.
3 *Persuasive*—characterised by appeals to a stakeholder public's values and emotions. Used when a problem is not recognised or considered important by a stakeholder public. Used to induce a stakeholder public to re-allocate resources.
4 *Promise and reward*—employs a coercive function and involves the exercise of power. Implies that the source of the message controls an outcome desired by the receiver of the message.
5 *Threat and punishment*—employs negative coercion and the exercise of power and threat. Implies that the source controls an outcome feared or disliked by the receiver. Useful when a stakeholder public's perceived need for change is low.
6 *Bargaining*—characterised by an organisational exchange of messages between communicators. Employs deception and withholding of information. Similar to Grunig's two-way model in that organisations and stakeholder publics have incompatible goals.
7 *Cooperative problem solving*—jointly defines problems and solutions to problems. Open exchange of information to establish common goals. Similar to Grunig's two-way symmetrical model in that there is a sense of interdependence.

To use these strategies effectively, corporations analyse all variables, both endogenous and exogenous, and make decisions on which strategies best fit an issue or event. For the media, or others attempting to analyse the corporation, the answer lies in **reverse engineering** the strategies the corporation has used. Reverse engineering, the dismantling of a product or process to see how it was made, can be effectively used to understand how corporations select communication strategy when there is no readily available information. Hazleton's strategies can be used to reverse engineer a corporation's media campaigns.

reverse engineering
the dismantling of something in the reverse order that it was constructed.

Linking theory to practice in the corporate sphere

Corporate media relations is circumscribed by issues and events as they occur in the present. It links its presence to anticipation of what might happen in the future and appropriates material from relevant case studies and practices from the past. Corporate media relations managers have very little time to apply research to anything other than the present. Corporate social responsibility, for example, was framed by corporate management in response to stakeholder activism. Stakeholders in this case were not identified by environmental activism or market opposition, but by investor stakeholders unhappy with the way corporations were managing their (investor stakeholder) assets. Investor stakeholders, through large, managed funds shareholdings, exercised persuasion and influence upon the corporate world with the result that genuine socially responsible policies have been developed and implemented. The impact of corporate social responsibility has been to enrich public sphere dialogue, both mediated and direct, and to enhance the image of the corporation through serious policy changes.

Recent research into the relationships between corporate practice and theory has come from England where Joep Cornelissen (2004) argues for a narrowing of the gap between practice and theory in the corporate sphere so that tensions can be analysed. In seeking a successful solution to the existing corporate conflict, Cornelissen suggests theorists might provide contextualisation and explanations for why practitioners do certain things rather than attempting to be instrumental. As it applies to the theoretical concept of theory itself this will lead to a clearer understanding of why some strategies and tactics are more appropriate than others and to a stronger interpretation of meaning that lies within an action or policy.

THE CHRONICLE: TENIX CORPORATION

How a large private contractor frames issues

For a large private corporation, the idea of building media relationships is as important as building relationships with stakeholders such as customers, governments, and suppliers. To this end, Tenix Corporation, a defence contractor and one of the largest privately owned corporations in Australasia, has a full-time media and public affairs department.

Media relations describes the state of the relationship between the company and the journalists who report on its activities. Building that relationship may take several forms, but in general it involves building personal relationships between the public affairs manager and journalists with whom the organisation is most often engaged, as well as ensuring that journalists with whom it is not generally involved know they have someone they can go to when they want information about the company.

As a private company engaged in business-to-business and business-to-government work, Tenix has a lower media profile than many other companies of comparable size, but it works in several fields that have considerable potential for creating controversy.

Tenix's process of building a media relationship is relatively simple. Public Affairs Manager Liam Bathgate introduces himself to the journalists with whom the company is most often engaged. He takes the trouble to determine their major interests in relation to Tenix's activities and, where possible, provide them with information relevant to those interests. He includes them on the guest lists for suitable company functions and responds to their information requests as quickly as he reasonably can, accurately, and with an awareness of the need for other stakeholders to approve material. If he cannot provide certain information, Mr Bathgate ensures that he explains why. He ensures that he is available (mobile phone) at all times and maintains contact through normal social functions.

For Tenix, the specialisation of its defence manufacturing is a valuable asset. The area is sufficiently specialised that Mr Bathgate personally knows all the Australian journalists on the round as well as many of the overseas journalists who might write about Australia.

When creating a media campaign strategy to support an issue or event, certain actions take place. According to Mr Bathgate, the type of campaign required will vary according to the goal and the people and stakeholders involved. 'In my area, such a campaign will usually be in support of a bid involving the company for a major contract. My role in campaign planning and implementation will vary depending on whether our company is the prime contractor, a teaming partner with another company or a subcontractor to another prime contractor. The strategy is determined in consultation with the person primarily responsible for winning the contract.'

The selection of tactics to support a campaign is similarly interesting. 'I will draw on news releases, backgrounders, letters to the editor, personality profiles, op-ed pieces and feature stories plus others as appropriate. It is important to make the point that I work in a continuum, and maintaining the value of our company brand requires consistency in relationship-building at all levels. You cannot just pull a set of rabbits out of a hat for every project and expect them to have credibility. You must have demonstrated your capability over a long period.'

To distinguish the company in a competitive market there are certain steps that the company takes to present itself to its target stakeholders. 'Generally, where we are the prime contractor, I start out with a list of key messages determined by the bid team, together with an analysis of our strengths and weaknesses and those of our rival bidders. The challenge then is to create fresh, informative and credible material that flows from that analysis. Again, this is part of a continuum of communications and marketing material, which enable use of our company branding to present a clearly recognisable face to the campaign.'

As part of the strategy, the creation of an event is useful to frame an issue. 'If I can, I will create an event to support the bid. It is a very useful way both to present the issue, and to continue the relationship-building process. It would typically not be for media alone, however, but for decision-makers and influencers as well. I try to include all of the following when I create an event: an interesting venue relevant to the goal we are pursuing, interesting speakers, a good guest list, appropriate hospitality (depending on timing—it would not be lavish, but good quality), media access to senior management, a clear statement of purpose, appropriate communications material, and an appropriate take-away gift.'

Media relations is strategically important for Tenix. According to Mr Bathgate, understanding how the media work and being able to credibly and reliably communicate information that meets the needs of the various media organisations is the basis of the job. 'If you can do that successfully, there is a good probability that the media will disseminate your messages. If you do not do that, there is a low probability that your message is even heard by the media, let alone disseminated, and even less desirably, a high probability that negative messages about your company are disseminated, by chance or deliberate action by competitors. Effective implementation of media relations also saves the company a lot of time and money.'

Corporate image

Corporate image and corporate content are different things that sometimes get confused in the minds of different stakeholders. Corporate image is the impression of the organisation held by a public (stakeholder group) based on *knowledge* and *experience*. We think the same way about corporations as about people. The *Economist* described the author of a new book about the Iraq war as being 'a decent man worthy of our trust'. When we think of corporations and what they do we should also think about whether they are *decent* and *trustworthy*. Corporate image varies between stakeholder groups. Media exposure uniformly increases stakeholder knowledge to achieve a correct impression. Corporate image is how we evaluate the organisation in terms of beliefs and behaviour. The closer a corporation comes to the beliefs and behaviour of target stakeholder groups, the closer it comes to a positive reputation (trust). The difficulty with an alignment of the corporation as having the same values and beliefs as the individual is in relative scale.

A corporation is a huge thing by any measure and the more it produces, the greater are its economy of scale and profit. Corporations are identified by large buildings, large factories, and large numbers of employees. So it is a paradox that they continuously try to equate themselves in size with average citizens, both in their selling and in their image. The clue to why this occurs and why a good media relations specialist will continue to promote it lies in corporations' ungraspable levels of sales and profits. We all want an Xbox or a PlayStation but if we start thinking that Microsoft has sold more than 22 million XBoxes and Sony has sold almost 100 million PlayStations, we are entering a different world. We need to think of Microsoft and Sony as friendly corporations that make things that we want, that we think are hot. If we think of them as mass producers of millions and millions of the same thing and of their profits being in the zone of numbers greater than millions—billions—then we cannot feel any direct relationship at all to the corporation. So part of the job of a media relations specialist is to keep the image of the corporation at a level that can be interpreted and meaningful to an individual citizen, while at the same time selecting and employing communication strategies that will increase the share price or **market capitalisation** of the organisation.

Reputation is made up of attributed values, including:

> **market capitalisation**
> the value of the material wealth of an entity as it is seen by stakeholders.

- authenticity
- honesty
- responsibility
- integrity.

Reputation also relies on trust as well as:

- innovative products and services
- a strong level of research and development
- effective corporate advertising, sales, and marketing.

Corporate identity is the symbols used in identification, which are:

- logo
- slogan
- livery (colours, design).

The more a brand name appears in the media, the more recognisable it becomes. We expect the University of Sydney brand name to be associated with trust and decency in its dealing with stakeholders (you and me). A media relations practitioner and a client want logos and names to frequently appear in stories.

THE CHRONICLE: MANAGED INNOVATION

How a small business frames an issue

Small to medium-sized enterprises focus resources on the primary goal of turnover. They are rarely in a financial position to engage expensive media relations counsellors. They find themselves engaging with media when there is a problem or crisis from which they cannot extricate themselves. They are rarely seen by the mainstream media to be worthy of investigation during times of normal operation. But the importance of media relationship building must never be underestimated by small and medium-sized organisations. It is axiomatic that if they are not seen during normal operations they will fail to be seen when they want to generate interest in an issue or event. Tens of thousands of small and medium-sized enterprises exist in Australia and New Zealand and they rely on a small advertising budget pitched mostly at B2B (trade) publications, to reach stakeholders such as customers, suppliers, and governments. A small business that devotes a percentage of its income to building a media relationship during normal business is in a strong position to increase engagement when an issue or event requires it.

One small business that has built a strong relationship with targeted media is Australian company Managed Innovation. As a management consultancy, Managed Innovation must compete with multinational corporations to provide a similar type of service, so it was important to be seen within the same business news pages that the competitors frequented. The company decided the strategy would be to present itself in one specific medium on the issue of innovation as an expert within the innovation market. Rather than pitch its campaign at a range of business-to-business magazines, it chose to focus on business-to-consumer publications and to focus on one in particular, *Business Review Weekly* (*BRW*). The campaign to present newsworthy material to *BRW* used standard tactics, such as news releases, profiles, and backgrounders, but it drew its success from the letter to the editor tactic. Every few months, the company responded to a story by sending a letter to the editor. Each letter pointed up the importance of the story and of the issue of innovation. Within twelve months the company had numerous letters published, including a letter of the week that won a handsome fountain pen for its author. The letter tactic led into the campaign with a direct correspondence between the company managing director and the editor of the magazine. It built a relationship that enabled the company to become a focus for the magazine when it required comment on any issue relating to innovation (see chapter 5 for details).

Managed Innovation was unable to devote a large percentage of its resources to media and public relations because it was a newly establishing organisation. It had built a reputation among a substantial number of manufacturing clients in Australia and Ireland. To increase its value it needed to introduce its services and expertise to stakeholders in other industry sectors. After researching the business-to-business and business-to-consumer magazine markets in Australia and New Zealand, Managed Innovation chose *BRW* as the vehicle. While Managed Innovation's strategy was bold, it could have achieved nothing. It succeeded because it used one important tactic over a reasonably long time: it was content to generate small degrees of interest and to build on the relationship at a manageable level. It successfully communicated the issue of innovation as an important aspect of business by focusing on the issue itself rather than on the expertise of the company to drive innovation. Managed Innovation did not make claims beyond its capabilities and it framed innovation as something that was acceptable to all organisations and to all levels of funding. It thus revealed the issue and itself as being interlinked with, but within reach and applicable to, all types of goals and objectives.

The success of the media campaign undertaken by Managed Innovation can be measured against an increase in client numbers. The success of future media campaigns can be measured against an increase in media relations research funding.

Public business

The life expectancy of a corporation today is less than twenty years. Change is due to mergers, acquisitions, and break-ups. Is there a difference between public and private corporations and business? Do the media view public and private differently? A public company must do certain things that are not required of a private company. Writing and producing an annual report is the one that interests us most. It is an operational task, usually undertaken by a media relations practitioner. An annual report is a media relations tactic and it is the public face of the company.

INNOVATION

EDITED BY SIMON LLOYD
slloyd@brw.fairfax.com.au

New and improved

It is hard to measure innovation within a company, but it starts with a workplace culture that encourages experiments and forgives mistakes. By Simon Lloyd

Innovation has become so important to growth that companies are making it a part of the key performance indicators for their staff. But this presents many challenges, because innovation is one of the hardest corporate functions or disciplines to define, let alone measure.

Clearly, the easiest measurement of innovation relates to new products. A product launch is invariably monitored for sales figures, giving managers an almost immediate indication of the return on the investment that was required to take the new product from concept to launch.

The problem with making innovation part of a key performance indicator arises when companies try to assess the effect on their business of internal, or process, innovation. Even harder is gauging the relationship between a company's culture — whether it actively nurtures innovation among all its employees — and the bottom line.

One school of thought says that if the company is growing and customer awareness and satisfaction with the product or service are high, then it is not necessary to measure internal innovation capabilities and performance as a key performance indicator. Counter to that is the notion that of all performance indicators, innovation needs to be a forward-looking measurement.

At an innovation forum organised by the consultancy Managed Innovation and Roche Pharmaceuticals in Sydney late last year, the adjunct professor-elect in scenario planning at the University of Technology Sydney, Oliver Freeman, told delegates that although business puts a lot of energy into analysing the past, it is equally important to devote time and energy to considering the future.

"Understand the key dynamics of change, its opportunities and its threats," Freeman said. "What could these mean to you and your organisation?"

The director of Managed Innovation, Allan Ryan, says: "Any company can easily measure product innovation as a past output, but when you are looking at organisational innovation, you have to use other measures that look forward."

Innovation, as far as company culture is concerned, is very much about individuals working within the organisation. Measuring their input, satisfaction and the results of their ideas is crucial to having employees who are enthusiastic about the company's goals.

Ryan says: "If an individual believes he or she is allowed to take risks and be innovative, then they are much more likely to do so than if they are part of an organisation that is risk-averse."

QUESTIONS TO ASK

What is the number of in-company entrepreneurs (people who have started a business in the company or before joining the company)?

What percentage of employees have been trained in innovation?

How many new competencies are being deliberately developed?

How many incentive schemes are in place to support innovation?

How many innovation mentors are there in the organisation?

What percentage of employees recognise a strategic focus on innovation?

What percentage of employees can name the innovation targets?

Is senior leadership directly accountable for the company's innovation processes?

SOURCE: STRATEGOS / WOODGIDE INSTITUTE

A tool that some companies in recent years have come to see as simplistic and even old-fashioned is returning to vogue among clever organisations that realise that without the right culture, innovation among employees is almost impossible. That tool is the employee survey.

The director of sales and marketing at Roche Pharmaceuticals, Kirsten O'Doherty, says her company is a strong believer in the role of the employee survey. In early 2004, Roche embarked on a cultural change programme that was designed to help employees engage more effectively in the innovation process throughout the organisation.

O'Doherty says: "Measuring the success of our innovation is really about measuring change in the organisation rather than the number of ideas that exit an ideas bank. As an affiliate of a large multinational we cannot do product innovation, so we are innovating in our business practices. We are trying to get an environment where people believe they can make a difference and that they can take a risk to contribute to the organisation, and that is very hard in a scientific industry."

O'Doherty says the employee survey is central to this process. Roche now conducts such a study each year, which encompasses attitudes to leadership and direction and staff engagement. "We call it a climate survey and it includes a lot of questions about decision-making processes and how people feel about their role within Roche."

Allowed to make mistakes

Measuring staff attitudes is only the first step in determining a company's current innovation capabilities and its potential. Knowing how to modify those attitudes, where necessary, is a second, important and often tricky step. This is especially the case if employees believe they have to come up with the biggest and best ideas to be acknowledged, let alone rewarded, by senior management.

Companies are wrong to promote this type of thinking, say experts in cultural innovation. Enlightened senior management promotes a culture in which employees are allowed to make mistakes in their pursuit of innovation. This attitude must be communicated most strongly from the chief executive.

The operational development manager

82 | January 19–25, 2006 | BRW.

Figure 7.1 *Business Review Weekly*'s article on innovation, 19–25 January 2006

shareholder
an individual, citizen or organisation that has some financial or other interest in something.

Public companies are organisations that are open to public scrutiny through their **shareholders**. Private companies are not answerable to shareholders, nor to anyone else, other than market forces. Public companies are listed on stock exchanges around the world. Stock exchanges list public company information that allows buyers and sellers in the market to trade company shares on a daily, weekly, and yearly basis. A share in a public company is defined as a proportionate right to participate in the ownership and profits of that company. A public company is usually valued by its *market capitalisation*, which is defined as the total value that the stock market attributes to the company. Market capitalisation is calculated by multiplying the total number of shares by the current market value. Corporate stockholders are part owners of a business, a business that has an investment value based on its *past* performance and *future* prospects. A private company is one that is held by an individual, group, or family in which all profit goes to the owners.

Private business

The majority of Australian and New Zealand business is small business, which is comprised of a single person manager and/or owner and various levels of employee numbers. Business is defined in relation to a number of factors, including sector of operation, number of employees, and turnover. Companies and businesses operate in different market sectors depending on their interests. These include:

- retail
- resources
- property
- finance
- tourism
- manufacturing
- engineering
- energy
- banking
- education.

Private and public companies, large and small, operate within these sectors in competition with each other. Large companies often have a number of businesses under their umbrella. Manufacturers make a variety of products, from toothpaste to car seat covers. Banks provide services such as insurance and superannuation as well as lending and investing.

Stakeholder perceptions

Corporate clients, the media, and the public have very different views and opinions about what corporations should do. Corporations exist solely to make profits. Public and private companies, unless they are not-for-profit organisations, have profit as their central focus. They make things to sell (products and services) for more than the cost of making them. Corporations are interested in the media when they can use it to publicise their products and services through advertising and editorial. They are also interested in *managing* criticism. Criticism most often appears in the media, so it is the role of the media relations manager to attempt to build better or stronger relationships between their client corporation or business and the media. Other things that media relations managers get involved with on behalf of corporations are:

- investor relations
- community relations
- government relations (public affairs)
- internal relations (employees).

All these create and build relationships with stakeholder publics—shareholders, for example, in investor relations—but for now we are only interested in the building of media relationships. We can, however, assume that media relations plays a role in informing all other stakeholders through the exercise of communication campaigns that include controlled or uncontrolled tactics.

How a business or corporation builds a relationship with the media is in part due to the nature of the financial transaction that is struck between them. Corporations and businesses underpin the media through the purchase of advertising space. Most of the media, as we know them, are products themselves of large corporations and businesses. We are interested in the process and objectives of relationship building between a business and the media. We can set aside for the moment the possibility that some corporations get more favourable treatment by the media because of cross shareholdings and other arrangements. There is never likely to be a negative story in *BRW*, for example, about a company or business owned by John Fairfax. Nor is it likely that Channel 9 news will run a negative story about Crown Casino or gambling in general.

Corporations and businesses prefer to avoid media scrutiny. Generally speaking, the media are perceived by them as being inaccurate, obtrusive, and dangerous. Yet left on their own, businesses and corporations have managed to produce:

- poisonous food
- eco disasters
- dangerous products
- poor services.

It is part of the role of the media to act, as they do with government, as a fourth estate, reporting with equanimity the actions of corporations and businesses. (In this, the media act like other agencies that assist in the regulation of business and government.) But corporations do not believe the equanimity part, so they seek to balance investigations into their activities with information that allows them to get on with what they are supposed to do—make a profit for owners and shareholders. Imposed between the investigating, information-seeking media and the withdrawn, information-withholding corporation, is the media relationship builder. It is frequently the case that media relationship builders have abandoned their employment in the media and moved to the corporate sphere. A high-profile example is Sydney journalist Christine Lacey moving from the *Sydney Morning Herald* to Channel 9, not as a reporter but as a media relationship builder. Lacey's reports in the business section of the *SMH* were *insider* stories about the world of the corporation that exposed all sorts of misdeeds. As a corporate communicator with Publishing and Broadcasting's 9 Network, her job was to sidestep such exposure.

Inhouse corporate counsel

Corporations retain media specialists inhouse as they are most qualified in building and sustaining good relations with the media. A large number of these specialists have worked as journalists and reporters and are recruited for the express purpose of sustaining relationships with their former colleagues. Strategically, this works very well in the short term. But, like those being recruited by corporations, their former reporter colleagues also move on. In contrast, the person employed by the corporation usually holds down the job longer. This may not have a serious impact on the relationship in the short term because the journalist-turned-corporate (hack to flack) still has street cred. It will take some time for this to change so that the former journalist looks outdated. But it will happen. Before it does, inhouse communicators need to develop strategies that will avoid the problem (see chapter 11 for more detail on managing risk).

One solution that worked well in the twentieth century was to continue to employ former journalists and build staff, so that some corporate communications departments now have large numbers of media specialists employed full time. This strategy still has relevance. Reporters in print, television, and radio are familiar with the differential between what they earn and what is made by practitioners in media relations. As the ethical gap between the two professions continues to narrow, so reporters and journalists are more inclined to make the transition to corporate communication. But this does not take account of the image of corporations as bad, and those who frame their media relations strategies as ethically unacceptable. The gap between journalism and media relations ethics may be narrowing, but there is still a genuine suspicion among media and other stakeholders that corporations are bad. Citizens who own shares in public corporations, for example, are not always happy with the way the management of their companies communicates. Corporate media relations counsellors must, therefore, develop strategies that build relationships with all types of stakeholders. But it is the media relationship that defines corporate communication because the media is the channel through which citizens obtain most of their information about corporations. While access to information framed on internet websites and in advertising is important to the way citizens shape images of corporations, they are closed entities: a citizen cannot, for example, walk through the front door of Microsoft in Redmond, Washington, and watch scientists cutting code for a new computer game. Corporations will argue that in the same way that citizens have access to governments through public galleries in parliaments, they have access to public companies through annual general meetings. But this access is limited to one meeting a year and is restricted to public companies. The large number of private corporations around the world have no legislative requirement to provide public access to their operations. As a result, it is incumbent upon the media to provide a balanced interpretation of corporate issues and events so that stakeholder publics can shape their behaviours and attitudes. It is equally incumbent upon corporate media and PR practitioners to provide information that can be interpreted in such a way.

What does a corporate media manager actually do to build these relationships with their former colleagues when the corporation they are now employed by is perceived to be a demon? Part of the role is to provide as much information as possible without compromising the organisation. Another part is defining information that may compromise the organisation, which may include sensitive technology that, if revealed, could gain some advantage for a competitor. It may include price-sensitive information that could negatively impact on an organisation's share price or it could be the design of a new handbag. The media are aware of the proprietary nature of business information. Reporters and journalists take this into account when investigating story material. Information about the way the media report issues allows media relationship builders to signal individuals and to frame material that fits. If a reporter is not on a distribution list or a media conference list, that reporter will be at a competitive disadvantage. Imagine for a moment being a journalist with a glossy, well-respected motor magazine and not getting an invitation to Germany to drive the new Mercedes Benz SLK500. Or being an editor on a glossy fashion magazine and not being invited to Fashion Week in Paris. These examples would revile reporters and journalists who eschew the idea of accepting corporate largesse, but they are a fact of corporate media relations. They play a large part in the competitiveness attached to media material. It is not on merit that particular material appears in the media, glossy or intellectual.

At this point an additional question arises. Can a reporter who has been receiving regular material from a corporation file copy with a negative angle if the corporation does something wrong? An example might be the global building-products corporation James Hardie. A content analysis of reporting on the corporation prior to the problems it encountered on the issue of funding asbestos compensation claims could be compared with the reporting after the issue became widely reported. It might also be a worthwhile exercise to analyse the individuals who reported on the company before and after to see if there was a change of attitude and the extent of the change (for an explanation of content analysis, see chapter 12).

A self-evident truth of media relationship building in the corporate sphere is that a media relationship builder will fail if they spend all their time and energy attempting to alter the attitude or behaviour of the reporter. Reporters display natural negativity towards corporations and businesses. They are perceived to be big, unfriendly, unnatural, environmentally insensitive, inhuman, and profit-driven. It is not within the scope of this book to argue the case for or against the relative merits of the corporation. Nor is it the intention to investigate which members of the media might fall into this category. It is, however, fair to argue that the job of the corporate communicator is to investigate which members of the media might be more likely to act antagonistically towards the organisation without good reason. In this, the corporate communicator must deal with the media in the same way as a government media adviser when confronted by an antagonist. An example is the state Labor government in New South Wales and its relationship with broadcaster Alan Jones. All the evidence points to Mr Jones acting as an antagonist on most issues and events associated with the state government. Leaving aside Mr Jones's own past political ambitions it is reasonable to suggest that a state government media adviser would not recommend spending time or resources in attempting to alter Mr Jones's opinion. There are other members of the media with whom engagement would be more successful for the state Labor government. Corporate media research will enable a media relations adviser to pinpoint who is likely to be objective in reporting corporate issue and events (see chapter 4 for a discussion of tactics that might be appropriate to investigating individual media people).

The business press and the antibusiness press

The business press usually writes about the issues and events that surround profit. The antibusiness press usually writes about how profit impacts on all other stakeholders.

Tom Skotnicki wrote in *BRW*:

> Transport Minister Warren Truss says that if Toll Holdings succeeds in
> its takeover of Patrick Corporation it should be prepared to act in the

national interest—that because of its dominant position it would need to maintain a wide perspective. Sorry minister, but the primary interest should be the interests of shareholders. A company has an obligation to other people insofar as this helps create a sustainable environment.

We can see from this example in which direction *BRW* leans. It would not be hard to assume that we could build a good relationship for our business with a journalist who clearly dislikes government and other intervention in the process of making a profit. Most business journalists believe in the primacy of the market. Any intervention—government, environmentalist, community group, employee—is bad for business. This is the standard in journalism—the first rule is don't take the side of government, no matter how reasonable the position may be. Reporters who cover business and corporations also play a booster role for organisations through their coverage. Business magazines and business television programs are less reliable in their investigation of corporations than are business newspapers. They tend to be easier to build relationships with because they require a constant supply of business stories to fill their pages. Business sections in newspapers, while they require material, are a little more flexible in page numbers, and, if necessary, they can be supported by the other sections in the newspaper. The only media with any real capacity to investigate business and corporations are public media organisations such as the Australian Broadcasting Corporation.

Stakeholder expectations of media reporting on business and corporations form three groups:

- media expectation—corporations act legally
- investor expectation—act legally + profitably and increasingly, act ethically
- environmentalist expectation—legal + ethical + socially responsible.

THE CHRONICLE: COSMAX PRESTIGE BRANDS

How a specialist agency business creates strong media relationships

As the media manager of a cosmetics company that houses over twenty different brands, Alice Hocking says it is her role to communicate the specific needs of each brand and its products to the company's stakeholders by using a multitude of media outlets. To ensure that the message she frames for the media is correctly received and interpreted, it is imperative that her relationship with them is strong. 'As I have chosen to work in a specific industry—beauty—I have been able to concentrate on building my relationship with core media stakeholders over time that has benefited communication of each of my brand's specific messages.'

For Ms Hocking, the first process in building a media relationship is understanding the specific stakeholders and identifying who or which media is needed to establish a relationship with so that communication will be seamless.

Once identified, there are a number of things to remember when establishing a new relationship:

1   Always respond to media enquiries as soon as possible.
2   Never promise anything to which you cannot commit.
3   Always supply above and beyond the amount of information the media require or expect.
4   Maintain your relationship with regular contact.
5   Where possible, offer exclusives to your key media.

'It is always advisable to know as much as possible about the media you are dealing with and their organisational policies so you can ensure that protocol is followed and you are conscious of anything that may be detrimental to the publicity you are trying to achieve.'

Allocation of budget funding to media relationship building is also important for the organisation. Ms Hocking suggests a budget forecast should allow a certain percentage of A&P [advertising and promotion] spending to cover any media relationship building costs.

'The key area in which I use my media relationship budget would be dining out. I take editors to cafes and restaurants for breakfast, lunch, dinner, or drinks. Occasionally, I will use funds to send a gift or flowers to thank them for a story they have written, or I will travel interstate to meet with them personally. Occasionally, when it is of the utmost importance, I will pay for a journalist to cover a launch overseas, which also helps build a strong relationship.'

Generally speaking, a new strategy is created for each media campaign, although Ms Hampton suggests there is sometimes a need to tweak them to fit a product's market. Strategy guidelines come from brand principles (who are based overseas) to ensure that the brand's image is upheld and its key requirements are met.

Depending on the importance of the product, and based on the A&P budget, a media campaign may begin with a launch event held three months prior to the availability date to enable glossy publications to coincide their editorial with the products on-counter date (as most glossies run to a three-month deadline). Before this, however, Ms Hocking says, she might provide an exclusive to a key journalist or publication that she believes will give the best editorial for the desired audience. This could entail inviting that journalist to the overseas launch, organising for them to have a one-off interview with a specific designer, or providing the journalist with more angles and information than any other publication.

If there is not a budget for a full-scale launch event, Ms Hocking says she will implement a soft launch where the product, news release, and any other information or images are sent to each of the specific media nationally. Some of the tactics used for a campaign launch include a news release, background information, a letter to the editor, a personality profile, or a feature story. Material is distributed as hard copy or email, depending on the situation.

To stand out in the sea of media material in the fashion and beauty world, Ms Hocking says it is important to recognise the value of a brand. 'Although most media don't have a lot of time for gimmicks as such, I ensure that all of our communication is presented professionally and in line with a brand's philosophy. Considering most of my brands have a designer element, the initial impact they make on the media must convey the brand's core values and designer image.'

In evaluating the success of media relationship building, Cosmax Prestige Brands uses Mediascape, a commercially available service that measures the dollar value of all of the publicity achieved for each brand on a quarterly basis. 'This has proved invaluable for measuring the success of each campaign. It has provided a lot of statistical information to my overseas brand principles as well as leading to potential new business opportunities.'

Corporate social responsibility

Corporate social responsibility is relatively new in rhetorical terms but it has been in existence in the Western world since the nineteenth century. It was influenced in the late twentieth century by the idea that corporations ought to be interested in more than the single entry bottom line of profit. If they were to actively pursue a balanced existence, so the line of reasoning suggested, then profit must live side by side with social equity and a concern for the physical environment in which the corporation existed. This thinking shaped **triple bottom line reporting**, the idea that a corporation must place equal value on its social and environmental position as it did on profit, and that it must report all three as results to stakeholders. While there is a strong rhetorical sense of triple bottom line reporting being communicated to stakeholders by corporations at the beginning of the twenty-first century, the idea of corporate

> **triple bottom line reporting**
> the combination of reporting three elements of an organisation to stakeholders; profit, environmental sustainability, and social responsibility.

social responsibility has its genesis in the tabling of legislation in England in the early nineteenth century. The Health and Morals of Apprentices Act, tabled in the British parliament by Robert Peel in 1802, followed concern that children living in poverty in London were being forced to travel to the north of England to work in new cotton- and wool-processing factories and to work at all hours of the day and night where no parent or other relative might be interested in their wellbeing. The idea that legislation was required to persuade those early corporations to undertake socially responsible measures for the wellbeing of their employees assumes corporations were interested in nothing other than profit. Similarly, legislation was required across the Western world in the twentieth century to secure corporate responsibility to ensure the wellbeing of the physical environment of the planet. Again, the corporation appears to have been motivated first by profit.

Corporate social responsibility is a catchy rhetorical device that embraces all the elements of triple bottom line accountability. It is the subject of international conferences and discussions in which corporate communicators present their credentials for sustainable business activity that is conscious of, and engaged with, the widest possible stakeholder interests imaginable. Thus it has tactical relationship building and framing objectives. But corporate social responsibility is equally a natural position for the large multinational company and the small domestic business. The idea that a corporation requires legislative proscription to act responsibly is no different to individuals being proscribed by law so that they will drive their cars responsibly: it has relevance to a minority. Like individuals, most corporations and businesses will exercise judgment in any given situation and act responsibly (leaving aside for the moment the idea that corporations and individuals would not pay tax if no tax law existed). Corporate social responsibility rests on the notion of value. It makes assumptions about equating corporate values with societal and community values. Part of the role of the corporate media relations manager is to sustain this relationship between corporate and societal values. But the idea that corporations will seriously think about long-term sustainable relationships avoids the reality of the short-term profit goal. Where once corporate profit reporting periods were as long as twelve months, in the late twentieth century the shorter reporting period—quarterly—became widespread. Corporations, like all competitive environments, live by their ability to sustain a **comparative advantage** and, in this, the shorter the reporting period, the happier the shareholders. Car sales, for example, are reported against monthly budgets and in the retail clothing sector, sales budgets and forecasts are reported weekly. The question that this raises relates to the sustainability of long-term environmental and social goals when short-term profits are a substantial requirement of corporate shareholders.

> **comparative advantage**
> the ability to create something more or less valuable than an alternative.

This is the issue for corporate communications experts in presenting corporate social responsibility as something more than a rhetorical device. The role of the corporate media counsel is to advocate at management level on behalf of all stakeholders, which includes corporate managements and boards of directors. The counsellor must weigh the objectives of the corporation with the objectives of all other interested stakeholders, including lunatic fringe groups. It is not enough to build relationships with corporate media, such as *BRW*, for example, and ignore fringe media such as *Crikey*. As we will see in chapter 11, ignoring fringe stakeholders can be perilous for a corporation or any other type of business. The difficulty for the corporate media manager lies in the personal perspective that one brings to the job and the reconciliation of personal values with corporate values. To reach a high level of achievement the media manager must be prepared to represent the interests of a variety of stakeholders to executive management and the board of directors. To do this, the board and management must place explicit trust in the professional capabilities of the media manager. All external stakeholders must place similar trust in the capabilities of the media manager to represent them.

8

Government and Politics

CHAPTER OBJECTIVES

- To learn about the role of media relations in government.
- To learn about the role of media relations in politics.

Some time before Australian Prime Minister John Howard turned sixty-four years of age, the Australian news media began speculating about his possible retirement. Newspapers, television, and radio framed the event against a number of possible scenarios, including the elevation of Treasurer Peter Costello to the prime ministership. Speculation about Mr Costello's ambitions to become prime minister occupied a vast amount of news media space and the turn of history allowed the approach of Mr Howard's birthday to dramatically increase the level of speculation. When that date passed with no retirement announcement—indeed, Mr Howard's government introduced a remarkable number of bills into the House after that date—the news media did not move on to some other event to fill the void. It continued its speculation to the point that it appeared to be obsessed with the relationship between the prime minister and the treasurer and the issue of when one would run away and the other would ascend to the throne. For the average citizen, this appeared to be a contest that was mildly interesting to watch in its unfolding and to speculate, with the media, on the result. An amusing front page headline and picture in the Sydney metropolitan daily, the *Daily Telegraph*, drew an interesting parallel with its speculation in late 2005 by suggesting the relationship was more than political, that it was in fact a 'marriage'. Such an analogy drew the relationship into a new sphere—one that resonated more with a wider number of average citizens as stakeholders who could relate to the idea of marriage and, ultimately, given the poor state of marriage in Australia, the marriage ending in divorce.

Viewed from another perspective—that of media relations—the idea that the media will devote enormous space and time to an event, such as a prime minister's birthday, and draw a connection between his age and the aspirations of another senior government minister, is a most effective campaign outcome. All the while the media were focusing on this event, it was setting aside more important issues and events, such as historic changes to Australia's industrial relations and security laws, which were effectively unchallenged inside and outside the Australian parliament. The strategy for the Liberal Party, as the senior coalition partner in government, was to frame and build on the media's perceived conflict between the prime minister and the treasurer. It worked well.

Defining media relations in government and politics

Politics and government are not the same. Media relations counsellors operate in both sectors but they do different things. 'Politics' is defined as the public life and affairs of government, the activities concerned with the exercise of authority and power, and the capacity to manage and maintain the affairs of a state. 'Government' is defined as the actions of governing, devising, and controlling policy and legislation, and the action of managing and maintaining the affairs of state. Citizens and other stakeholders, including media, frequently confuse the two. For the purpose of this book, politics will describe the strategies used in campaign development by candidates for elected office. Government will describe the strategies and actions of those elected to government and opposition. In politics, media counsellors develop campaigns and strategies for candidates to influence and persuade two primary stakeholders: the media and constituent voters. The strategies and campaigns developed by governments retain the media as primary stakeholders, but shift their focus to the wider electorate. They are interested in a greater number of stakeholders than just the citizen as eligible voter. The media and citizens are still primary, but additional stakeholders also move into the frame, including opposition or shadow governments, backbenchers from their own party or group, independents in parliament, unions and other industrial organisations, employer organisations, charitable and not-for-profit organisations, as well as myriad community and interest groups (for a discussion of community and interest groups, see chapter 9).

Media relations practitioners building campaigns for political candidates frequently remain with the candidate after election to government or opposition. Alternatively, candidates may engage the expertise of agencies with political communication experience. In Australia and New Zealand, successful candidates have framed media campaigns in conjunction with media individuals, who then shift from media to politics. In government, media practitioners arrive from a number of places. Some are seconded from government departments where they are permanent employees, a large number are enlisted from media, while others arrive from the corporate sphere. They all operate at a number of levels within politics and government. Within the corporate sphere they are usually referred to as corporate communicators or public affairs managers. Within politics they are called campaign directors. Within government, they become media and policy advisers.

There are a number of contests that are important to media relations practitioners in the political and government spheres. The first is the role of the campaign director in assisting a political candidate to get elected. Until a candidate is elected, the nominee is just another citizen. At this level, the important contests are between the candidates as competitors and the media as stakeholders reporting the election campaigns. Once elected, a candidate becomes a member of a government, a member of an opposition, or an independent. The candidate may sit in either the upper house, or the Senate (senator), the lower house, or House of Representatives (MHR) at federal level, or in legislative assemblies (MLA) and councils (MLC) at state level (except Queensland), or in local government chambers as a councillor. Here, the contests become more complex. As an elected representative, the individual is interested in a wider number of stakeholders, including constituents, media, and other elected representatives. The role of the media practitioner shifts in focus. While it remains important to sustain strong media relationships, equally important relationships must be built with local constituents and wider stakeholders, such as other governments, international organisations, and nations.

Government

Introduction

Governments send information to citizens through a huge variety of channels for a huge number of reasons:

- to stop the outbreak or spread of diseases (health message)
- to warn about travel to dangerous countries (tourism message)

- to alert citizens to the possibility of terrorist threats (security message).

In democratic countries, governments provide information to citizens to improve their wellbeing. The model used by governments to disseminate news and information is known as the **public information model** (Grunig & Hunt 1984). This means governments think about the information they provide to stakeholders as being useful to them. The objective is to inform citizens (primary stakeholders) about what the government is doing on their behalf. To be successful, governments engage directly with citizens through advertising and indirectly through the media.

> **public information model**
>
> the second of James Grunig's excellence models; the action of providing information, usually from government or other institutional sources, to wider stakeholder publics.

Local governments (local council):

- send newsletters to residents
- send news releases to local newspapers
- hold press briefings with local newspapers
- run a mayoral column in a local newspaper
- run a mayoral talk-back program on local radio
- buy space in newspapers to advertise land developments
- run websites to provide general information.

State governments:

- hold press conferences to make announcements
- hold daily press briefing sessions
- send news releases to metropolitan newspapers
- send media backgrounders and news to radio stations
- run advertising campaigns about issues
- run websites to support media information campaigns.

National governments:

- construct public information campaigns
- hold daily media briefings
- run websites to provide information.

International governments (United Nations):

- run and own radio stations to spread information
- run and own television stations to spread information
- run and own websites to support other owned media.

All these things can be described as part of the media relationship building process because they provide media with an enormous amount of background and specific information. Like corporations, governments use media relations to build an image and an identity. From the other side of the picture, stakeholders use the media to attempt to influence or persuade governments. For the moment we are interested in the way governments use the media.

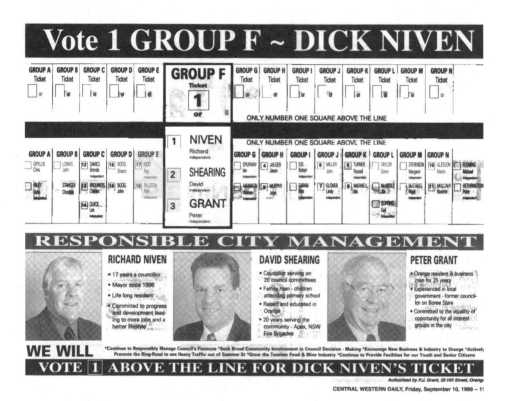

Figure 8.1 How-to-vote advertisement

THE CHRONICLE: THE *WEEKLY TIMES* NEWSPAPER

Why the media choose certain frames

In late 2005, an independent suburban Sydney newspaper, the *Weekly Times*, published a story about railway station upgrading. It was a story used directly from a news release from the office of Mr John Watkins, member for Ryde and Transport Minister in the New South Wales state government. Opposite the story, on the same page, was a paid advertising column from John Watkins applauding the new rail timetable. The same column thanked the local community for its support since Mr Watkins became deputy premier of New South Wales some weeks earlier. The *Weekly Times* is an independent newspaper that survives on government advertising. In Gladesville, Hunters Hill, and Ryde—the newspaper's distribution area—there is a large population of old and retired people. They read the *Weekly Times* almost religiously. And they read the paid advertising columns from politicians in the same way as they read news stories. There is a level of trust attached to the material they read. They believe there is some integrity attached to the messages. So. How does a Labor politician such as Mr Watkins build a good media relationship with the *Weekly Times* when evidence points to the newspaper being historically a strong Liberal Party supporter? Part of the answer lies in the long-term nature of the relationship and the understanding that exists between individual politicians and media at local level. While it is relatively easy to 'dis' a government because it's a big, faceless organisation, dissing is not as easy at a personal, local level.

Framing issues and events

One model of government relations that frames public relations involvement in government in terms of the ability of the organisation to build stronger relations with the public is that conceived by US scholar John Ledingham. Ledingham's (2001) model is not new (see Botan 1993; Wilcox et al. 2000; Maloney 2000), but it provides a strong counterpoint to the argument that governments fail to acknowledge the existence of community within the public sphere unless that community is perceived to hold institutional power. Ledingham follows Kruckeberg and Starck's (1998) dictum that public relations focuses on the restoration and maintenance of a sense of community, and thus revisits the argument put by Australian political scientist Ron Wild (1974) that public relations is government derived, or at least the relationship between governments and their publics is, rather than a contemporary generalist view that it is a management function within a corporate environment interested only in the goal of financial profit.

Ledingham's research, conducted in a US midwest metropolitan centre not unlike many regional Australian cities, attempted to examine the drift of residents from one neighbourhood to another and to identify public perceptions, attitudes, and choice behaviours for local government planning. Its purpose was to attempt to find a link between community and public relations and to test an earlier model, the Bruning–Ledingham Relationship Scale of social exchange theory, relative to the relationship model. The research found that when a partnership was enacted, there were standards of expectations of each other. If the standards are not met, there will be less satisfaction and less possibility of behavioural change.

Government media advisers

Earlier criticism of the emergence of the political communicator in the guise of the media relations counsellor came from Habermas (1989), who argued that the birth of persuasion and influence transferring from the honorific avocation of the politician to the paid professional brought about the structural transformation of the public sphere. For Habermas, the restrictive within a society circumscribed by communication produces observable limitations, the consequence of which is a communicative–theoretic model in which 'actors orient their own actions by their own interpretations' (Habermas 1987: 118). Such is the position of politicians as actors through either an interpretation of their own actions or an interpretation by a second actor (media adviser) of the interpretation of the actions of the politicians. The reliance of a communal interpretation of communicative action and the relativisation of utterances within a valid framework presents the politician with a logical direction in which to enact an election campaign.

Government ministers build relationships with the media through personal engagement and through permanently employed media advisers. A ministerial media adviser's job is to build and maintain a relationship with specific reporters, journalists, and editors and to field calls from the media at all hours of the day and night. A state government minister's media adviser, for example, is expected to know everything about the media and the people who work in them. A media adviser builds a profile of a media individual by inculcating everything the individual writes or broadcasts so they have a feel for the direction the individual will take on an issue or event that relates to the specific ministerial portfolio the adviser is responsible for. Media relationship building for the ministerial adviser requires knowledge of every aspect of a portfolio and the ability to provide information that will be considered valuable and newsworthy.

THE CHRONICLE: THE NEW SOUTH WALES GOVERNMENT

How a media adviser builds a relationship

When a ministerial media adviser develops a campaign around an issue or event, it is done in consultation with other ministerial staff and the minister. Decisions about the development of a media campaign to support an issue or event are made in the same way that a media adviser makes decisions in the private sector. A ministerial media adviser will create a campaign around an issue or event using the same tactics available to general counsellors. The most frequently used tactic is the news release. News releases are distributed to individuals in hard copy, by internet, and, increasingly, as text messages. Ministerial media advisers receive text messages and calls from journalists and reporters in response so the whole communication process can be achieved anywhere.

There is one important difference between a ministerial media adviser and a general media relations counsellor. A ministerial media adviser rarely makes a comment on the record on behalf of the client. The role of the adviser is to remain in the background. It is a dialogic process—the adviser deals with the media on behalf of the minister—but within the public sphere the minister appears as the prolocutor.

Part of the relationship building process occurs when the adviser attempts to persuade a reporter or journalist of the news value of an issue or event. An interesting example occurred in December 2005 in the southern suburb of Cronulla in Sydney when tensions between ethnic groups were beaten up by the media into issues of race and terrorism. New South Wales Premier Morris Iemma made public statements about the issue of race and terrorism, and about the events that had occurred. During the week that the issue and events had news currency, the premier's rhetoric altered perceptibly but was carried widely and positively by the Sydney media. It was the result of the premier's media advisers being in constant contact with specific media, most notably the *Sydney Morning Herald* and television news reporters from Channels 9 and 7 that the message being delivered by the premier shifted from crisis to leadership.

Much of the time of the ministerial media adviser is spent in using experience rather than theoretical strategy to manage the media. As well as acting as the director when there is a communication crisis, the adviser is locked in to what has become known as the *permanent campaign*—the political image and reputation campaigns of the individual who is seeking always to be re-elected. Thus, there is a need to understand the two-pronged nature of the work. On one hand, the adviser is building relationships with the media and framing issues and events so that they will resonate with stakeholders beyond the media—various stakeholder publics. On the other hand, the adviser is building reputational capital for the minister that can be drawn upon at the next election. The difficulty in balancing the two is experienced nowhere else in the media field.

The adviser does not usually waste time attempting to build relationships with media who are openly hostile to a government's policies. In the New South Wales example, the premier's media adviser would spend little time anguishing over how to build a relationship with a talk-back radio program host if the host had been a political opposition candidate at some time in the past. There would be no opportunity to build a relationship, no matter how an issue or event was framed.

In the field of media relations, the job of ministerial media adviser is one of the most exciting and rewarding in the short term. The clue to longevity of working life is secondment from a permanent position within the public service. The alternative is to take the risk of being unemployed if the government loses the next election.

Politics

Political media relations

Most people find politics difficult, complex, and boring when compared to the simplicity of their household budget or normal daily decision-making processes (Kavanagh 1996). But when they do become politically aware and begin to grasp the complexities, voters tend to show more interest in the image of a party than in its policies (Schumpeter 1976). Early analysis of political communication was concerned with the role of democratic processes and outcomes (see, for example, Lippmann 1922;

Packard 1957). This early literature made a strong contribution to the understanding of contemporary political communication. It provided a secure base from which scholars in emerging fields, such as journalism, media relations, and public policy, expanded, relating their work in turn to the disciplines of economics, politics, and sociology. An examination of political communication from the viewpoint of democracy requires an analysis of various components relative to the public sphere. Mayhew (1997) attributes the origin of scholarly writing on political communication (as public relations) to Habermas in the 1950s and 1960s. Prior to Habermas, observers took a more generalist view, at once analysing and providing practical advice on lobbying, publicity, and advertising (see Bernays 1928; Goldman 1948). But Habermas's work should be viewed in the light of even earlier influence in the development of rhetoric as a historical precedent for public relations and as the true base on which modern political media relations—as a science of influence and persuasion—is built (see, for example, Aristotle's *Rhetoric*). Political media relations is used in its historical position within the political paradigm rather than in its contemporary position as a function of marketing and management. Political media relations has a number of potential modernist starting points, most notably the Eisenhower election campaign of 1952 in the USA. Eisenhower adapted quickly to the arrival of television that year, rejecting the traditional whistlestop train journey in favour of mass message delivery through the new medium. There is a similar starting point in the UK, and, with a later date, in Australia, where television was introduced in 1956.

Approaching the marketing argument

If marketing relies for its existence on the identification of aggregates of preferences in determining potential sales of goods and creates a framework in which these aggregates are measured against the supply of goods and services from industry, political public relations relies for its existence on values, opinions, and attitudes that are almost impossible to aggregate in an attempt to find a state of equilibrium that can, in contrast, be measured against the supply of **redeemable tokens** from politics (Maloney 2005). This is not to suggest that marketers, in their pursuit of equilibrium, have abandoned politics. On the contrary, there appears to be an increased quest to discover a state within the polity from which profit can be derived. For most marketers, particularly in the global pursuit of diversification that occupies the minds of multinationals, politics is the measurement of risk against taking up occupation in a country. It is the risk associated with a change in government policy that may adversely impact the operations of a particular organisation or corporation that is their sole interest (Keegan & Green 1997). Low political risk is equal to higher

redeemable tokens
forms of metaphorical currency that can be traded for votes; promises based on some future investment in political capital.

potential investment. For developing countries eager to grasp foreign exchange, there are avenues of pursuit that embrace the political media relations option—presentation of the country as a sound investment base—when in fact its political instability is less than assured. This argument presupposes a position relative to the selling of politics and its market-driven nature. Marketers attempt to reach the goal of equilibrium, gaining exponential advantage, but the constant change in values or adoption of new values outside the marketer's sphere of influence reduces any attempt to achieve a state of permanency. If this is the case, it raises the question of how a political media relations counsellor can represent certain interests within an increasingly dynamic framework using persuasive argument so that public opinion and attitudes are influenced at the ballot box. An additional question concerns the level of marketing that can be applied to a political media relations campaign in conjunction with a persuasive argument, whether the argument requires the support of marketing tools and tactics, or whether the argument can stand alone and alter the balance. An argument could be put that a politician presenting individual legitimacy and policy veracity through a spokesperson loses the right to be seen as the main actor. Witness the relationship between independent federal MP Pauline Hanson and adviser Mr David Oldfield during the 1998 Australian federal election campaign. The outcome of the campaign was the success of Mr Oldfield's personal ambition to gain a seat in the New South Wales parliament. Mr Oldfield, as a political media relations counsellor for the Pauline Hanson campaign, presented his own image as equally or more important than that of Ms Hanson (Kingston 1999).

If, as Mayhew argues, a contemporary political campaign is crafted along the same lines as a marketing campaign, there is justification for the number of consultants offering campaign solutions. It is not, however, a simple step from making an assumption about the use of marketing tools to conclude that marketing has subsumed political campaigning within its economic framework. Marketing is, by its nature, based on tactics designed to sell a product or service. Certain marketing tools that have made a successful transition to the political sphere include direct mail, telephone surveys, database management, and list selling (Mayhew 1997). But, overall, the measurement of effective marketing campaigns cannot be assumed to equate with a similar success in the political field, for a number of reasons. Marketing is economic. Politics, on the other hand, is a sociological discipline. There are tangible factors outside of financial considerations that impel a stakeholder towards a particular political direction.

As part of the process of commodifying politics, political media relations has turned in recent years to the use of marketing and marketing communication tools to assist political campaigns. The use of tools such as market research, and evaluating specific demographic groups of journalists and editors, is now a ritual part of national election campaigns in Western democracies. The use of marketing tools has a different effect on a stakeholder electorate to that of the employment of media relations and advertising. Advertising provides direct image comparison. The candidate who uses the local newspaper to advertise a policy, accompanied by a picture, allows the electorate to read its own message into the image. Media relations campaigns that include the dissemination of published material such as newsletters also provide a relatively direct relationship with the electorate. Marketing tools, on the other hand, are perceived by the electorate to be tactics that are unfair or unscrupulous because the electorate is unsure when these marketing tools are being applied.

Contemporary politics: approaching candidature

Politicians and candidates require the services of political media relations because of the diffuse nature of contemporary politics. Historically, candidates for representative office may have followed the path through party work, and in so doing gained the requisite skills to become an actor in the parliament. Whether a candidate became a successful actor was determined by the level of knowledge gained as a rank-and-file party member combined with the degree to which a candidate applied himself or herself to the task of winning various policy campaigns. Party membership most often began through familial ties and friendships. For the contemporary candidate a wider number of avenues are open, including induction into a party with no formal or informal training within the ranks.

The modern search for high-profile candidates in the business, sporting, and academic communities has created a change in structure of the development of candidates. Quite frequently, candidates enter the political arena on a specific mission, often one that has no political component and has equipped the elected representative with no political skills or knowledge of political theory. For these candidates, the potential for election is increased if they have the financial capacity to invest in the employment of a political public relations expert, one who can provide all the necessary information for them to present a strong campaign to the electorate. Candidates often enter the arena unequipped, intent on campaigning on what they believe to be their individual merit. Most of these candidates are content to show a public face at one poll, gaining the votes of immediate family and friends. They generally disappear from the political arena, never to return. Thus we have a situation in which candidates will present their credentials as they relate to their places of employment, their community affiliations, or their family. It is not unusual for a candidate to run on a platform of family, work, and church. Candidates who rely upon intuition to win office—those who believe they only need to nominate to gain enough votes—do not win. Intuition and a feeling for the electorate may provide the initial impetus or motivation to nominate, but only the development of a strategy and the application of tactics within the strategy will impel that initial motivation towards elected representation. Australian political scientist Richard Lucy's analysis of the 1965 Liberal campaign for the state seat of Manly in New South Wales provides early evidence of a cultural infiltration and a naïve belief in the role of intuition as an important factor in campaign development, along with a simple misunderstanding of the distinction between propaganda and persuasion (Lucy 1968).

First Rural Transaction Centre for Eugowra

In a real coup for Cabonne Council and Calare, the Prime Minister John Howard opened Australia's first Rural Transaction Centre in Eugowra on October 29th, 1999.

The centre contains outlets for Medicare, the Reliance Credit Union, Centrelink and other services including the internet. It is the first of 500 planned Australia wide to compensate for the withdrawal of major services from smaller regional communities.

The effort Cabonne Council put into securing funding for the Eugowra Centre helped the Council win two prestigious Regional and Economic Development awards at the 1999 Australian Local Government Association's National Awards for Innovation. Ω

Dear elector

I hope that you all managed to survive the changeover to the year 2000 without too many hiccups, either Y2K or diet induced!

It is now approaching four years since I was first elected to Federal Parliament and I hope I have been able to show that an independent can represent an electorate perhaps more effectively than a party member.

If I take a position on any issue, whether it is the GST or the Republic I do so for what I regard as sound reasons. However, my staff and I provide help and advice on issues and Government policy whether I personally agree with it or not.

Late last year I suggested to the Remuneration Tribunal that a realistic way of setting MPs' salaries should be found, and nominated the Male Average Weekly Earnings index, by which age pensions are set. The tribunal accepted my advice in part, but decided to use a higher base figure, Total Adult Average earnings.

This is what I objected to, not so much the increase in MPs' salaries which created all the headlines. Although the benchmark is still not ideal, at least any future adjustments are now tied to real workplace earnings, not some elite salary of senior bureaucrats or judges.

The mobile phone issue is still raging, with serious question marks over the effectiveness of the new CDMA system.

Please fill in the survey on the back page to help us keep pressure on Telstra and the Government for a truly "equivalent" replacement for analogue.

PETER ANDREN

Figure 8.2 A standard newsletter used to communicate with stakeholders

THE CHRONICLE: NORTH SYDNEY COUNCIL

Environmental media relations: Campaigning on a limited budget

Local government communicates its policies to a variety of stakeholders through issues and events that have been developed as campaigns. North Sydney Council, a local government authority with responsibility for an interesting mix of residential accommodation and highrise offices, communicates its messages to the media and other stakeholders in a number of ways. It has a strong environmental policy, so each year it runs a variety of environmental campaigns. There is an assortment of stakeholders to whom it pitches environmental messages, including local businesses, schools, community groups, and residents. Campaigns seek to raise awareness, alter attitudes and behaviours, and focus on a range of issues, including biodiversity conservation, water conservation, waste minimisation, and energy conservation. The environmental campaigns are managed by staff from the environmental services department; media relations are managed by the communications department. The two departments work closely in framing messages to stakeholders but the communications department is responsible for media relationship building.

A council such as North Sydney is mostly interested in local media, although some issues and events attract the attention of metropolitan media as well. Some of the media objectives for North Sydney Council include:

- meeting regularly with the editor of local newspapers the *North Shore Times* (*NST*) and the *Mosman Daily* (*MD*)
- meeting with reporters on the *NST* and *MD* on an annual basis for drinks
- maintaining warm relationships with relevant journalists
- forming relationships over time, in particular with a reporter who stays in the position for a long time
- dealing with all types of media—press, radio, and television; press is regional and local (the *MD* covers more council stories than other media).

According to the council's communications manager, Ms Sandra Moore, the longer a reporter stays with a medium the more chance there is of developing a strong relationship. 'We don't go out of our way to create a relationship with media. More often they come to us for stories.'

North Sydney Council has a research focus that includes an important Habermasian concept: its communication and environmental department staff follow and listen to media gossip from friends who work in the media. Habermas argues that the coffee house and its conversation (gossip) was the original site of public sphere development of communication media. Its use by council staff reinforces the continuity of gossip as a valuable research tactic. Council supplements and confirms any gossip research with a media monitoring service which it obtains monthly. Both these research techniques assist it to build profiles of media individuals although it does not do so formally by preparing case files on individuals. Clipping and filing media mentions is another standard research and evaluation technique used (see chapter 12 for a discussion of media mentions evaluation). Council also follows relevant news stories on a daily basis using *Newslines*, an online service.

While North Sydney Council has no formal budget for media relationship building, it uses a different strategy for each media campaign. To begin, it determines who its stakeholders are and the best way to reach them. It then investigates which journalists and media outlets might pick up the story that underpins the campaign issue or event. For its Footprints project—a sustainable living campaign for 20–35 year olds—the *Sydney Morning Herald* was targeted for media coverage. According to Ms Moore, the *SMH* is recognised as having a high level of readership among this age group. For its Energy and Water Forum, a number of alternative communication vehicles were investigated. As well as local media, council pitched its campaign to regional media and environmental contacts, including universities, to publicise the forum through their networks. Council wanted delegates from a wide range of social backgrounds and age groups.

As for most organisations, some of North Sydney Council's tactics work better than others under certain conditions. The council disseminates news releases, then follows up with journalists' requests, sending photographs and, if it is required, undertaking deeper background research.

According to Ms Moore, if it is a good story she will simply send out the news release: 'We know it is going to get picked up. If it is going to be so easy, we work the phones. Sometimes we use a third party advocate to sell the story, [a] high-profile industry expert, or celebrity or community member. Our stories are people focused. We rely more heavily on the quality of the story to sell to the media. We use the people angle to sell it. We use standard tactics, including news releases, background information, letters to editors, opinion pieces, feature stories, and personality profiles.'

Ms Moore says the delivery of material will depend upon how the media wish to receive it and in what format. 'To make it stand out we use our personal relationship with reporters. We will make an introductory telephone call about an issue or event, so that makes it more personal.'

As part of its planned media and public relations environmental strategy, council creates events around campaign issues. Past campaigns include:

- Green Power Poster—a design competition (2005)
- Footprints Project—the media were invited to an event to talk to participants (2004)
- Eco Pets Campaign—a photo opportunity with local pet owners (and pets) (2003).

Council evaluates and measures the success of its environmental media and public relations in a number of ways. One is its use of MASS Com Audit, a tool that measures the percentage of media releases published and attendance at media events (if the purpose is to publicise a forthcoming event) (see chapter 12 for more detail on evaluation).

Ms Moore describes the relationship building process as controversial:

We have a policy that representatives from the communications department can talk to the media. Council staff respect the professional skills and advice that are offered by the communications department. The problem that the department has is getting communication materials on time. There are a lot of internal clients, so there are a lot of needs and wants within council which makes the job very complex. The relationship with the media is very good and constructive. We make a point of not criticising reporters and journalists, and respect the conditions under which they operate. Council has the capacity to understand the position of the media. Our role is to present a story that will add value to the organisation. We present a story that best fits a medium's style and required information. However, as a government organisation, we would not go any further than that. We do not attempt to buy a voice in the media.

Political communication campaigns

For the politician, the main functions of communicating politics is to affect the allocation of resources and to avert, divert, or convert social change (Nimmo 1978). The most important issue facing a candidate at an election is the capacity to develop a legitimate communication campaign, then to implement it. Election campaigning requires an adaptive mechanism that can be triggered each time a new or favourable communication idea emerges (Kavanagh 1996). Political media relations rationalises persuasive strategies and tactics apprehended from advertising, marketing, and corporate public relations. Thus meaning can be ascribed in terms of a single issue or mandate, as it parallels the notion of candidate as product. Taking the metaphor further, this sets up a campaign to develop micro specialisations as complex as strategies for the counteraction of negative advertising campaigns. On the other hand, some elements of election campaigning have not altered significantly since the beginning of the twentieth century, even the end of the nineteenth century when leaflets and posters were the primary sources of campaign publicity. One important element of a strong campaign is the capacity of the candidate to accurately interpret the needs of the various stakeholders within the electorate. A candidate should be prepared to meet with as many stakeholders as is physically possible within the campaign timeframe.

Politicians and candidates need to be aware of the presence or otherwise of specific media with whom they wish to have or develop a relationship. As a reporter on a Sydney suburban newspaper in the 1980s the author attended a media event at the Australian Nuclear Science and Technology Organisation's facilities in Lucas Heights. The federal Opposition spokesman on science and technology, Mr Andrew Peacock, along with several other lesser politicians, was to attend the briefing. When Mr Peacock arrived, he immediately walked straight up to me and asked directly if

I was from the metropolitan press. When I replied in the negative, Mr Peacock abandoned me and the group of reporters I was standing with, turning away to go into the facility. It occurred to me later that it had been my clothing that had alerted him. I had on a coat and tie, not customary attire for a suburban reporter at the time. What this demonstrates is the simple hierarchy politician's employ when timing is critical. There was no value for Mr Peacock in gaining coverage in the suburban press. His interest was in making a negative comment at a higher level about federal Labor government policy on science and technology.

Candidates spend an inordinate amount of time developing a campaign yet frequently they are frightened by the reality of implementation. They find it far easier to present themselves in what they consider to be their everyday attitude with the concomitant expectation that voters will see this as a positive image of the person that somehow reflects a similar level of policy. Minimalist communication of this nature appears to be normative in regional electorates in Australia and New Zealand. There is a strong belief in the notion that word of mouth is more important than publicised policy statements, and that electors will osmotically transfer what is in the mind of the candidate to themselves without possibility of misinterpretation or ambiguity. There is also a belief that what has worked in the past will work in the future. The maxim 'If it ain't broke don't fix it' applies to a majority of candidates. The problem for the majority is their incapacity to see the result as a win or a loss (there are no second placegetters in this game) and to apply all their resources to being elected. As British political scientist Dennis Kavanagh (1996) suggests, it is the subordination of all goals to that of election victory that marks off the territory of the real political candidate.

There is a paradox in the assessment of candidates who present an unadorned image in that it resists Mayhew's argument for the injection of the political communicator between the candidate and the public. An interesting position Mayhew takes is that of deductive reasoning, or syllogistic argument, and its relationship to the redemption of tokens. It is, he suggests, standard practice in advertising or political persuasion to imply positive position but not specify exactly how promised benefits will materialise. This technique can be found in the advertising campaigns of most political candidates in Australia and New Zealand at some time or other. The technique is applied best in print media, hence the large number of candidates who invest in advertising space in local regional, and suburban newspapers, supplying pictures of themselves with a short caption promising a wide range of benefits for stakeholders. This suggests that citizens are unable to grasp the superficial nature of this type of persuasion, eager as they are to elect a candidate on the basis of implication and the redemption of a candidate's tokens based on narrow or ill-defined reputational capital.

THE CHRONICLE: THE MEDIA AND THE CANDIDATE

How an unknown citizen framed a media election campaign

Let's look at how a relationship gets built between a medium (editor, reporter, or journalist) and a politician. It's a bit like a sporting competition. We go out and compete, we have respect for a skilled opponent, we meet again in the second round, and we know a bit more about the competitor's capabilities. We get to know their weaknesses but at the same time they know ours and we build further mutual respect. The same thing happens before a politician enters the political arena. There is a local contest between a political candidate and the local media (sometimes, the local reporter follows the candidate into parliament by becoming the member's media adviser). To get a sense of the personal and how it invades the political sphere we can investigate the campaign of a candidate at a local government election in Australia. Let's call her Olivia. She had no media experience. She had a few beers at the football one day and talked to her partner about how she thought the local council was not very well represented. Olivia's partner, who had also had a few beers, said 'Why don't you run for election then?' Olivia, who was by now unable to concentrate too well, agreed (too much sun, too much football—nothing to do with the beer). Her partner thought he knew a little about how to construct a political campaign and a little about how to build a media relationship to support the campaign.

This is what happened. Olivia got elected. How did she do it? And how did she develop the media relationship during her first four years on the local council? Her relationship with the media was good. She had run the distance so the media (competitor) had respect for her. She made some big mistakes, but the media chose not to expose them (for a number of reasons), so she developed respect for the media. This is the part of the story we call 'ritual performance'. The media know certain things have to happen and political candidates know certain things have to happen. There are rules and referees. In this, politics is the same as a tennis match.

The campaign

Let's look at Olivia's campaign and media relationship building tactics. She made her decision in March and the election was in September. Her best girlfriend said, 'You haven't got a chance, don't waste your time.' She based her assessment on a number of things:

- not born in the town
- not a member of any community group
- not well known in the community.

This stopped Olivia for three months; she didn't regroup until May. Her final decision to run was based on her idea that the existing council was not looking after the wider interest of the community. She was not a member of a political party, so she decided to run as an independent. At the close of the poll there were thirty-three nominations for the fourteen council seats. Olivia's campaign platform was ideological. Her campaign slogan (to build her image) was 'Family, Community, Honesty, Integrity'.

She called herself a 'true independent' because other candidates calling themselves independent were really members of the two dominant parties. She came up with ideas that she thought might get some media coverage. Of the thirty-two other candidates doing the same thing, only fourteen of them were already well known.

Olivia's ideas included:

- tree preservation
- a popularly elected mayor
- pathways for indigenous citizens
- above-the-line voting
- a disaster recovery plan.

Boring. No one was interested. She sent her ideas as news releases to newspapers, radio, and television. No one used them. She decided to publish her own newsletter, found some newsagents who would distribute it, and someone who would write and publish it.

ABC radio thought this was a novel idea and ran a story about it in its morning news bulletin, which was followed by an interview with Olivia about why she had to resort to such an unusual tactic. Once it ran on ABC radio, a newspaper picked it up. Once the newspaper picked it up, a television station rang to do an interview about one of the specific ideas (voting). Olivia finally got coverage because she moved outside the ritual. The coverage kept going because she was able to provide good information about her issues and reduce the media's knowledge gap on issues such as above- and below-the-line voting. The television reporter was not afraid to admit that she knew very little about the issue and that was why she had not picked up on it to begin with. (The same reporter went on to work on political news in a national news network.)

The importance of the non-ritual tactic was the turning point of the campaign. But its importance is lost in the fact that campaign research had not identified that certain media people lacked knowledge of above- and below-the-line voting. The television reporter had read what had been published in the newsletter and revealed that she had had more 'trust' in this than the same story in the news release because it had been 'published'.

The second stage of Olivia's media relations campaign was to buy a small amount of advertising space in the local newspaper and a couple of spots on television. In order to so she had to raise some money and, in this, she was very brave: she asked people directly to contribute to her campaign. As a result, a restaurateur gave her $500, a few people Olivia met in the street on Saturdays when she was out campaigning gave her $10. Some other candidates spent between $2000 and $4000. One candidate spent $25 000. Olivia spent $1000.

9

Community, Not-for-profit, and Interest Groups

CHAPTER OBJECTIVE

- To develop an understanding of the role played by organisations other than governments and corporations in the sociopolitical sphere.

Corporate and government organisations are distinguished by their activities. Organisations that lie outside the fields of corporate and government activity are less easy to define. Some are subject to legislation that allows them to be tax exempt, but this is not a clear way to delineate them because this taxonomy includes groups as different in structure and purpose as employer groups, such as the PRIA, and charitable organisations, such as Burnside Uniting Care. It also includes organisations devoted to worship. Others, groups that form for specific purposes, such as in opposition to an issue or event, and then disband, also fit within this taxonomy but they are equally difficult to delineate because they emerge and fade, often as quickly as the issue or event they formed to support or oppose.

One differentiating element of the organisations or interest groups in this category is profit. Unlike with corporations, the most important stakeholders are not shareholders, and profit is not the primary goal. But this does not help to differentiate them from government, which also has diffuse primary stakeholders other than direct shareholders. An additional hurdle in the defining process lies in the widespread and conflicting use of the word 'community'. As an adjective, it creates meaning: community centre, community health, community leader, community hospital, community care, community worker, community service, and so on. It is also used rhetorically by politicians and other prolocutors to define a sense of place, or a sense of togetherness. Its common definition is 'an organised political, municipal or social body; a body of people living in the same locality; a body of people having religion, profession, or other identification in common'. This is part of the reason it is so important to the media relations process. While 'community' may have ceased to exist in reality, the perception is that the word can provide a sense of belonging.

Figure 9.1 Public Relations Institute of Australia meeting

Ideology

Community, not-for-profit organisations, and interest groups need to have an ideology, which gives them their reason for existence. Ideologies come in all shapes and sizes. Among the most common and most easily identified are:

- liberalism and conservatism, which both vie for dominance in the Western world
- socialism, with its path towards liberty and choice
- feminism and its positive recasting of political language
- green ideology as a buttress against all others.

Ideology is the shaping of ideas to form a coherent argument that will justify actions. An ideology is a call to action to affect change or a counteraction to retain the status quo. Organisations outside the corporate and government spheres adopt ideologies, frame and present issues around those ideologies, and attempt to persuade and exert influence on governments, corporations, or other organisations.

An attempt has been made to taxonomise all organisations that fall outside government and corporate spheres (Demetrious & Hughes 2004). But the convenience of this typology fails to acknowledge the paradox of the special characteristics of such organisations as well as their contemporary adherence to conventional media relations strategies and tactics. Of more importance is the acknowledgment that the organisations themselves need not be categorised in any meaningful way. If taxonomies are required, they should be measured against the frequency and use of strategies and tactics applied by individual organisations. Research of this nature will provide similar evidence of their intentions to that of corporations and governments when their policies are measured against strategy selection. An understanding of the nature of the organisation and its ideology through an analysis of its strategies and tactics leads to an understanding of its policies.

Community ideology

A community ideology is shaped by its surrounding *built* environment. **Communities** are a subset of society. They exist within systems and structures predominantly as part of the built, rather than the physical, environment. Thus, community ideologies are appropriated from whichever reality is dominant within the system or structure. Hippie communities in the 1960s argued that their ideology created policies of self-sufficiency within the physical environment, but the argument was specious because the communities that were established required systems and structures that ultimately overwhelmed the physical environment to become part of an alternative built environment. Twenty-first century community ideology tends to take elements of any number of existing ideologies and shape them to suit an individual community purpose.

Identifying community

Any attempt to understand and define community and community organisations is not helped by the number of activities labelled 'community' by governments. These constructions are designed to tie governments to the citizen's requirement for a sense of place (Meyrovitch 1985), to promote government as the benevolent social underpinning, the centre of the Habermasian sociopolitical public sphere. To overcome this opaqueness, other labels have been used by organisations and groups to differentiate them. But these labels have also come under scrutiny because of the possibility of alternative meanings being applied to them. 'Special interest group' is one example; equally ambiguous is the not-for-profit label.

community
a group of citizens; citizens organised into a political and/or social group.

The idea of community as an overarching philosophy is not new in the Western world. Collective social responsibility has existed side by side with the idea of individual advancement since the Renaissance. Towards the end of the twentieth century it emerged as communitarianism and gained support from among some European scholars keen to interlock individual liberty and human existence with the notion of a 'pluralistic web of communities' (Etzioni 1998). This idea was not founded on the principles of communism or on other ideals of communal society. Rather, it has its basis in the idea that while individual rights are important, they confer on the individual a duty to support and maintain each other within the sphere. For community groups, this is the central strategy in relationship building: the transference of the individual relationship of trust and support to other stakeholders, such as the media (Wilson 1990). It is such an important part of a strategy that it has been adopted, ironically successfully, by corporations and governments (see chapter 7, Corporate social responsibility). For media practitioners, this is the core competence of community and the clue to why community groups are better at building media relationships and why they are successful in framing issues and events. The greatest difficulty confronting a community group lies in its ability to fund a campaign. But this is not the case for all community groups. Indeed, funding can be forthcoming from the most unlikely places.

Figure 9.2 Cover of Hornsby Shire Council *Community Report 2004–2005*

THE CHRONICLE: UNITINGCARE BURNSIDE

How to get media coverage for community social justice issues

UnitingCare Burnside is a child and family welfare agency working in disadvantaged communities in New South Wales. Through services such as family counselling, out-of-home care for children and young people, and educational support and development, Burnside aims to protect children from abuse and neglect, break cycles of disadvantage, and improve life opportunities. Underpinning all Burnside's services is a deep concern for social justice and positive social change. This is demonstrated through a commitment to research, policy development, and advocacy with the aim of influencing governments and other decision-makers to make the community a just and safe place for all children, young people, and families.

The media work of the organisation is actively managed to complement lobbying and advocacy strategies, and is used as a means to highlight issues of concern that affect the people who use the services.

According to Ms Sandra Black, senior manager for social justice and communication, media relations at Burnside operates within the social justice, partnerships, and communication areas and interconnects with the areas of social policy and advocacy, research, quality assurance, and income development. These areas work together to provide the background information, evidence-based research, statistics, and latest innovations in service delivery to ensure credibility and accuracy of the media statements released.

Burnside's strategic plan sets key priority areas around its core services, and assists in forming the framework for the development of key messages, which, in turn, set the agenda in relation to issues commented on in the media. The aim is to be a credible source of information for the media on issues relating to disadvantaged children, young people, and families.

Burnside works to achieve a credible reputation with media by focusing on core issues and activating media selectively, characterised by strong statements that are regarded as newsworthy. Critical to the success in this area is the role of the chief executive officer as principal spokesperson who articulates the issues and the potential solutions concisely and with impact. Other spokespeople within the organisation are nominated according to the issue and their expertise in the area as appropriate. Often the expert is a person who uses Burnside's services. Alliances with other stakeholder organisations are actively pursued to strengthen lobbying strategies and provide increased power to key messages in the media.

Monitoring and analysing the media on issues that appear as news and how they are reported is an important part of Burnside's media work. This assists in targeting informed journalists, and provides information about which media to avoid. The approach taken will depend on the issue, timing, and what is determined as most effective.

A targeted media release and/or phone call or email to selected journalists is the primary tool; however, letters to the editor also provide an effective forum for commenting on relevant issues on the media agenda. If a media release has widespread distribution, background information is often supplied, particularly about the organisation.

Ms Black says one area that requires continual investigation is media enquiries to Burnside:

> Unsolicited enquiries from media are met with assistance as far as possible once an assessment is made as to the reasons behind the enquiry. We analyse possible scenarios based on what we can supply. Often, a story may not eventuate but this work is seen as an important part of developing trusting relationships, and results in Burnside becoming the first point of contact in the future to comment on issues relevant to the sector.
>
> Relationship building also occurs with the media departments of other organisations similar to Burnside and we frequently become the contact point for specific information. A recent example is legislation around return to work for parents with school-aged children. It generated interest from journalists seeking comment from those potentially affected. They contacted the sector's peak organisation who referred the journalists to Burnside media.

Social issues media

According to Ms Black, one of the challenges in social issues media is coming up with new and interesting angles on what can often be ongoing issues within the industry. Being passionate about a social justice issue does not on its own translate into a newsworthy item that will capture the imagination of journalists:

> One of the ways Burnside achieves media attention is through its innovative research agenda. The needs of children in out-of-home care research project [conducted by Burnside] in collaboration with the University of Western Sydney's Social Justice and Social Change Research Centre, presented an opportunity to obtain positive media and reinforce one of the organisation's key priority areas.
>
> This was the first piece of Australian research that included the participation of children voicing what they needed when in out-of-home care.
>
> Other key points were the link with a reputable university research centre as a major stakeholder, the research recommendations that would change the way services in out-of-home care would be delivered using a child's perspective, and the challenge issued to an established service system.
>
> We decided to prerelease the report to one journalist who is well regarded in the reporting of social issues in news and who also writes opinion pieces for a large Sydney metropolitan daily.
>
> The tactic provided the journalist with time to read the report and put together a story that would be released on the same day the media release was sent to other targeted press and radio. The result was a more indepth story that appeared in the major daily newspaper on the same day as radio interviews with the researchers.

This was a positive outcome for Burnside in achieving wide media coverage and reinforcing the relationship already developed with a key social issues journalist.

The report was also placed on the internet and more than 1000 hits were achieved on the day of the media coverage.

Ms Black says requests for presentations at industry conferences also occurred as a result of the media coverage.

An unplanned consequence of the media attention was the acquisition of a number of new stakeholder supporters for the organisation, including an ongoing community business partnership to assist children in out-of-home care.

Not-for-profit ideology

A not-for-profit ideology is shaped by the objective of support and assistance. It would be fair to say that most not-for-profit organisations adopt liberal or conservative ideologies. Their status as not-for-profit organisations means they generally work closely with governments to achieve their goals and objectives. Governments in the Western world are either liberal or conservative. Not-for-profit organisations operate within a systems and structural environment. Many large not-for-profit organisations have a bureaucratic structure similar to that of governments. Smaller, less bureaucratic not-for-profits, such as the PRIA and the PRINZ, rely for their continued existence on the support of unpaid professional volunteers. The boards of directors of not-for-profit organisations are comprised of volunteers, as are the thousands who contribute time and energy to doorknock appeals and other continuous not-for-profit activities. The ideology of the not-for-profit organisation is thus grounded in support and maintenance of others over self.

Identifying not-for-profits

Like governments and corporations, not-for-profit organisations have stakeholders. Not-for-profit organisations are subject to a different tax regime to corporations and other for-profit businesses. In this they differ from community groups. Not-for-profit organisations have access to limited funding. They have the media as a stakeholder the same way as a corporation or government does. They seek to gain media coverage for their issues and events by understanding how the news media work. But they have a much-needed advantage: they use the model of relationship building to establish their issues and their organisations as valid. The Salvation Army, for example, and its annual doorknock appeal get plenty of media coverage. Reporters are unable to place a negative spin on this activity. Not-for-profits ask newspaper managers to insert free ads when space allows. This is part of the relationship building process. Some not-for-profit organisations arrange an event on a regular basis to provide additional support they believe is required for an activity—Clean Up Australia Day, for example. Others get involved in events that may have no perceived finishing point. Not-for-profits are frequently government funded.

THE CHRONICLE: NATIONAL PRESCRIBING SERVICE LIMITED

How a not-for-profit organisation deals with the media

National Prescribing Service Limited (NPS) is an Australian government-funded organisation with interests in health and medicine. NPS views media relationship building as integral to effective public relations

For NPS, media relations is about how the organisation is viewed by the media and how it views the media. It is important to work with the media, and to know where in the market the not-for-profit is viewed by them—whether it is seen as an industry leader, a new player, or a lobbying organisation. For NPS, the process of building a media relationship involves getting to know the media well (key players, audience demographics, special interests), running media education events, arranging one-on-one liaison, pitching its story appropriately and well, making regular contact with journalists and reporters, and networking.

As part of its continuous media research, NPS undertakes internet searches of individuals, tracks their careers and interests, and analyses their style in their articles. In researching media organisations it analyses audience demographics, circulation, readership, ownership, features, and regular supplements. Its research does not extend to building profiles of media organisations by using proprietary databases or stock-exchange data.

NPS's budget for its media relations is embedded in a wider corporate public affairs budget. It includes investment in media education: tip sheets, sponsoring conferences and awards, and media events with an educational focus. Such events might be a breakfast and face-to-face meetings. It also includes meetings with each of who the organisation considers to be key journalists.

According to NPS senior public affairs manager Fran Hagon, NPS uses many different tactics when building a media relationship. Tactic choice is dependent upon the type of strategy, but it could include news releases, background information, letters to the editor, personality profiles, community service placements, op ed pieces, feature stories, fact sheets, links to further information, copies of resource documents, and supply of an organisational profile. It sends press kits in hard copy and other material by email. It claims to have a strong relationship with the media it uses because it builds relationships with specialist media in the health and medical fields, and provides evidence-based information that is reliable and independent of the pharmaceutical companies.

When the NPS creates a campaign strategy it does so around a single message with a different PR strategy each time.

An example is its *Common colds need common sense: they don't need antibiotics* campaign, which is run annually. 'We plan a different PR strategy each year. Its target in 2005 was parents and carers of young children so we hosted an event at a local kindergarten with a high-profile media person as guest of honour.'

As a relatively newly established organisation, NPS has invested wisely in building a media profile. Awareness is still not as high as the organisation would like it to be, but it adapts its strategies to maximise impact and awareness. It is driven by organisational goals and objectives and identifies media opportunities through matching interests. It uses framing to build its media relationships by targeting specific media.

'Media are targeted. We individualise our media releases for each target audience,' said Ms Hagon. The benefits in these relationships are that the media come to us for ideas, comments and spokespeople.

To measure the success of its media relations, NPS uses specific methods of evaluation, including media monitoring and analysis, formative and summative analysis, and techniques such as focus groups, telephone polls, and content analysis.

Interest group ideology

Interest group ideology is shaped by self. It is the binary opposite of not-for-profit in its pursuit of the assistance of others. Self-interest or self-reliance is the underpinning of conservative ideology but most interest groups would deny this attachment. Like community and not-for-profit organisations, self-interest groups situationally adopt partial ideologies. A green ideology is most suited to interest groups. It might be either green as socialist or green as anarchist. Whatever its basis it has as its core the relationship between human being and nature (see Freeden 1996). Thus, interest groups most often appear to oppose issues or events that they perceive to be out of alignment with natural phenomena. For the mainstream media, this is also a natural ideological position and provides the basis for good relationship building and makes framing issues and events easier for those referring to themselves as **special interest groups** and organising around a green ideology.

Identifying interest groups

An interest group is defined as a group of people sharing a common identifying interest. The difficulty for media relations is that this label also applies to individuals with a common interest in property, shares, or other asset classes, placing them in the category that defines itself by profit. Interest groups usually form around an issue and unform upon resolution of the issue. These groups are not usually subject to tax and other laws as they generally have no legal status.

An example is action by a group in St Marys, New South Wales, to stop development there of an Austrailan Defence Industries' munitions site as a large housing estate. These communities are often referred to as 'special interest groups'. An interest group can organise itself within a corporation, for example, to get a better deal on tea and coffee. We tend to refer to 'community' activity as such when it transcends the boundaries of special interest and when

> **special interest groups**
> a group of citizens who form for a specific reason or action.

it is less spontaneously organised. It may need to have an organiser, or a facilitator, but ultimately, there is a good chance it will continue for some time once it is formed. A special interest group, on the other hand, will most likely disband after the required issue or event is completed, whether satisfactorily or unsatisfactorily. One way to determine whether a community group is also a special interest group is to examine whether there has been activity after the initial campaign.

Media coverage is part of the answer to the question of how an interest group exerts power. Media coverage takes the issue or activity to a wider number of stakeholders and stakeseekers. It may not always mobilise individuals to join the action, but it will have a better chance of changing behaviour and attitudes if it is diffuse. Most interest group actions differ in terms of the influence and persuasion they bring to bear along with the resources that are required and their social and political implications. Availability of socioeconomic resources results in considerable differences in levels of participation. University graduates are twice as likely to be involved in interest group activity as those with only secondary education. There is also a variation in involvement among occupational and income groups.

Interest groups most often form for a single purpose, among them the following examples:

- to oppose a land development
- to attract funding for a swimming pool
- to stop development of a motorway.

Interest groups form to take action either against an activity or to promote an activity. Grassroots groups formed out of objection to an activity are rarely well funded. Without professional assistance they frequently fail to achieve their goals, aims, and objectives. The difficulty with this is that most grassroots groups adopt a position from which they are set up to fail.

They have:

- an elementary understanding of the political process
- an elementary understanding of institutional power
- a belief that media will naturally assist in their campaign.

THE CHRONICLE: INLAND MARKETING CORPORATION

Presenting all the facts in a long investigative feature story

To establish a powerful position that may not be in accordance with the real value it offers, an interest group can use a media and PR strategy to develop special rhetoric to position itself to take advantage of favourable media coverage and influence public opinion. I refer to this as a *mezzanine strategy* because it elevates the interest group or organisation to a point that is indeterminate but obvious. Mezzanine status, from the Latin *medianus*, meaning 'median', places an interest group above other groups or organisations that operate at a low level but below corporations, government, and the media at elite levels. This higher level is unachievable for interest groups but they need to elevate themselves above grassroots groups operating at ground level.

Such was the case of an interest group known as the Inland Marketing Corporation (IMC). This organisation, as we will see below, was established for the purpose of shipping fresh produce from inland Australia to Asian markets more directly than by traditional methods. In the process of establishment, the IMC employed a media relations strategy that positioned it at a level far above its value. It subsequently succeeded in gaining substantial media coverage of its issues and events, an objective that enabled it to inflate its position and use that to garner support funding from public organisations.

Brief background to the issue

The IMC was a regional development initiative of four central-western New South Wales councils. In 1995 four councils centred on the Lachlan Valley—Parkes, Forbes, Lachlan and Cabonne—combined, each investing $2000 in the concept of inland export marketing. This initial small capital investment assisted in securing the beginnings of ownership of the concept that was competitively being considered in Victoria and Queensland within similar primary producing districts. The four councils became the client stakeholders.

The IMC media relations campaign set out to define the organisation in media terms through ownership of the issue of transport and logistics of fresh export produce, specifically, to Asia. The idea for an inland marketing organisation close to the eastern seaboard, with responsibility for coordinating air-freighted exports of fresh produce to Asia, was promoted in 1994 within a federally funded local enterprise government framework to investigate regional economic development. The investigation showed that such an organisation was viable. A report on the potential demand for export crops to Asia intersected with the investigation. The IMC engaged a consultant to write a business plan and to develop strategies in harmony with the original federal government. The proposed operations were focused on reconstructing a Second World War airforce base at Parkes as the centre of its Asian export operations from which fresh food could be flown directly to Asian markets.

In the next few years the IMC lobbied successfully to obtain funding from federal, state, and local government of $4.5 million, $600 000, and $775 000 respectively prior to the launch of a wider local government investment strategy.

An information memorandum from the IMC to regional councils dated 27 April 2001 stated that the IMC concept was founded by its managing director and interim chairman, Alex Ferguson. Directors were Julian Hercus, an aviation consultant and former deputy chief executive commercial of Qantas Airways; Ric Simes, chief economist and executive director; N M Rothschild, former senior economic adviser to Paul Keating; Norman Hunt, managing partner of Hunt Partners, lawyers; and John Chudleigh, former principal of Orange Agricultural College. By its own recognisance, the IMC was 'established with the aim of developing new and exciting opportunities for farmers and regional communities in Australia'. This was the starting point of the IMC's political PR campaign in which the construction of images that take the rhetorical token to be self-contained requiring no redemption or explication, is overlayed with its economic campaign. It is difficult to determine what exactly is meant by 'new and exciting opportunities for farmers', nonetheless, the abstract images continued, with the IMC promising to introduce 'innovative solutions for export marketing and transport of agricultural products'. Images of boosterism and positivity substituted for realism throughout the campaign, culminating in the publication in the New South Wales *Government Gazette* of the IMC as a legitimate investment vehicle for local government.

The campaign strategy

The IMC campaign was so powerful that special rhetoric altered state government policy and placed the burden of responsibility for investment in the organisation on local government, regardless of discursive processes normally undertaken in the public sphere. Rhetorical foundations of the campaign to lock in funding from local government were revealed on the organisation's website in which it claimed local government was instrumental in establishing the IMC as the driving force behind regional communities. The website offered a claim that the founding four councils had support from 'over fifty other councils throughout New South Wales', which, *prima facie*, was accurate. It was, however, a falsification of the scale of the involvement of councils, a claim that was perpetuated by others with a vested interest in the development as the campaign evolved.

Of the 102 councils in New South Wales with the potential to invest in the IMC scheme, sixty ignored the offer, eleven rejected it, and sixteen accepted it before the deadline of 31 August 2001.

Between 1995 and 2000 a number of reports reflecting the IMC's advantages were prepared on the organisation's behalf; others were less favourable. The *Asimus Report* rejected the probabilities raised by the IMC that it would increase exports and find Asian markets. Asimus received representations from local councils and regional development authorities 'stressing the importance of infrastructure investment in regional economies and the importance of such investments as catalysts for economic growth'. Asimus acknowledged the importance of the issues of economic growth but concluded the rhetoric did not outweigh the reality that there is a 'need to seek investment in projects which are likely to **yield** high returns at relatively low risk'. The implication was that the overall IMC venture was high-risk and low-yield. The *Asimus Report* had been prepared as a response to a feasibility study by the Centre for Agricultural and Regional Economics (CARE) and DJA Maunsell. On publication of the negative *Asimus Report*, CARE and Maunsell argued the IMC proposal was based on a 'holistic' approach to construction of a freight facility and in the context of 'the opportunities available to Australia to maintain and expand our market share in trade in Asia and elsewhere, especially in perishable products'. By establishing ownership of the idea of fast freight of fresh produce to Asia, whether it did or did not have any basis in reality, the IMC captured, through a strong emotional appeal of economic rhetoric, the interest of government and media. It had a special effect on the New South Wales government but, while it had no direct political interest in investing financially in the central-west region, it assisted in the creation of the strategy that would persuade local government of its merits. The IMC tactic of using a third person to frame a positive argument was successful.

yield

the return from a campaign relative to the maximum theoretical return obtainable.

Linking opportunities

The rationalism frame for economic issues in regional Australia has been well documented. Its deep commitment at an institutional level (local, state, and federal government, industry groups, agribusiness groups) precludes regional media from any real investigation of alternative frames. Regional media must be seen to be committed to the same economic rationalism because it wants to be seen to be supporting community values, goals, and objectives. The IMC saw this as a prime opportunity to develop its rhetorical position. It would be difficult for the media to argue against such a good proposition, even if it were able to demonstrate that some of the tactics being used by the IMC may have been unethical. Economic growth for regional Australia was a conservative policy agenda that resonated with regional news organisation audiences; to reject it was to court disaster. The IMC was guilty of nothing more than exploiting the existing media frame that favoured economic growth at the expense of public discourse.

This was the start of a supplementary IMC campaign to position itself as a powerful organisation, with the interests of the wider community as its goal. The supplementary campaign involved it repositioning itself so that it would be seen to be equal in value and stature to those primary stakeholder organisations it was approaching for additional funding: state and local government in New South Wales. In this it was concerned with building relationships that highlighted its value and equality relative to the primary stakeholders.

Orange City Council involvement

One primary stakeholder that was concerned about the issue of direct local government investment in the IMC was Orange City Council in the central-west of New South Wales. At a city council meeting held on 21 June 2001, the business papers included an item outlining the strategy from the New South Wales government allowing councils to invest in the IMC. It recommended council invest $48 000 in the IMC as a B Class shareholder, a strategy that had been put to 102 councils throughout New South Wales. The business paper provided no evidence to suggest that other councils had accepted the offer. Advice from two senior staff was for council to accept the offer because it tied in with council's management plan for leadership by local government in regional communities.

Prior to the meeting, one councillor sought independent advice on the efficacy of council using ratepayer funds for high-risk investments. The advice was that council's best interests were not served by investing in what appeared to be a high-risk strategy. The councillor took the advice to the meeting, with an additional argument that included misuse of ratepayer funds and lack of scrutiny of the investment by council prior to a decision. Despite his best intentions, the approval was granted on 5 July after being held over on his appeal.

The IMC media strategy

The IMC disseminated news of its activities on its website and directly to media organisations in the expectation it would receive favourable coverage. In June and August 2001, news releases were distributed highlighting the strategic intent of the IMC relative to its attempt to position itself as a legitimate organisation at mezzanine level. In the first release it praised an Australian Industry Group (AIG)–Commonwealth Bank survey stating that '[the report] reinforces the strategies of the Inland Marketing Corporation [and that] the IMC fully supports the findings of the *Industry in the Regions Report*'. Using third-person support for an issue or event is a standard tactic.

IMC support for the AIG survey pivoted around the AIG argument that industry substantially added to the net wealth of regions and that, 'through using local resources and selling to markets outside the region, including export markets, regional industry provided a solid base for local economic development and ongoing growth [and that] to ensure the future of regions we need to encourage regional industry to be more competitive through investing in human and physical resources; to be more outward looking by developing export markets'. The AIG report surveyed 635 businesses that had a combined turnover of $9500 million and employed 40000 people. It covered twelve regions in Queensland, New South Wales, and Victoria but did not include the central-west region of New South Wales, the district in which the IMC had located itself. The AIG findings were published at a time when the federal government was focusing closely on attempting to revitalise regional markets.

The AIG is itself a powerful interest group and thus exists in an institutional sense at a high level in Australia, so it should come as no surprise that the IMC support for the AIG report was a clever positioning strategy. Alignment with another powerful interest group (no matter that it was self-generated) provided support for the proposition, from the media viewpoint at least, that the IMC was also powerful.

While the AIG survey focused on industry, an earlier report from the Central West Economic Development Group (CWEDG) determined that 'the profile of the central west region … is typical of most Australian rural regions with lower family income levels, skills levels below the national average and international standards, a significant departure of youth, and economic dependence on rural enterprises'. The CWEDG report stated the central-west region was unlikely to ever be a substantial supplier of manufactured product, locally or internationally, other than rural 'value adding'.

In these terms it was paradoxical that the IMC chose to locate in the central-west. On the one hand, it was attempting to gain government support to assist in economic regeneration, but on the other, strong evidence suggested infrastructure appeared to be too narrow to support development in either the long or short term.

A second IMC news release dated 24 August was a direct response to an *Australian Financial Review* story published on 10 July in which reporter Lisa Allen claimed sixty of 102 eligible councils had ignored the IMC offer while eleven had rejected it outright. The story was headed 'IMC spreads from border to border'—an allusion to a diffusion and strength across New South Wales in its pursuit of local government investment. This was neither accurate nor reflective of reality. The article began by stating that IMC shareholders 'truly represent a significant proportion of inland New South Wales'. It quoted Alex Ferguson as being 'delighted with the response to the … share offer [and that] the positive response clearly illustrates most councils are committed to finding new opportunities for growth in their region'. There are no substantiating figures in the second IMC news release. There is an allusion to a significant proportion of councils taking up the offer when in fact by the date of the final extension, 30 November, fewer than half had accepted. Following publication of the *AFR* story Ferguson contacted Allen's editor demanding an apology for publishing misleading information.

The news releases issued by the IMC are normative in their attempts to provide a positive frame on the information surrounding the issue of investment. Responsibility for investigation and substantiation of the information lay with the media. Journalism, being a dynamic process rather than a static phenomenon, routinises the unexpected, thereby enabling organisations such as the IMC to present strategies in the context of existing policy, in this case, economic rationalism.

Figure 9.3 IMC newsletter, *Quarterly Update*

The news release becomes news

An analysis of how the media dealt with the news releases from the IMC is instructive. For the media in the central west, particularly the local newspaper the *Central Western Daily* (*CWD*), the IMC issue appeared to be problematical. *CWD* reporters routinised the unexpected (the high-risk, ratepayer-funded investment) by initially reporting the issue without regard to alternative contextual analyses or investigation of unintended consequences. The newspaper policy was supportive of regional economic development, so that was the context. Television and radio in Orange provided limited news coverage of the issue but no feature interest in the story prior to the 5 July council meeting and only limited news follow-up after that date.

Initially, the story was not picked up by the *CWD* as a lead-in to the 21 June council meeting, as would normally be expected of an issue of the magnitude of the IMC investment. But following the 21 June meeting articles written by *CWD* council reporter Nick Redmond and regional affairs reporter Mark Filmer appeared.

Additional persuasive tactics

An important tactic from the viewpoint of a media relations practitioner is the use of the space in a newspaper that is provided for officials and elites such as the op ed pages, letters to the editor, and leaders. An additional important space is that provided to individuals. In the case of the *CWD*, the mayor is given a weekly space to report on council issues and events. As we can see from the IMC example, it is not difficult to get the official to provide support for an issue or event. Traditionally, the mayor's column appeared each Wednesday of the week following a council meeting. It was a normative example of Grunig's public information model of strategic communication. It was effectively and consistently applied to inform citizens of council decisions after the event. In 2001 the model altered. Public information post-event was replaced with a pre-event threat and punishment model. The mayoral column disappeared from the Wednesday edition following the council meeting to re-emerge in the Wednesday edition immediately preceding the council meeting. The IMC investment proposal appeared in the mayoral column on Wednesday, 4 June, the day prior to the independent councillor's appeal being debated in council. The mayor reflected directly on the appeal, suggesting it would be lost in the chamber. Space in the *CWD* devoted to the mayoral column is unpaid-for community information space.

The process of influencing public opinion indirectly—by presenting the opinion of a high-profile, powerful, elite public figure prior to debate on an issue of public importance—reinforces the object of the debate, the outcome of which is justified in any follow-up material and generated as a further reinforcing mechanism of public opinion. *CWD* coverage is limited to reports of activity rather than of process and policy.

The function of becoming the printed diary of the home town is what a newspaper must aspire to fulfil if it is to be a newspaper, but it is also a vehicle with which to communicate the means of social influence. American journalist and political communicator Walter Lippman's argument, that a 'stereotyped shape assumed by an event at an obvious place that uncovers the run of the news [and that] the most obvious place is where people's affairs touch public authority', resonates with the transfer of the mayoral column in the *CWD* from a 'post-match roundup' to a 'pre-match roundup'. Justification for the transfer may be supported by the principle that the public is more interested in information prior to an event and the Mayhewian logic that spectacle is a persuasive means of influence, but it is more likely that it fitted the strategy of the IMC.

An exciting opportunity; change legislation

While high-risk investments are an accepted function of a market economy—more often associated with large profits and spectacular collapses—there is an interesting public relations dimension to the changes made to the Local Government Act that enabled the IMC to actively seek investment of council funds.

For a number of years the New South Wales government had devolved responsibility for state-based issues to local government, including law and order and waste management, so there was a precedent for an alteration to legislation to allow local government to invest in additional activities. (In New South Wales, responsibility for local government legislation is taken by state government within the department of local government, which is, effectively, a branch of state government.)

A story in the *AFR* of 28 June 2001 by reporter Lisa Allen cited a Public Accounts Committee (PAC) statement that Minister for State and Regional Development Michael Egan misled the electorate by not disclosing to whom the department was granting money. Information from the PAC statement supported a New South Wales Audit Office report on the need for greater disclosure. The Audit Office argued that investment of public money demanded public accountability. The independent Orange City councillor pursued this line of reasoning in the IMC case. He argued that it was not good enough to accept a ruling handed down by the state government without public discussion.

In pursuing this argument, the independent councillor was adopting the line taken by Allen in the *AFR* following the PAC report. He found a link between the Department of State and Regional Development and the Department of Local Government and believed collusion existed between the departments' ministers, Egan and Harry Woods, and that Egan had been persuaded by the IMC to seek a change to the Act that would force local government to invest in IMC. There was an incentive in this for the state government, too. The proposal relieved the pressure to invest outside the Sydney metropolitan area—a course it was reticent to take—placing the burden of responsibility on local government.

The actions of the IMC show that a small organisation can pursue a public relations strategy that will position it at a level where it is perceived to be more powerful and valuable than it really is. A mezzanine strategy frames an interest group in such a way that stakeholders take at face value its symbolic capital (see chapter 2 for a discussion of Bourdeau's symbolic capital). But it must also take into account any opposition to the strategy. In this the actions of the independent councillor are instructive, revealing that while the IMC was developing its strategy, a stakeholder opposed to the idea was also working to influence and persuade media stakeholders and others within the public sphere. Publication of the IMC story in the *CWD* on 26 June provided the independent councillor with the evidence he needed to extend his own campaign if he were to gain support for his resistance to the investment. He contacted Lisa Allen at the *AFR* and provided background information on the issue. He also outlined to her the questions he would ask in the chamber if his appeal were upheld. Here we have both the interest group as stakeholder building a relationship with the media and a stakeholder opposed to the issue also building a relationship. Both stakeholders became sources for the reporter.

Allen followed up the lead from the independent councillor and the following Tuesday, 10 July, a piece with the headline, 'Councils ignore $5m stock offer' appeared under her byline in the *AFR*. Allen's story was well balanced. She made contact with the IMC chairman, Alex Ferguson, Dubbo city mayor, Allan Smith (Dubbo rejected the offer), and presented information on the number of councils that had agreed to accept the offer, those who had rejected it, and the number that had ignored it. The information on the number of councils ignoring the offer motivated Mr Ferguson to respond with a letter to the *AFR* editor claiming inaccuracies in the story. Lisa Allen framed the story around the independent councillor's argument that local government was being required by the state government to invest public money in a high-risk business when the state government itself was not prepared to invest larger sums. Dubbo Mayor Allan Smith was quoted as saying he wanted to see some evidence of how the $6 million in federal funding had been used as, other than marketing brochures, a business plan had yet to be produced.

Third person support

In conducting its issue campaign, argument by enthymeme was the IMC's objective. It persuaded its investors through the presentation of token arguments that suggested a positive outcome but failed to specify how they would be achieved. But its success was achieved by securing the support of a prolocutor, a third person with a large stock of symbolic capital. In public relations terms, the main actor in the IMC case was the IMC itself. But it had successfully persuaded a federal member of parliament, Peter Andren, to act on its behalf. Andren had been a newsreader at the local television station for twenty years before becoming an MP. He had successfully contested three federal elections, so his support of the IMC was invaluable.

In acting on behalf of the interest group, the basis of Andren's argument was that the IMC was vital to the economic growth of the central west and that regional development in industrial and commercial terms was the spearhead of such development. This argument was not new. Economic development outside the Sydney region, in the greater part of the state, was devoted to agriculture, mining, forestry, and fishing; very few major industrial developments in New South Wales had occurred outside the Sydney region. This made the argument from Andren and the IMC more persuasive for its economic potential, which was enormous: if the strategy worked, the community of the central west stood to benefit substantially.

Strategy success but venture short-lived

Inland Marketing Corporation's success in persuading a few local councils in New South Wales to invest ratepayer funds in its high-risk, low-yield proposal was directly derived directly from its capacity to present itself to institutional stakeholders and the media as a mezzanine actor of almost equal stature. By adapting powerful rhetoric to its own special non-redemptive tactics, and by drawing on its knowledge of the relationship between market-driven media and economic outcome-driven government, it succeeded in persuading decision-making stakeholders of the merit of its strategy.

The independent councillor's opposition strategy was unsuccessful. His limited experience of politics and media prevented him from pursuing his investigation into the IMC investment proposal to its fullest extent. While *AFR* reporter Lisa Allen was capable of researching information on the number of councils and those interested and uninterested, the independent councillor found the time constraints on investigation of such minor details overwhelming. He was also professionally ignorant of elementary investigative procedures: whom he might contact to obtain such information. His campaign was overwhelmed by powerful institutions and by a naïve assumption that placing an issue in the public sphere, through the media, would lead to public debate and a balanced outcome.

Global public opinion reflects a requirement of governments to improve delivery of services, achieve greater levels of resource use, remove themselves from areas where they have little expertise, and generally remain in the background while self-interest and economic considerations move to the foreground. When a government acts in some way towards an issue or event, then it does so as policy or, more correctly, as public policy. The act or action taken by the government is seen to be public policy. The IMC was capable of persuading and influencing government and media to the extent that its strategy was accepted in the policy sphere without real investigation. It was a minor interest group that applied a successful mezzanine relations strategy, but it failed to carry through. In 2004 the IMC registered for bankruptcy.

10

Timelines and Budgets

CHAPTER OBJECTIVES

- To understand why a well-researched budget is important to a campaign.
- To become familiar with the concept of timelines.
- To develop an understanding of the technical requirements of campaign planning.

In earlier chapters we have been concerned with objectives and setting up a campaign proposal and strategy so that both the agent and the client feel confident in a successful outcome. But campaign proposals, objectives, and actions can only be successful if they are constructed within well-designed and planned time scales and within manageable budgets.

Time scales—deadlines—do not pose much of a problem for the media relations practitioner. Historically, practitioners made the shift from journalism where the practitioner lives and dies by the deadline. The professionalisation of the field, with practitioners emerging from university and technical courses, is equally rigorous about deadlines: examinations and other assessments must be handed in before a deadline or the student risks being penalised. The same situation exists in the professional world of the media relations practitioner. Much of the work undertaken on behalf of clients is in building relationships with media, and the media works to rigid deadlines.

The requirement of a campaign to include a budget—funding—is more problematical. Financial input requires a level of skill not usually developed in someone interested in writing and other creative industries. But the well-crafted budget can mean the difference between a client accepting and rejecting a campaign proposal. It also means a media relations counsellor moves from being an expert in one area to needing to understand other areas. The shift marks off the territory of the media relations expert who needs to become focused on business objectives.

For inhouse practitioners, budgets will be supplied by finance departments. The level of spending on an issue or event will have been discussed across departments. A media relations expert will have provided input into the discussion based on research into the requirements. For a media event to launch a new policy, a corporation, for example, might have costed venue hire, actors, refreshments, entertainment, travel expenses, and accommodation. The client in this case will be the management of the organisation and approval for spending will come from that direction.

The preparation of the budget as part of the complete campaign strategy will be no different to the campaign proposal between an independent agent and a client. A budget compiled for a client must be transparent and include all possible cost contingencies.

Timelines and their importance

If media relations campaigns require a slogan it might be '*Carpe diem*'. Timing issues and events so that they have the most impact is vital to the success of any campaign. Understanding when to schedule them is the job of the media relations expert. In this the practitioner must deal with a number of variables. Most notable among them is how the client perceives the running of the campaign. A good client will leave an agent to get on with the job. An interventionist client has the potential to create havoc during crucial times. So the first thing to deal with in campaign scheduling is the role of the client. If the client is to act as spokesperson for an issue or event then the timing of the speaking engagements must be discussed early. Media relations practitioners have been known to create their own mini crises by not communicating with a client, and then discovering that a scheduled date for a client to speak to a media conference in Sydney coincides with the client being in New York.

Timelines and the timing of tactics can be achieved in a number of different ways, but they all relate directly to the relationship that has been built between stakeholders and the meaning that the frame has attached to the issue or event. Sometimes tactical timing is subject to risk and crisis (see chapter 11). A media campaign may have scheduled delivery of an important client announcement on policy that is evaluated as having a news value that might place it between pages one and five in a metropolitan daily newspaper and as a television news piece that might make the second ten minutes of a metropolitan news bulletin. It is scheduled for a weekday when there is unlikely to be much competition in the specific field. But the news item is dropped at the last minute to make space for the murder of a prominent politician. Exogenous variables are part of the daily routine of the media relations practitioner.

Campaign time planning requires a media relations practitioner to have a wide knowledge of what is occurring in the social, political, and economic spheres around a campaign. A corporation that increases its capital and its share price by relying on the production and distribution of rock music is going to schedule the release and sale of new albums by its popular bands to coincide with seasonal events, such as Christmas or summer holidays, to have optimum sales impact. A media relations campaign must be considered in the same seasonal, environmental, and situational terms. A government set to announce an unpopular policy will do so when the media are occupied with other more important events. A popular policy, on the other hand, will be scheduled to gain maximum media exposure at a time that reflects the best electoral advantage for the government. The reaction to such a tactic might be that governments and other organisations should alter unpopular decisions so that they become popular. But this is a symptom of market-driven policy rather than responsible policy.

There are a number of ways of representing campaign timing. The most common in media relations campaigns has been appropriated from management. It is the chart designed by management consultant Henry Gantt in the late nineteenth century. It is still known as a Gantt chart and it serves a solid purpose in being able to graphically represent every possible thing that needs doing in a campaign. It is a chart in which a series of horizontal lines shows the items that have been completed at certain times during the campaign against what was planned. A more sophisticated representation has been appropriated from engineering. It is the critical path method of analysis.

While a graphical timeline representation of a campaign can be a valuable measurement tool, not all campaigns require such sophisticated mechanisms. A client requiring one-off media coverage of an event does not need the added cost of a Gantt chart. An agent can arrange to write and disseminate event information without drawing up a matrix: a simple calendar will do the trick. It is when a campaign takes on multiple tactics, stakeholders, and occurs over one long period or several time periods, that the Gantt chart comes into its own.

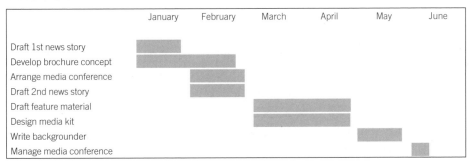

Figure 10.1 A typical representation of a Gantt chart

THE CHRONICLE: UNITED NATIONS MILLENNIUM DECLARATION

Constructing a global timeline for a major event

Imagine for a moment a campaign to gain widespread stakeholder support for a reduction in global poverty. Before such a policy is announced by an organisation as important as the United Nations, a number of things need to happen. One of the first is that someone must draw up a schedule of issues and events that relate to the announcement. The goal of reducing world poverty relates directly to the achievement of objectives in a linear fashion around the world over a prescribed period of time. It is underpinned by the rolling out of tactics that can be achieved within the allotted timeframe and within budget. The original announcement, as one of the Millennium Declarations of the global organisation, was viewed in two ways. It was seen by one side as a triumph of humanitarianism and a goal that should be embraced by all stakeholders, and from the other, as a goal that might be partially attainable but not within the proposed timeframe. Fortunately for those around the world living in poverty the view that prevailed was to attempt to do something quickly rather than slowly. But this exposed the organisation to the need to draw up one of the world's biggest Gantt charts. The timeline was so complex, and the number of elements that required definition so great, that it became a campaign in itself.

Within the United Nations, the Department of Public Information takes responsibility for delivery of messages to stakeholders. Using the Millennium Declaration as a guide, one of the core messages being disseminated is that of the eradication of poverty. A timeline for the strategy used by the department includes scheduling news releases, publishing hardcover books, producing radio programs and television news material, writing and producing internet material, publishing a quarterly magazine, *Africa Recovery*, running an annual international media seminar on peace in the Middle East, and an annual Palestinian media practitioners' training program. These are just a few of the tactics required to execute an effective campaign on the issue of global poverty. But the timing required by the United Nations is the same as that needed by a local community group keen to get some media coverage of a church fete.

Different ways to present timelines

As briefly discussed above, there are different methods of representing and scheduling campaign tactics so that they have the desired impact. A timeline is a linear approximation of each stage of a campaign. It has a starting point and a finishing point. A starting point might be when a client engages an agent to write a news release. It might be when an agent decides a story needs telling and wants to find a client with whom to match it up.

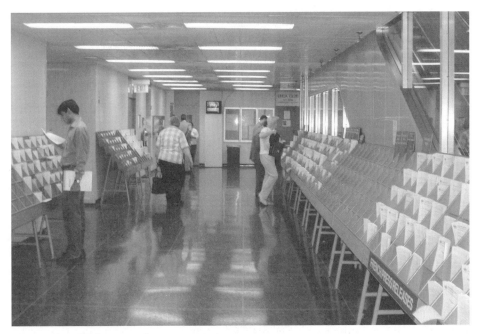

Figure 10.2 UN press releases

Example 1

You run a media relations consultancy. You get a call from someone in the Queensland premier's department asking if you can meet with the premier's media advisers. You attend the meeting and discuss how you might assist in getting stories in the *Courier Mail* that reflect a favourable image of the premier. Before you leave the meeting, the media advisers agree that you run a campaign. Your timeframe begins *now*.

Example 2

You are watching television on Tuesday night, *Last Man Standing*. There is a lot of stuff going on about sex and short-term relationships and blokes, but not much about the consequences of the relationships for the women involved. You run a media relations consultancy. You know of a number of organisations that are involved in women's health issues, including counselling pregnant teenage girls who have been rejected by family and friends.

You go into the office on Wednesday and begin:

- making a list of the possible clients
- identifying the issues
- researching the program's producers and writers.

Your timeframe begins *now*.

Matching timelines to budgets

In the first example there is a clear timeline and, consequently, a clear cost. The premier's department will ask you to supply costs, either a cost per hour or a cost for a complete project. You go back to your office and work out a budget for both based on:

- an hourly rate
- a project fee.

An hourly rate budget is one based on how many hours it will take you to complete all the tasks and reach your goal. A project cost means the same thing but might be structured in a different way. An hourly rate might be expected to include only the costs of writing the material. All additional costs will be your responsibility. An hourly rate is, therefore, usually higher than an hourly rate in a project cost.

A project cost might include all additional costs such as:

- transport costs for you to attend meetings
- your computer, facsimile, and telephone costs
- meetings you organise with reporters and/or editors.

An hourly rate can often work better for you if the work is short-term. If you are taking six hours to write four or five news pieces and one backstory then you might charge $300.00 an hour, which would include initial briefing sessions. However, if the premier's department asks you to submit costing for a longer-term writing strategy, such as writing a piece a week for the next three months, you might choose a project cost:

12 weeks × 6 hours = 72 hours × $300.00 = $21 600.00 + briefing session + disbursements = $25 000.00

Over the longer term you might want to reduce your hourly rate to make it appear more attractive and add *oncosts* to reach a similar figure.

In the second example it is not so clear cut. You might need to take a risk on pitching for something that a potential client does not know that they need. This is called a **loss leader**. It leads you in to future income, but you need to take a loss for it to be effective. You will be able to factor your costs into your later income, but initially, you are out there taking a risk (for more on risk assessment and management, see chapter 11).

loss leader

something done for less than the real fee that will assist in making the object more appealing.

But, like Bruno's relationships in *Last Man Standing*, it may come to nothing. In this case your budget development begins twice: first, when you think about the costs associated with bringing the issue to a client, and second, when the client starts paying you for coming up with a good idea.

THE CHRONICLE: BEGA VALLEY SHIRE COUNCIL AND BEGA DISTRICT NEWS

Government and the media collaborate on a timeline for street theatre

Towns and cities across the world conjure issues and events for the purpose of identifying them as special. Spectacular events become embedded in our minds as being part of those towns and cities: New Year's Eve in New York, Dragon Boat Race in Hong Kong, and Cherry Blossom Festival in Tokyo are examples that resonate and draw visitors from around the world. But they do not happen without complex organisation. They are not random; rather, they are campaigns designed to have a relaxed feel so that they appear to blend with the life of the town or city. Some sites base their entire existence upon planned issues and events. Citizens and visitors to the site have difficulty separating the construction from the spontaneous. In other places, the spontaneous culture has been adapted to become an event of some magnitude rather than simply a local act, Mardi Gras in Rio de Janeiro and blues music in New Orleans being but two obvious examples. The capturing of the local spirit or emotion attached to such festivals is how other towns and cities attempt to generate their own cultural emotional interest to create economic value for their sites. To achieve success, there is a high level of organisation and stakeholder agreement required.

In Bega, in southeastern New South Wales, stakeholder agreement and organisation has created an interesting version of street theatre that embraces the whole town. *Art in the Streets*, as it is labelled, provides space for local artists and craftspeople throughout the holiday month of January. Works are displayed in shops, other buildings, and public spaces. Artists are freely identified at the launch of the event, and throughout the month they share their thoughts and techniques with interested citizens. The event has a number of stakeholders: the local regional art gallery, the chamber of commerce and industry, a local tourism committee, the local council (for official approval), and, most importantly, the local newspaper. The event receives regular endorsements from the local public broadcaster leading into and during its life.

It is the involvement of the local newspaper, the *Bega District News*, that is of most importance to the success of the event. The newspaper publishes a twenty-four page A4 colour calendar of the event and develops the timeline. Twice a week the newspaper works to publication deadlines so it is familiar with the requirements of being ready for such an event. The most important element of the timing is the completion of all the works that will be displayed. Creative work is not usually something that can be completed for a specific commercial deadline so the organisers need to know in advance what is available. This adds an element of spontaneity. The event requires a timeline based on:

- availability of spaces
- completion of works
- early publicity.

This is a relatively simple event, yet to be successful it requires visitors other than locals to enter the public and private town spaces and to linger long enough to spend money. It is the role of the local media to talk up the event. A local newspaper today, as it was when Walter Lippmann described it in the early part of the twentieth century, is a **chronicle** of events that happen in a town, a diary that provides

chronicle

a record or register; a narrative account of issues and events.

information but at the same time investigates actions and issues that are out of place. The requirement of local newspapers to subsist by selling space for advertising locks them into a booster role when such events are conceived and planned. Events such as this thrive on early publicity and endorsement. It would be unthinkable anywhere in the world for a newspaper to consider attacking such a normative event. It will always provide support until such time as an issue emerges demonstrating the need for investigation.

Figure 10.3 Promotion by the *Bega District News* of the Bega *Art in the Streets* festival

Budgets and financial planning

A budget is defined as a periodic estimate of expenditure or, more simply, the amount of money needed for spending on a specific object or task. So the budget for a media campaign is a statement of account between an agent and a client. It represents the tangible financial investment a client is prepared to make to reach stakeholders. For an agent, it must represent an image that reflects other business investments made by a client. It must be presented in such a way that it is easily recognisable and able to be interpreted quickly and accurately. In other words, a budget is not something to be taken lightly, despite the general feeling of dread it may invoke in those less numerate.

A good starting point in working up a proper budget is to add up all the tangible elements. Tangibles are the mechanisms that will put tactics into play. If an agent is planning to hold a media conference, then the tangible elements will include:

- venue
- computer technology
- refreshments
- prose material.

The first elements are simple. Every hotel in the central business districts of cities competes for conferences and events. A list of hotels, telephone numbers, and expected attendance numbers will be a good starting point for research. Media material is a little more complex. As we have seen, an agent can charge an hourly rate for writing and producing material, or a project rate. If a decision is made to charge a project rate and the figure turns out to be less than the agent expected would be needed, there is not much chance of alteration during the course of the campaign.

In planning a campaign's finances, an agent must take into account all types of activities and tactics that will lead to the successful completion of the campaign. For this to happen an agent must be fully aware of and conversant with a number of technical aspects of the production of written and broadcast materials. An agent can enlist the service of a print broker, for example, to factor into a budget the cost of producing and printing a glossy brochure or an annual report, but a general working knowledge of the process of production is important to have so that neither the agent nor the client are charged more than necessary. It is also important to be able to communicate with service providers in the language of the business. Knowing what a *pica* (pronounced pie-ka) and an *en rule* are will make life easier for the agent when dealing with a printer or a typesetter. A campaign budget should include a final cost for a brochure or other printed material but it does not need to include the printer's cost breakdown to the agent. An additional cost, referred to as 'a loading', should be added by the agent for managing the printing and production process. As well as writing media material, some consultancies use inhouse production to design and layout media material; others use specialist bureaus. Other production processes that require high levels of technical knowledge are radio and television broadcast news releases and features. Production of a television community service announcement for a client requires an agent to have a working knowledge of camera techniques and digital transfer technology.

A standard campaign budget

Media relations income, for a standard agency, is generated from fees to clients. Fees generally include all those things that are required to run a campaign. The same applies to inhouse practitioners. Any number of costs can be included in a campaign budget, and will depend on the range of issues and events under consideration. One cost that is omnipresent is the amount charged for writing. As this is the most time-consuming element in most campaigns (if we include the cost and time for researching prior to writing) it is a substantial part of the budget. Writing can be costed anywhere from a one-page news release to the writing of an annual report or a book. A one-page news release might attract a fee of anywhere between $100 and $1000 plus additional research costs. Estimates for budgetary purposes are also used by inhouse practitioners to measure against success.

Other budget items might include:

- research
- venue and equipment hire
- transport
- design and printing
- mailing
- stationery.

Preparing and laying out a budget is a business function. On a standard graph, budget items are laid out on the left-hand margin under headings and subheadings. On the right-hand margin, estimated costs for each element are laid out in a column with subtotals for each subsection. A venue for a media conference, for example, may supply technology and refreshments as part of the overall venue hire. Large hotels charge for using their technology and charge a cost per head for attendance, but leave aside a charge for a room. These costs can be budgeted as a single item or separated to show the client their specific costs. There are several readily available software programs that will assist the agent to easily perform this task.

A budget for a media relations campaign is not much different to a budget prepared by a group of friends going on a surfing holiday. All the things they need to buy are worked out around a few beers the day before departure—new tyres for the SUV, wax, CDs, food, petrol, a swag for Liz—are categorised and costed, then determined against existing funds. The same thing happens for a campaign budget for a client. The cost is worked out against funds or, in the case of a new client, possible funds.

Pitches for new campaigns and new clients are slightly different. A budget for a new client should be closely discussed with the client before preparation. It would be unwise to pitch a $1 million campaign budget to a client who had a perception of the costs being 50 per cent less. The most important thing to consider when preparing a budget is the cost of the activities involved measured against the client's capacity to invest in the campaign and the potential success of the results.

THE CHRONICLE: STELLAR*CONCEPTS

How to develop a client budget

Stellar*Concepts, a medium-sized agency, works with consumer and B2B clients to build media relationships and frame issues and events so that they are relevant to all types of media. To achieve success in media relationships, the agency works closely with clients to develop budgets and timelines that reflect a client's interests as well as an understanding of media requirements.

In most cases, Stellar* works with clients on a rolling retainer basis, managing a twelve-month budget that is, typically, split into agency fees, expenses, and other PR activity. The agency works in accordance with their clients' financial year planning, strategy, and budgeting, and is provided with a brief and budget in June each year. Stellar* responds to this by developing a twelve-month plan and budget. Stellar* is provided with a total budget and asked to respond with a recommended breakdown based on the total sum to include fees and all other activity, including events, sponsorships, and media activity.

The first step in developing the budget is to set up a workshop that involves the client's marketing staff and its marketing agencies, such as its advertising and media buying agency to review business and marketing objectives for the coming year. This allows Stellar* to brainstorm and plan its strategy and weight activities and budget according to business and marketing priorities. The second step is internal agency brainstorming, which involves all Stellar* account team people and senior management. It uses a creative brainstorming method that helps to generate original and newsworthy ideas. Once these ideas are developed they are filtered and costed within the confines of the allocated budget. Stellar* then constructs a strategy document that is accompanied by a budget breakdown with most, if not all, activities, including a media relations component. The strategy document includes a number of measurement criteria, including a media matrix (matching actual stories against projected stories, coverage, key messages based on business or product priorities), as well as ongoing MEDIAudit and projection of other deliverables.

A typical strategy and budget (with percentage weighting attributed) includes:

- fee and expenses at 50 per cent of total budget with activities that include strategy and development with quarterly update on progress towards measurable objectives
- planning, organisation, and implementation of the *program*
- organisation and media activity
- sourcing and negotiating sponsorships and sampling opportunities, including writing and submitting sponsorship concepts and proposals

- developing proactive story angles, media liaison, and editorial placement; typically, they will work with their clients to set some clear measurable publicity outcomes on an annual basis against which they can be measured
- reacting to same day news and monitoring competitor activity
- copywriting and distribution of a minimum number of news releases per year
- product launches to key media and other stakeholders that Stellar* refers to as 'influencers'
- sponsorship allocations, including cash sponsorship, media entertainment, and events
- a budget allowance for product sampling based on the wholesale unit cost of the product for distribution at events selected.

An important part of the strategy response to the client's brief is the development of a timeline for all media activities over the projected twelve-month period. This forms the basis of Stellar*'s regular work-in-progress meeting with clients and is usually submitted in a template format developed by Stellar* using Microsoft Excel.

	A	B	C	D
1	SAMPLE PR BUDGET			
2	Prepared by Stellar* Concepts			
3	Please note that all items are ex-GST			
4	ITEM	UNIT COST	QUANTITY	TOTAL
5	Total PR budget including fees and activity	$ 192,000.00	1	$ 192,000.00
6				
7	Agency fees @ 50% of total budget			
8	Monthly retainer @ $8000 per month	$ 8,000.00	12	$ 96,000.00
9	Monthly expenses @ 15% of fees (but charged on actuals)	$ 1,200.00	12	$ 14,400.00
10	Subtotal			$ 110,400.00
11				
12	PR Activity			
13	Sponsorships			
14	Sponsorship cash investment	$ 50,000.00	1	$ 50,000.00
15	Split over 4–6 events throughout the year			
16	Sponsorship product investment - based on sampling 500 products p.a. at unit cost of $12 per product	$ 12.00	500	$ 6,000.00
17				
18	Events			
19	Events, i.e. product launches, trade shows, key influencer activities, media events, including catering, beverage, themeing, venue hire, stunts, etc.			
20	1 x product launch	$ 20,000.00	1	$ 20,000.00
21	2 x media events/trade launches	$ 10,000.00	2	$ 20,000.00
22	Allocation for additional media/key influencer/client entertainment throughout the year	$ 5,000.00	1	$ 5,000.00
23				
24	General publicity placement			
25	Press kit development	$ 2,000.00	1	$ 2,000.00
26	Photography to accompany regular rollout of media stories	$ 5,000.00	1	$ 5,000.00
27	Media site visits	$ 2,400.00	1	$ 2,400.00
28	Subtotal			$ 110,400.00
29				
30	GRAND TOTAL			$ 220,800.00
31				

Figure 10.4 A typical budget graph

The cost of writing, designing, and printing

A media relations practitioner will be commissioned to write news releases, backstories, features, and the narrative section of annual reports, as discussed in earlier chapters. Practitioners may not be expected to design and layout complex publications, nor to have the expertise to print them, but at each stage of the process, the more knowledge one has of the process, the smoother the ride to completion.

Let's say we have been asked by a large organisation to present a proposal to write, design, and print a glossy, four-colour annual report but this year the client wants to produce it as a book as well as a digital video disk (DVD). There are a number of ways we can tackle this. We can commission a writer, a designer, and a printer to provide costs for each component. We can add a management fee and submit the proposed budget to the prospective client. This is what we would do if we were a small agency because our time is better occupied pitching for new business and servicing existing clients at a management level than sitting in the back room acting out our technical and creative fantasies.

On the other hand, we might be an even smaller consultancy in which there is just us: two people with writing and design skills who are very good at news releases. A large number of consultancies in Australia and New Zealand operate this way. Most have specific skills—writing, design, management—but rarely do they have all the skills bundled together. To do so would mean having been trained as a reporter, a copy subeditor, a layout subeditor, a typesetter, a printer, and a manager. Whatever the situation, we are going to require the services of other professionals at some stage in the process. For the process to run smoothly and successfully we need to know something about it technically.

The knowledge a printer expects media relations people to have

Printers create all types of media for clients. The list might include annual reports, brochures, flyers, and press kit folders. But it also includes video packaging CDs and DVDs. Printing is a complex technology, but most printers suggest that a good relationship can be built between a media relations practitioner and a printer if the practitioner has a good grasp of printing technology, especially design and layout, but also the technical specifications that go together to create a printed product.

Summit Printing, a company with interests in compact disk manufacturing, DVD technology and four-colour printing and packaging, produces all types of media for clients. One of its more interesting tasks is the manufacture and inking of music CDs and DVDs. This process is automated, but it requires a media relations practitioner to understand the technologies and costs involved if they are to use the technology effectively as part of an issue or event. So it is important to include a breakdown of costs in a budget. A knowledge of the design, film, and printing processes also enables a media relations practitioner to contain costs. Print brokers will take on the task of managing a print job, but the additional cost of management may be prohibitive. In commissioning a media relations expert, it is reasonable for a client to expect a high level of understanding of all stages of the design and production process.

According to Summit Printing Sales Manager Peter Cottam, a standard printing job will require a media relations practitioner to submit a number of pieces of information that will then be costed by the printer. Manufacture and printing of a CD or DVD will be slightly different.

A standard print job will require:

1 quantity (the number of copies to be printed)
2 supply of artwork (on disc or as an emailed file from PC, Macintosh, or ISDN)
3 final size—flat and/or folded
4 type of fold—roll, Z, gate
5 stock—paper, board, gloss, matte, satin, offsets, and weight of stock in grams per square metre (gsm)
6 colours—1, 2, 3, 4, 5, CMYK, varnish
7 product description—leaflet or flyer, folder or brochure, poster, presentation, folder
8 self cover, plus covers and page numbers if it is a booklet
9 coated—machine varnish, celloglaze, UV varnish
10 packaging description—boxed, shrinkwrapped, on pallets
11 delivery instructions—one delivery address, multiple delivery.

This is a standard list of requirements for the printing stage of the job. Additional requirements include the type of artwork, film, and proofs that the job demands. The size of the job should cause no undue stress; apart from cost, printing one copy is no different to printing 500 000 copies in terms of the design and writing.

The quantity printed will include *overs* or *unders*, which is the number that is either underestimated or overestimated by the printer when the paper for the job is purchased.

perfect binding
a way of joining together the pages of a publication such as a magazine or book; glued on the spine rather than stapled.

The supply of artwork is the way the designer presents the written material to the printer, either as a Mac or PC disk or as an email attachment. The material will probably have been designed using either InDesign or QuarkXPress.

Size relates to the dimensions of the finished book. It could be standard A4 with **perfect binding** or it could be **saddle stitched**, both of which are methods of holding the pages together. Size also requires you to indicate whether the book is **landscape orientation** or **portrait orientation**, meaning whether the pages are read vertically or horizontally.

> **saddle stitched**
> a method of joining pages in a book or magazine by using a number of staples inserted in the spine.

Type of fold means the book can have an additional page as its covers (covers are referred to as outside front, inside front, outside back and inside back), which is called a gatefold.

Stock is the type of paper, its weight, and its feel. Weight is referred to in grams per square metre. A standard A4 leaf is around 80 gsm. An annual report might have paper stock as heavy as 140 gsm, which can be glossy or matte finished.

> **landscape orientation**
> the placement of a page layout so that the width is greater than the height; derived from pictures of natural scenes.

A four-colour annual report means a printer uses the four available colours of cyan, magenta, yellow, and black, also known as CMYK (where black is designated by the letter K). A fifth colour, usually a specific colour selected from the standard for measuring printing colours, the Pantone Matching System (PMS), usually the colour designated as a corporate colour, might also be needed in the process. A client will provide its specific PMS colour for all print jobs and the printer will match

> **portrait orientation**
> a way of placing a page so that the height is greater than the width; see landscape orientation.

it exactly. A colour chart showing every PMS colour can be bought from any art or stationery shop.

The book can be printed in two parts, the covers and the pages, depending upon the weight of paper for both. The covers might use a heavier stock than the pages, and usually does. Whatever the case, they will be printed according to the type of machine the printer has. It might print sixteen pages in a run or thirty-two. The number of pages will always be expressed as multiples of four, either including or excluding covers.

For the DVD that accompanies the hard copy report, the printer will require some similar and some additional information, including:

1 quantity
2 number of colours on label
3 type of packaging—cardboard sleeve, plastic tray, jewel case, easypack
4 sleeve and/or booklet
5 number of pages for booklet
6 number of colours for booklet and/or sleeve.

The additional investment for the DVD will be in the production of the video images and voice. Video production and broadcast production, unless a media relations practitioner has specific expertise, should be factored into the budget as an outsourced component of a campaign. Like design and production capabilities, if a practitioner has expertise, it can be employed resourcefully to produce the video or broadcast components of a DVD.

Figure 10.5 Packaging CDs

Part 4

Evaluation and Assessment

11

Risk, Uncertainty, and Crisis: How to Identify and Manage Them

CHAPTER OBJECTIVES

- To learn to identify risk and uncertainly in media relations.
- To understand the importance of managing risk and uncertainty.

Successful media relationship building requires skilful management. Designing and constructing media campaigns is the first step in the process. Managing the campaign to a successful conclusion and being able to evaluate its success are the hallmarks of what Grunig calls 'excellence' in public relations. Problems may arise during the **formative stage** of a relationship building campaign but only the implementation will bring out the potential risk or crisis. In this chapter we are interested to learn not so much about how to avoid crisis as how to recognise risk and uncertainty and to manage the resultant exposure. When these two scientific principles are understood and built into a campaign, the risk or

formative stage
the early stage of a campaign where ideas are being developed.

uncertainty of a crisis will be lessened. We are also interested here in the idea of crisis as it relates to media rather than wider stakeholders. A media-related crisis can result from all types of activity, from something as complex as the unintended release of sensitive commercial information to a simple behavioural or personality issue between a client and a media organisation or individual.

Part of the reason for the increase in unnatural disasters that have had an impact on media relations experts is the short-sightedness of business and governments in the pursuit of profit and other direct stakeholders' influences. Short reporting and budgeting periods require a narrow focus. Looking closely all the time does not allow for a long view towards what might become a problem and how to avert it. Issues and events for all types of organisations can become problems and problems can become emergencies or crises if there is no long view. This short-sightedness is something that affects more than organisations. It has the capacity to affect countries and global issues and events such as monetary values and prices (see Snooks 1998). Historically, global stock markets have altered when there is no long view of economies. The difficulty for media relations practitioners in taking the long view is that the organisations that employ them require short-term goals and objectives to be met on a rotating basis. As I have mentioned elsewhere, where once a short-term goal might have been measured against a yearly profit and long-term objectives against a five-year plan, now short-term goals are measured weekly and a long-term objective is too long if it extends past six months. A media relations practitioner must, therefore, be as prescient as a medieval sage, the irony of which is barely concealable. For the media relations practitioner, a balance must be reached between knowing what is likely to divert an organisation from its course and what avenues can be pursued to manage a diversion.

Emergencies and crises cause uncertainty, ambiguity, and disorder. They have the potential to destabilise a regime or social order, to threaten life, or at the least to cause surprise and irritation. A crisis is not always unnatural—the threat of an avian influenza pandemic, for example—but for an organisation, any crisis can have dire consequences. How the media—as a primary stakeholder—investigate and frame crises and how they differentiate natural and unnatural crises is the focus of this chapter. We are also interested in how other stakeholder publics shape their opinions of organisations that are the subject of crisis or emergency, but they lie beyond the media.

Media linguistically differentiate between natural and unnatural crises. A natural occurrence is framed as a disaster, while an unnatural disaster is a crisis. This is not unreasonable and it has broad ramifications for how an organisation responds to both. For an organisation, being the central actor in a crisis creates core problems while being a peripheral actor in a disaster can create core benefits. An organisation, for example, that provides financial and other aid in a natural disaster such as an earthquake or flood, builds reputational capital with a wide number of stakeholders, including the media. An organisation that fails to financially invest in the diversion of a disaster, avian flu, for example, loses reputational capital first with the media and then with stakeholders as its lack of involvement is more widely reported.

It is the duty of the media to investigate and report natural and unnatural crises and emergencies for a variety of reasons. Natural disasters and emergencies, such as floods, earthquakes, and bushfires, are generally reported first as straight news related to loss of life or property. After the event, investigation widens to embrace possible causes and effects, and to apportion blame. In the event of a crisis, communication plays a vital role in averting potential increases in loss and has attached to it certain models that have become known as 'crisis communication' (Heath 2001). When organisations are confronted by crisis they must explain, deny, or justify their policies and existence, redeem their image and reputation, and reposition themselves competitively after the event. For the media, a corporate or government crisis is a signal to attack the legitimacy and credibility of the organisation. Depending upon the severity of the crisis, it might also provide an opportunity to attack on a broader front, implicating other organisations and individuals within the immediate sphere of the organisation in crisis.

Some years ago, a South Australian food manufacturer and processor was bankrupted by the death of an individual who ate its processed meat. The media enquiry into the corporation investigated government controls and regulations on processed food as well as the circumstances that allowed the corporation to manufacture deadly food products.

A media attack on credibility and legitimacy must be managed by a media professional. For a food manufacturer that kills a customer, there is no denying responsibility for the crisis. It must be explained in those terms. There can be no justification. But explanations and taking responsibility are not always simple, and rebuilding media relationships after a crisis are not always possible. As Australian scholar Steve Mackey (2004) points out, a crisis can link a place or time in the minds of stakeholders forever. It is no coincidence that Osama bin Laden's terrorist organisation chose September 11 2001 as the date on which to etch its horror into the minds of Americans. (The telephone emergency phone number in the USA is 911.)

The media and an interpretation of crisis

Media thrive on crisis, emergency, and disaster. Even the most innocuous, mediocre, weekly suburban newspaper gets hot and heavy when disaster strikes. A tree falling on a car in a storm will generate hundreds of column centimetres attacking the local authority for not being vigilant and pruning the trees before they had a chance to squash someone's property (private property rights feature in eight out of ten news stories in local weeklies), and five times out of ten, there will be someone who deserves to take blame. The other 50 per cent of the time media frames material as if there is implied blame: someone is accountable but is opaque in the overall investigation of the crisis. For the media, the individual who is attempting to frame the crisis—the source—is not always viewed as objective. A local council media relations officer, for example, in providing information after the event, might be seen to be providing a one-sided view of the crisis. Under normal conditions, the relationship building between the media and the council media relations officer might be significant as a local weekly newspaper relies heavily on council material for its news copy. The difficulty for the council media relations officer is in being seen as an unreliable source during times of crisis when the council's position might not reflect the level of agitation that the newspaper requires.

Organisations frequently apply investment to natural disasters to sustain reputational capital but that does not mean that it will remain as a credit with a stakeholder. Unlike a bank in which deposits can be made and withdrawn, reputational capital has a short shelf life. The media will rarely recognise an organisation is in credit.

Figure 11.1 At work in a newsroom: an editorial meeting at the *Central Western Daily*, Orange, N.S.W.

What do you mean, risk?

Risk, which can be defined as exposure to injury or loss, is something we expose ourselves to every day of our lives. The media exacerbate the image of risk through news of issues and events to which we are naturally risk-averse. Murder, car crashes, and shark attacks are all events that we, as citizens, wish to avoid. But they are a part of the world in which we live so we will expose ourselves to the risk of encountering them if we go out late at night, drive motor vehicles, or swim in the ocean. The older we get, the more we see risk as something that might have a direct effect on us. In our twenties we take extraordinary risks with our lives, our careers, and our finances. Nothing will happen to us. In our thirties we take fewer financial risks but we still think we are physically bulletproof. By the time we reach our forties (if we haven't taken too big a physical risk and been killed) most of us have a mortgage and our career has become very important, so we take fewer financial and job risks.

When we begin a media relations campaign we expose a client to potential injury and to potential loss. It is the duty of a media relations practitioner to manage risk so that any exposure to injury or loss is minimised. This assumes a level of risk in all issues or events. The goal is to reduce risk to a manageable level. Media relations is mostly about risk avoidance. But this assumes that risk can be avoided. What we are interested in is managing risk and reducing uncertainty. We are interested in how we can reduce risk and uncertainty for our primary stakeholders, the media and the client.

There are four stages of risk and uncertainty:

1   when we deliver a campaign proposal to a client
2   when we send out material to the media
3   when there is a knowledge gap
4   when our frame does not match the media agenda.

How a client perceives a proposal

The media relations client is the stakeholder of greatest importance. Without a client a media relations campaign does not exist, as it is the client who pays the bills. It is important to keep a focus on the importance of the client, not only because they pay the bills, but also for the simple reason that it is their issue or event that secures and nourishes the existence of the media relations specialist. If there is no client, there is no issue or event. Even so, the importance of the client must be considered on balance with the existence of all other stakeholders. Balancing stakeholder requirements can be problematical. If a client is motivated and becomes overenthusiastic about an issue or event, it can have a detrimental effect on a campaign issue or event. A client who thinks a news release should be distributed before the completion of adequate research into an issue or event requires counselling as much as a client who is reticent about media engagement. A client will be more attuned to the risk associated with their business than with the risk attached to media engagement. (In this chapter, as discussed elsewhere, the idea of client and agency is attributable to all media–client relations, regardless of whether they are inhouse or agency.) They will be naturally risk-averse when considering investment in media relations campaigns unless they have had positive experiences. Not all clients have wide media relations experience and some may have had a negative experience. So there is a level of risk attached to the delivery of a client campaign proposal. We need to know the probability that our media relations proposal will not be rejected by our client. We need to assess the level of risk we involve ourselves in when we put a proposal to a client. Here, we begin to understand theories of persuasion and influence and how they motivate a client to accept a proposal and that we will implement the proposed strategies.

We can define risk simply as danger and exposure to the possibility of loss.

A client will not be keen to engage with a campaign proposal that includes a high level of risk. An example might be a decision to send material to a newspaper about an issue that has the potential for the reporter to investigate it further and write a negative story. Even if the probability of a negative story were 30 per cent, the client might be unwilling to take that risk. Clients will accept the details of a campaign proposal if they believe the risk is manageable. It is the duty of a media relations professional to persuade the client that the risk is manageable.

How the media perceive client material

Getting over the client hurdle is the first stage in managing media relations risk. The second risk for a media relations practitioner is in the sending of material to the media. There is plenty of evidence that the majority of news releases are neither read nor acted upon by the media receiving them. I calculate that on any given working day in Australia the media—that is all newspapers, radio, television, and internet organisations—receive around 500 000 pieces of information that could be labelled 'news releases'. They arrive by email, facsimile, and hard copy from governments, corporations, agents, charities, community groups, special interest groups, unions, educational institutions, small businesses, sports clubs, community clubs, other media, conventions, conferences, hospitals, agriculturalists, churches, animal welfare organisations, and individuals. In New Zealand the volume is not as great but that is simply because the population is smaller.

THE CHRONICLE: INVESTIGATING REAL NEWS

Why journalists hate news releases

Imagine, then, that you are a journalist with a tight deadline. You are working on a really interesting and newsworthy story and beside you on your desk is a half-metre-high pile of A4 paper. Some are single sheets, others are three or four sheets stapled together. They all have a headline at the top of the page followed by well set out, thoughtful copy concluding with all the necessary details for you to make contact with the person sending the material. But they are of no relevance or interest to you or your medium. So they sit there for a few more days until you take some from the top of the pile, give them a cursory glance, then drop them in the waste basket. The next afternoon, when you arrive for your shift, you boot your computer and discover there are seventy-three new pieces of material that have been emailed to you unsolicited. Your deadline for the interesting, newsworthy copy is later that evening. You highlight the top email, click on the bottom one while holding down the shift key, and trash the lot. (Pity, there was an apology from an old boyfriend in there, but hey, he should have sent a text message.) The only thought you give to the news releases is the irritation they cause.

This imagined example is the cause of great concern for the media relations practitioner, but there is an equally destructive element within the media that is less well known. Part of the contemporary Australian and New Zealand media culture is the act of dismissing news material from media relations practitioners out of hand. It presents practitioners with a grave risk: the possibility that no matter how interesting and newsworthy a news release might seem to them, it will not even be looked at, let alone investigated, by the journalist because it is seen to be evil. The demonisation of the news release draws its strength from the notion that journalism is an investigative activity requiring objectivity and freedom. Among the media, the news release is there to be reviled and its producers to be smirked at and abused as being lesser human beings.

Unless the news release has an appropriate seal. For the media relations practitioner an acceptable seal is the difference between high risk and low risk. A client with a seal that produces reputational capital runs far less risk in the presentation of media material than one with no reputational capital or developing capital. But in the constantly changing media world, a seal that is right one day may not be the right seal the next. An example might be the name of the governor-general at the top of a news release, or the Australian coat of arms. Prior to 1975, the office of the governor-general stamped on the letterhead of material sent to the media would guarantee positive investigation of its content. At the beginning of the twenty-first century, the same letterhead is likely to receive negative comment among its media recipients and the possibility that the issue or event in question will become a story with a negative angle. In just one generation, the risk for the office has dramatically altered. Similarly, the logo of multinational building-products corporation James Hardie at the top of a news release may generate a flurry of criticism within a contemporary newsroom whereas at the beginning of the 1990s Hardie was the darling of the stock exchange and of the residential building boom in Australia. There are hundreds of examples of Australian and New Zealand organisations increasing the risk of poor media coverage simply by being who they are.

This, they understand

In the examples above, the media has an image of the organisations with which they are engaging. An additional risk for the media relations builder outcrops when the media has some knowledge of an issue or event but not enough to make an informed decision about its newsworthiness or its potential story angle. Implementation of knowledge gap and sense-making theories is highly valuable in reducing the risk at this stage of a campaign.

Knowledge gap theory is closely related to framing theory. Without a certain degree of knowledge about an issue or event a journalist is likely to act in the same way as an unguided missile: the result can be equally devastating for stakeholders and innocent bystanders. Journalists and reporters are not above running with story angles that they are barely across. Deadlines and shallow source research (the internet is the main culprit) force individuals in all types of media to run with material that is often shaky in its veracity. Knowledge gap theory assumes that communication has the capacity to transfer meaningful information that can be interpreted in such a way that the gap that existed between what the individual already knew and what is received will be substantially reduced. Successful knowledge gap reduction is reliant upon dialogic communication between stakeholders at a level where interpretation cannot be mistaken. It has cultural, political, and economic significance. It requires the media relations practitioner to build a strong research profile of all media with direct consequences for a client. We take a risk sending material to a reporter when we know nothing about them. There is a greater probability that the reporter may expose us and our client to danger if they choose to use material in a way we did not anticipate.

THE CHRONICLE: AVIAN FLU AND INFECTION CONTROL

How to assess risk in a client

Your client is guest speaker at a conference on infection control at a time when avian flu is being reported narrowly and in indeterminate ways. Some newspapers frame it so that it appears to be something that is happening in China; others take a broader view and anticipate that it could have a wider effect in the longer term. Also in the conference panel session is a reporter from a well-respected metropolitan newspaper. Based on your research, your client knows a bit about the reporter's work and its significance to the avian flu issue, so you frame your client's speech to acknowledge its importance. At the last minute the reporter becomes sick and asks a colleague to attend in her place. Neither you nor the client know much about the replacement reporter and, as the announcement of the replacement is made immediately before the conference session, you have no time to do any research. The client makes a good presentation but all the interpretation pitched at the advertised reporter is wasted because the substitute reporter is from the other side of the political divide. She makes a point in her speech of taking your client to task over comments about the media.

In this imagined example, knowledge gap reduction will make no difference to the way the reporter perceived your client because she was politically opposed to his position no matter how much she knew about his view of the issue. Under normal circumstances the client could have minimised the risk of exposure by lessening the uncertainty. The late change to the program created a heightened level of risk.

The reward outweighs the risk

Let's look at risk from another angle. When is it worth taking a big risk because the potential yield will outweigh the problems? Here are some examples:.

- British Prime Minister Tony Blair and the sexed-up dossier that lead to suicide.
- US President George Bush announcing that weapons of mass destruction existed in Iraq.
- Australian Prime Minister John Howard announcing tighter security legislation.

There are distinct advantages in undertaking a media relations campaign in which risk is a major factor but the benefit, if successful, is larger. Here are some questions:

- Was the Australian federal government campaign to introduce a goods and services tax risk-free?
- Was the campaign to legislate against compulsory student unionism risk free?
- Should governments undertake only those campaigns that are risk free?
- Should governments create policies that they say are good for the electorate no matter what the cost?
- How do governments frame these campaigns for the media as primary stakeholders?

Measuring risk in a media campaign

A decision is subject to risk when there is a range of possible outcomes and when there are objectively known probabilities. But risk is not uncertainty. Uncertainty is a number of outcomes to which objective probabilities cannot be assigned.

- How can we measure risk in media relations?
- If we can measure risk, can we then manage it so that we have a favourable outcome?
- How much risk should a public company be involved in and, should it put itself at risk, what are its duties to its shareholders?

Tossing a coin or buying a savings bond are decisions subject to risk since there is more than one possible outcome and the odds can be calculated. We took a risk in continuing with our client's speech (in the example above) in the face of uncertainty over how the substitute reporter would react. (Keep in mind though, that the reporter was not the primary stakeholder—200 health professionals were.)

A risky situation is one in which one of the outcomes involves a loss. In business we may not feel we are taking a risk if an investment had two outcomes.

- Outcome 1 = a profit of $100 million.
- Outcome 2 = a profit of $50 million.

But this is a situation involving risk. Objective probabilities often cannot be assigned, so many situations called risky are actually uncertain. Uncertainty exists when there is more than one possible outcome to a course of action but the probability of getting any one outcome is not known (the form of each possible outcome is known). If the probabilities of obtaining certain outcomes are known, then this situation is one of risk. Let's think about the gamble involved in tossing a coin. We can be certain it will fall either heads or tails. The probability is it will fall either heads or tails so there is no uncertainty. But there is risk because you might back one outcome and you might lose. Let's change the rules. Suppose instead of tossing a coin, we hinge the gamble on some action or event the outcome of which could not possibly be known: a person with orange hair will walk into the room we are in and that person will be a member of the National Party. Since we are not likely to know the probabilities of these two events—the orange hair and the National Party membership—the problem facing us is one of uncertainty.

The distinction is that:

- risk can be insured against (underwritten)
- uncertainty cannot be insured against.

In the corporate and political spheres, in which media relations experts play a major role, any financial strategy needs to take into account the relationship between risk and return. The greater the risk the greater the return, or *yield*. In media relations the yield from a strategy is an important measure of the acceptability of that strategy. If a client accepts that a high level of risk will return a higher yield, then a campaign strategy can take on the higher risk burden. Another measure of acceptability is the risk that the organisation or corporation faces in pursuing a particular strategy. This risk can be assessed as part of an evaluation of specific options. At the broadest level an assessment of how the capital structure would change is a good general measure of risk (which is why media relations is often seen as a cost rather than a benefit).

Three ways to assess risk

The three most prominent methods of assessing risk in any communication are:

- sensitivity analysis
- simulation modelling
- stakeholder mapping.

Sensitivity analysis is a useful technique for assessing risk during strategy development. It is also referred to as 'what if' analysis. It allows all the important assumptions underlying a particular communication strategy to be questioned and changed (if necessary).

Key campaign assumptions may be that:

- people will quit smoking
- kids will eat healthy food
- people will vote for us
- a corporation will sell 5 per cent more goods or services.

Sensitivity analysis asks what the effect might be if a media relations campaign changed the balance by 1 per cent, rather than 10 per cent. Would these figures alter the decision to pursue the strategy?

Simulation modelling is useful in strategy evaluation. It has limitations for media relations because it requires large amounts of high-quality data concerning the relationship between environmental factors and organisational performance (internal indicators and external indicators).

Stakeholder mapping analyses the political agenda for an organisation. Stakeholder maps are valuable tools in assessing the:

- likely reactions of stakeholders to strategies
- the ability to manage these reactions
- the acceptability and risk reduction of the strategies.

Crisis? Yes, there is a crisis

Crisis is a word that is used too frequently by media relations practitioners. Like many other emotive and defining words, it has been devalued to the extent that it has come to mean anything that is upsetting or offsetting. In this it has settled close by its Latin derivation meaning a decision or judgment, an issue or event—a *turning point*. Crisis can occur anywhere and at any time: leaving home without a pocket handkerchief was the turning point—a crisis—on which Bilbo Baggins the Hobbit found himself away from the Shire. It can be defined as a vitally important stage in an issue or event, a judgment, or a decision, in political, economic, cultural, or personal terms. A point on which a decision or judgment turns, on which an issue or event becomes successful or fails, goes to the core of understanding what media relations is all about. The US presidency of John Fitzgerald Kennedy lurched from one crisis to another; to name one specifically, the *Cuban Missile Crisis*. It is rare for a crisis to receive a proper name. If we think about it another way, it would have been named the Cuban Missile Event, but that would have had far less impact with the stakeholder publics to which the name was pitched (by the media).

In media relations terms, crisis is most often linked to reputation. Books devoted entirely to crisis management overflow from the shelves of university libraries. Crisis has been characterised for media relations purposes as having the potential to threaten life, safety, and structural existence (Bains, Egan & Jefkins 2004). It collapses time so that urgency adds weight to its value. Its very existence focuses the minds of media relations experts around the globe so that campaigns are developed to prevent it from spreading or to get over it (Fearn-Banks 2002). A publicly listed corporation might be said to be in crisis when its share price continues to fall. A government might be said to be in crisis when proposed legislation fails to gain approval in parliament or when it fails to contain racial disturbances—in late 2005 the governments of France and New South Wales, to name two very different regimes, were both in crisis due to racial events. A not-for-profit organisation might be said to be in crisis when a chief executive's contract is terminated on discovery of embezzlement.

According to US scholar Kathleen Fearn-Banks, a crisis has a five-stage lifecycle:

1 detection
2 preparation
3 containment
4 recovery
5 evaluation.

The vigilance of the media relations manager can mean the difference in the first stage of crisis development. I am referring here again to the turning point of an unnatural issue or event as crisis. It is the unnatural issue or event that occupies the media relations manager because it has a direct impact on reputation and image. Early detection or warning offers an opportunity to divert a crisis and halt its lifecycle at Stage 1.

The idea that reduction in risk and uncertainty can reduce the probability of an issue or event turning into a crisis was discussed above. There will, however, because of the very nature of political, cultural, and economic events and their relationships to individual behaviour and attitude, be a crisis that gets past Stage 1. If we assume this to be axiomatic, then we must have in place a plan to deal with the eventualities of the issue or event turning.

Action films have been around for a long time and provide an example of a turning point. The first of the genre was set in the American west where cowboys herded cattle. The action always included a cattle stampede. Rustlers would fire pistols into the air and the steers would run away, frightened by the noise. Cowboys guarding the herd would take off after it and, at some point, would turn it from a dangerous path and calm it to a walk before rounding it up. The turning point was always the most interesting part. The *detection* of the potential crisis was hearing the gunshots. The *preparation* for dealing with the crisis was staying in the saddle. *Containment* became the turning point and *recovery* was when the herd slowed to a walk. *Evaluation* happened after the dust settled. The range boss would count the number of dead cowboys and the number of missing steers, and decide how much damage the crisis, or event, had caused.

For the media relations manager the preparation stage is much like staying in the saddle. Chapter 4 outlined the importance of providing all contact details to relevant stakeholders when disseminating news material. During a crisis, the importance of visibility and availability is vital to the successful management of the crisis.

THE CHRONICLE: EVENTS TAKE A TURN FOR THE WORSE

How to avoid a hostile media pack

Sometimes the best preparation will not alter the level of seriousness of the crisis in the minds of the media. In New South Wales in late 2005 the premier, Morris Iemma, found himself engaged with a hostile media over a racial event that occurred in a southern Sydney suburb. Sydney is world renowned for its beaches and beach culture but it has very few that are easily accessible by public transport. One accessible beach is Cronulla, in the Sutherland Shire; it is accessible by train. During most weekends in summer, crowds arrive by train and make the short walk to the beach to sunbake, surf, and relax. In December 2005 a lifesaver—a volunteer who patrols the beach to assist surfers in distress—was attacked by a group of men whom the media claimed were of Middle Eastern origin. The details of the attack provided by the media were sketchy but one thing remained clear: the media were looking for someone to demonstrate leadership.

The attack on the lifesaver provoked an uncoordinated, unprofessional, but highly effective campaign—using mobile telephony—against the ethnic group perceived to be responsible. During the following week a mobile telephone message was circulated among a large group of people appealing to them to gather at the beach to defend it against 'un-Australian' practices. On the day of the event, at the appointed time, a large number of police prevented any further violence, but the media played up the event as an indication of the lack of leadership and authority being shown by the New South Wales government. On commercial radio the day after the event Premier Iemma did little to demonstrate that his government was in control of the present situation and that a turning point in racial intolerance had been reached. For the media, it was a good example of an organisation failing to use the Five Steps model to avert or control the crisis. Additionally, the event had the potential to threaten lives and safety, and to cause damage to property. One could argue from this that the state government ignored the potential in the crisis, but in reality it detected, prepared, contained, and recovered from the crisis. In the evaluation stage the media and the government differed in their conclusions. Part of the reason for the media's negative evaluation of the event might be residual.

A crisis has the potential to elevate the image and reputation of an organisation, but the media do not always apply equanimity to single events or issues. In the case of the New South Wales government, certain sections of the media have residual anger and cynicism about events and issues that they feel the government has poorly managed. Large issues, such as hospital and health care mismanagement, roads and traffic developments, and water quality and supply remain on the media agenda, so a smaller event such as a racial disturbance can be easily locked into the same frame to suit the prevailing conditions. The premier may have remained visible and available during the Cronulla crisis but it was not enough to restore or rebuild reputational capital.

Image and reputation: restoring symbolic capital

The restoration of image and reputation after a crisis is a complex process. Each is a different thing, requiring different approaches. Image is defined as a likeness, a mental representation of something, or the characteristics of an organisation or individual as they are perceived by stakeholder publics. Image derives its existence from perceptions and a representation of the external. It is the representation of the external that distinguishes the image of the individual or organisation.

Reputation, on the other hand, is distinguished by the condition of being highly regarded or held in esteem—or not. Reputation takes its existence from the actions that an individual or organisation pursues rather than the representation of the external. Reputation is also differentiated from image by being built over a period of time, while image can be created momentarily.

Corporations and other organisations invest heavily in image building through advertising and other marketing strategies. Image can thus be built on false perceptions, while reputation requires an assessment of an organisation's or individual's behaviour. A detailed discussion of the external image of an organisation or individual is outside the dimensions of this book; however, we are interested in the way the media deal with organisations or individuals when they are perceived to have tarnished their images or reputations.

The reputation of Australian cricketer Shane Warne as a world-class spin bowler was not damaged by certain off-field actions by Shane Warne the spin bowler. His reputation as a spin bowler remained intact to the extent that he retained his place in the Australian cricket team. His image as an individual, however, and as a role model for boys, was severely damaged by his actions. During the crisis in which Shane Warne found himself—a married man making sexual advances towards a woman who was not his wife—the media conflated image and reputation, blurring the lines between external image and professional action. The reason Warne retained his place in the Australian cricket team related to how the Australian Cricket Board saw his *reputation* and differentiated it sufficiently from his *image* to conclude that stakeholder publics would make the same differentiation. Similar crises arose for the National Rugby League as individuals and groups damaged the image of the game of football by association but maintained their positions within various teams due to their reputations as footballers.

The difficulty for organisations and individuals when a crisis occurs is the restoration of image *and* reputation. Crisis management asserts that image must be developed, maintained, and protected, and that after a crisis occurs image must then be restored. But image cannot always be protected.

Surfing the crisis wave

Crisis management as a media relations activity reflects on the idea that crisis has a starting point, and can be determined, managed, and evaluated in rational terms. As mentioned in the preface of this book, rationalisation of public relations strategies and tactics fails to acknowledge the strong emotional nature of engagement between and among individuals and organisations. The media, on the other hand, have strong attachments to emotional appeals on behalf of their stakeholder publics: readers, viewers, and listeners. It is simplistic to assume that a list of actions to be undertaken by a company spokesperson during time of crisis will help maintain or restore image or reputation after the event. While it may assist the organisation or individual in engaging with other stakeholders, as we have seen from the Cronulla example above, the media have a very different approach to the issue. Crisis management cannot be viewed from the perspective of the media relations practitioner alone and in a rational way. A crisis ignites dormant emotions and inflames behaviours and attitudes out of all recognition with a rational strategy.

A crisis management strategy for a media relations practitioner might include provision of clear and unambiguous information, but for the media, there will always be news value in the interpretation and immediacy of the crisis. Part of the requirement of a news story is that it has colour, so a reporter who is provided only with factual information will attempt to create emotive meaning around the rational. This usually involves finding someone who has been directly affected by the crisis and, if not, someone who is indirectly involved.

Media will engage in attack journalism if they perceive a crisis is not being played out in accordance with certain rules and actions related to reputation restoration. The orthodox taxonomies of reputation restoration are:

- denial
- evasion
- irritation reduction

- correction
- rapprochement.

Denial is obvious and to be avoided, yet it is most often the first thing an organisation or individual uses. 'I didn't do it' is a common phrase employed by individuals, even when they are caught in the act, and organisations that believe blame can be redirected away from them at all times. Individuals within organisations will deny responsibility for all types of actions, happily shifting blame to colleagues or other stakeholders.

Publicly, organisations that deny blame create an enormous risk of continued media attack. In some cases the objective of denying blame or responsibility is strategic: it provides an organisation with additional time in which to frame an alternative strategy. In these cases organisations and individuals will embrace the *correction* and *rapprochement* categories in parallel, after they have had time to regroup. Politicians are famous for their ability to deny, then feel self-loathing, followed closely by correction. They usually disappear from view sometime soon after a crisis, citing family and other interests to be pursued. In the corporate sphere, high-profile chief executives from some of the largest multinationals are serving members of penitentiaries, having first used the denial strategy. In some of these cases, pursuit by the media has been the turning point in the individuals being charged and incarcerated.

Even those organisations that are perceived to have a strong reputation can be embroiled in crisis and choose the wrong tactic for reputation restoration. The United Nations oil for food strategy is a good example.

THE CHRONICLE: THE UNITED NATIONS OIL FOR FOOD PROGRAM

Working through a media image crisis

In what became known as the oil for food crisis, the world's leading humanitarian organisation, the United Nations, caused itself to become immersed in a crisis that should never have existed, then presented tactics that it knew had to eventually be exposed by global media. It was a crisis that severely damaged the image of an organisation that had built its reputation on exemplary conduct.

The Oil for Food Program devised by the UN was an ethical and well thought: out strategy that allowed Iraq to use a portion of its large petroleum export revenue to purchase humanitarian relief. The program began in 1996 as the West imposed economic sanctions against Iraq over its human rights abuses. In the first five years of operation, the program generated US$127 billion in humanitarian supplies (UN News Centre). The UN found itself in crisis over the program when it was revealed in the media that high-level UN staff had provided sensitive tendering information to rival bidders in the aid program and that the secretary-general's son may have been working for a company with direct involvement in the program.

An investigation of the UN's news releases, all of which are published on its website, reveals that the organisation, despite its pre-eminence and highly valued reputation, used each one of the available taxonomies in a vain attempt to restore its reputation after the revelations of its activities in the *New York Times*.

Denial

We can see from a release dated 28 April 2004, that Secretary-General Kofi Annan did not deny the allegations outright, but attempted to reduce the heat in the crisis by saying some of the allegations were 'outrageous'.

Evasion

While there is no evidence that the UN attempted to evade the crisis, news releases issued on 1 and 8 December 2004 show that there was an attempt to divert attention from the issue with tactics such as a vote of confidence in the secretary-general from UN staff and the General Assembly respectively. A day later, on 9 December, a further diversion came from an endorsement of the secretary-general by the US government.

Irritation reduction

In May 2004 the secretary-general publicly announced his support for the establishment of an independent inquiry into the allegations. In so doing, the UN sought to reduce the irritation that was becoming constant through media investigation of all those associated, directly and indirectly, with the program. A further irritation reduction occurred on 13 October when the UN announced it would fund the independent inquiry from money remaining within the program after it ceased operating. Irritation reduction increased in the new year. In January 2005 the UN pre-empted the independent inquiry's finding with an announcement of a full management review of the organisation. Such an announcement could lead nowhere other than to correction and rapprochement.

Correction

To begin the correction process in retrieving its reputation, on 3 February 2005 the secretary-general announced that disciplinary action would be taken against officials involved in the program. To correct the action, the UN announced five days later, on 7 February, that it would take disciplinary action against two highly placed staff members, the head of the program, Benon Sevan, and the deputy director of the Security Council Affairs Division, Joseph Stephanides. Both were given two weeks to respond to allegations of misconduct. On 1 June 2005 the secretary-general announced that he had terminated the employment of Joseph Stephanides from the UN; Benon Sevan had already retired.

Rapprochement

In August 2005 the UN began embracing the rapprochement stage of the crisis by announcing a review of its procurement procedures. Later, at the World Information Summit in September 2005 in New York and in press material in December 2005, it agreed to establish an ethics office so that crises such as the oil for food scandal would never again emerge. To demonstrate that it was serious about its ethics in the future, and that it had completed its rapprochement, the proposed ethics office was to have independent oversight and auditing function.

Figure 11.2 United Nations journalist office's at UN Plaza, New York.

12

Measuring Successful Relationships: Approaches to Research Methods

CHAPTER OBJECTIVES

- To understand the principles associated with accurate campaign measurement.
- To develop an understanding of the importance of evaluation to media relations issues and events.

Evaluation and measurement are important elements in the increasing professionalisation of media relations. The development of measurement techniques has signalled the intentions of professionals in the field to think and act in a serious way and to maintain transparent cost-effectiveness with client stakeholders. Evaluation is the *fourth stage* of the strategic development of a media relations campaign. But, as we will see, it is not limited to the end of a campaign. If it is correctly undertaken, it provides valuable signals all along the campaign trail.

For evaluation or measurement of campaign success to be taken seriously it must be considered in a systematic way. There is always room for emotive evaluation—a room crowded with journalists providing a standing ovation in response to a client's speech is a good emotive measure of success—but it should run parallel with rational evaluation if a client is to see it in terms of a return on investment.

When thinking about evaluation, a media relations practitioner must always keep in mind the needs of the client and how the client's organisation measures its own success. The overlap here with sales and marketing measurement is palpable. In media relations it is difficult to move far from the notion that an increase in sales is a measure of success. Increased sales means increased profits. Most organisations operate on the basis of increases in output rather than decreases in output, whether they are profit-driven or otherwise. Part of the reason that evaluation and measurement have become important to media relations lies in the fact that, in the past, poor measurement techniques meant the activities that define media relations were subsumed under a marketing umbrella because marketing could be successfully measured against sales. Other business activities—supply, design, manufacturing, and distribution—are all measurable components within some type of business model. So are sales and marketing. But up until recently, media relations activities were a grey area and thus considered cost centres rather than profit centres. The result was that media relations activities were the first to be sidelined when the business cycle was in a downswing, and the last to be added in an upswing, along with other cost centre activities such as labour and raw materials.

Media relations activities still suffer the ignominy of being attached to marketing and sales in many areas of business, but organisations that understand the value of media relations measured against successful evaluation and research techniques are growing substantially in number. In the USA and Europe, media relations activities as a separate entity within the business model have been highly valued since the last quarter of the twentieth century. In Australia and New Zealand the transfer of the activities to a field divided off from marketing and sales is taking a little longer, but is at least moving in the right general direction. The idea of emotive measurement circumscribed by a piece in the *Australian Financial Review*, for example, is being supplanted by a more professional approach to evaluation as a rational business technique.

In general business, the percentage of income devoted to research and development (R&D) is a measure of the success of the business. In media relations, the realisation that spending on R&D has a direct positive effect on the bottom line is yet to have a serious impact.

Evaluating media relations

While there is a variety of measurement techniques available for media relations evaluation, it remains a constant among Australian and New Zealand practitioners that the Message Exposure Model is still king in the media relations subfield. I will discuss it below, along with the alternatives. Selection of an evaluation model is primarily a function of the issue or event under investigation, and the type of media relationship that has been built around it. A media relationship developed at global level and including the *New York Times*, the *Economist*, the *Times*, CNN, the BBC, and *Asahi Shimbun* will require a different measurement model to that developed at local level around the *West Australian* and ABC Perth. But we are also interested in the evaluation of media relations and how it fits with overall public relations measurement.

When we think of media relations, we focus our attention on one stakeholder group, the media. So we are mostly interested in the success of published or broadcast material. When we think of public relations we include a number of additional stakeholder groups. The success of the relationship building campaign with these wider stakeholders is measured using different models, but the relationship of the models to each other and the relationship of the stakeholders to each other remains of primary importance to the campaign. We will discuss each model below with a focus on the detail in the media relations evaluation process.

What is evaluation?

Evaluation is an essential component of any communication campaign. It improves the probability of achieving program success. It is the systematic application of research procedures to understand the conceptualisation, design, implementation, and utility of media relations campaigns. Evaluation determines:

- effectiveness
- achievement of goals
- efficiency of goals.

How media relations campaigns reach and influence their intended targets is part of the evaluation process. Evaluation specifies explicitly the goals and objectives of the campaign. If we specify our objectives it is possible to create a media relations campaign that will meet the objectives. The first step in evaluation is to see if we met our objectives.

Evaluation should be conducted in three phases:

1 formative
2 process
3 summative.

Formative identifies and assesses the motivation for the existence of the campaign. It embraces all the activities that define the extent of the campaign and consists of gathering data on possible strategies. It includes what we may already know about the media. It investigates factors—endogenous and exogenous variables—that have the potential to interfere with desired goals and objectives. It informs our campaign at its beginning.

This brings us back to objectives. Let's revisit them. Objectives are a prerequisite for evaluation. Objectives are goals expressed in measurable, concrete terms. They are not abstract. Goals specify means and results; objectives specify nuts and bolts. We cannot engage in a theory-based media relations exercise without considering goals and objectives; conversely, we cannot seriously consider the relationship between media relations goals and objectives without being theoretical, because theories underlie all goals and objectives. Objectives are expressed in practical terms but in a variety of ways. The level of specificity will depend on a client's willingness or ability to collect specific data. There is not much point in specifying objectives and collecting data that will not be used later in a campaign. Outcomes the client is interested in should be the first reference point for creating objectives.

Some guidelines for developing objectives might be as follows:

1 Don't confuse process with outcome:
    – media relations practitioners do process
    – stakeholder publics do outcomes
    – media objectives focus on outcomes.
2 Develop objectives that reflect the various stages of an issue or event.
3 Objectives that focus on stakeholders are outcome goals.
4 Objectives that focus on the campaign are process goals.
5 Use action words to describe objectives.
6 All objectives should be goal-related. Don't create objectives in a vacuum.
7 Recognise that objectives are hypotheses based on a theory about why the media relations campaign is expected to influence stakeholders.

Objectives can then be expressed as stimulus response statements; the media relations campaign is the stimulus and the stakeholder's reaction is the response.

Let's return to evaluation. The goal is what we want, the strategy is how we make it happen. The objective is the goal in reality rather than theory, and the tactics are what we do to put the objective into action. When we talk of objectives, we talk of actions. When we talk of tactics, we talk of the order in which the actions take place. US scholar Don Stacks, building on the work of Broom and Dozier, suggests goals are long-term campaign outcomes, that which we strive to achieve as an overall result, while objectives are specific and directly related to campaign outputs (Stacks 2003).

There are a few simple questions that we should be asking as we build a checklist for evaluation against objectives:

- Was the campaign adequately planned?
- Did the media understand the message?
- Did we reach all stakeholders?
- Did we reach the objectives we set?
- Did we reach the goal of the campaign?
- Did the campaign fall within budget?
- What unforeseen circumstances affected the campaign's success?
- How could the campaign have been more effective?
- What steps can we take to improve future campaign success?

Formative, process, and summative evaluation

There are three stages during the life of a campaign where it is reasonable to assume that some level of rational evaluation will occur. An issue or event may begin with an emotional charge—the ignition that fires it up—but if it is to be sustained and meet the client's goals and objectives, then it will need to be rationally evaluated throughout its life.

Formative evaluation

As might be expected, *formative* research and evaluation begin at the start of a campaign. They form the basis of the direction the issue or event might take. Research into the cost of an event might cause a media relations counsellor and a client to re-evaluate the event before it actually comes to life. This type of research is crucial to keeping a client's media relations campaign within an acceptable budget. It is also important at the formative stage of a campaign to know exactly what is likely to occur as the campaign takes shape. Emotional appeals can be valuable during the process stages of a campaign but rationality and clear-headedness are vital requirements in the early stages. Client issues and events (see chapter 10) are inexorably linked to budgets. The formative evaluation stage of a media relations campaign will benefit unconditionally from research that includes the relationship of budget to objective outcomes. The most important aspect at this point in design is that the campaign research and its related findings fit with client objectives. This is the formative evaluation stage of the campaign.

Process evaluation

Process evaluation is an interesting concept. For most media relations practitioners it is perceived in the same way that a journalist or reporter perceives it: a natural capability driven by experience moves the campaign from its inception through to its conclusion. Experience is the most highly valued component in any profession. It is the difference between successful outcomes and mediocre outcomes. It provides a smooth path through formulation, development, and conclusion of any issue or event, but it does not always allow for revolutionary change. Imagine for a moment the media relations practitioner situated in the middle of the twentieth century. The Second World War was defining politics, economics, and culture. The user-friendly Macintosh computer was thirty-five years away from being invented, and the internet, well, it would have been unimaginable. Now relocate that same practitioner at the dawn of the twenty-first century. By now the practitioner has a huge amount of experience, but most of it is of little value because this person is technologically illiterate as well as being unfamiliar with all types of business and cultural practices. The practitioner's experience would be less than useful. The importance of experience and change cannot be underestimated, but the addition of process evaluation to the media relations campaign catalogue draws the field towards a higher level of acceptance.

Process evaluation can be easily defined as the measurement of objectives that are reached throughout the life of a campaign. It may be that an issue or event is not defined by the media coverage that is attained at its conclusion; it may be part of the strategy that early coverage provides an evaluation point. Coverage in a B2B magazine, for example, might provide a measurement of acceptability levels that could be expected in wider media coverage.

Summative evaluation

Evaluation at the completion of an issue or event is known as summative evaluation. It is defined as the sum of the research and campaign activities that made up the issue or event. As process evaluation measured campaign success against measurable objectives, summative evaluation should measure the success of a campaign against goals (discussed in detail in chapter 3). In this section we are interested in the methods we can use to evaluate the success of a campaign. The difficulty with summative evaluation lies in the different ways that goals can be described by the media relations practitioner and by the client.

Methods of media relations evaluation

There are three reliable and widely used methods of evaluation in media relations. I refer to them as *Three M Evaluation*, the three ems of media relations: *metrics, message exposure*, and *media impressions*. When used in conjunction with each other they offer the most reliable set of formative and summative measurement tools presently available.

Metrics

This method of evaluation has been adapted from linguistics and psychology. It is also known as psychometrics. Its goal is to uncover and interpret specific characteristics about groups of reporters, journalists, or other media workers. It is also applied by public relations practitioners to the observation and interpretation of other stakeholders. Metrics relies for its value on the interpretation of characteristics associated with individuals that have been extrapolated from their written or spoken work. I have discussed this more generally elsewhere in the book, but it is now important to define metrics in more specific media terms.

Metrics is most valuable as a method of interpreting a journalist's characteristics so that a media profile can be built of an individual or a group who may display similar characteristics (see chapter 6 for a discussion of media profile use in relationship building). When used in conjunction with media impressions and message exposure, metrics supplies the third pillar of establishment for media relations evaluation. Metrics has its basis in content analysis (see later in this chapter). The use of news source databases, such as Lexis–Nexis or Factiva, is crucial for the full realisation of media metrics. News databases provide the key to metric evaluation of large-scale analyses. They may not play an important role in smaller metric analysis—psychological interpretation of a single reporter on, say, the *Adelaide Advertiser* over a period of a few weeks—but their value when applying large-scale measurement is enormous. Let's say a reporter has been writing for the *Australian Financial Review* for more than twenty years. From an archival database we can extract full texts of everything that reporter has written. We can then code the material against predetermined scales, which might be as simple as the level of hostility the reporter displays towards the subject being written about, or they might reveal the level of anxiety, dismay, revival, or hope that the individual composes around the subject.

The measurement and evaluation of psychological characteristics in humans is not new. What is relatively new for media relations is the application of psychometrics to investigate the work of the media and from it draw inferences and make predictions. By making accurate psychometric measurements of the work of certain reporters or journalists, it is almost impossible to create a media campaign that will fail. Metrics relies for its success on constants within the psychological functions of humans and the capability to respond to persuasion and influence. No matter how large media workers' claims to high resistance to persuasion and influence, they are nonetheless human and hold attitudes and opinions that can be influenced. Media workers as a group may respond less positively to certain stimuli—gifts or gadgets attached to news releases, for example—because they have become inured through cynicism, but they exist within a state that Katz (1960) identified as needing to be pleasantly situated while at the same time developing a defensive mechanism to protect them from issues within themselves and their environments that they do not wish to face. Katz applied this to all people, not just media workers. If we add to it the argument by Stiff and Mongeau (2003) that people are capable of insulating themselves from emotions through the way they view objects and situations, then we have a valuable insight into how reporters and journalists situate themselves.

THE CHRONICLE: EVALUATING PERSONAL ASSURANCES

How to measure what is said against what is done

You have a friend who has been living in a Victorian west coast town. She owns a coffee shop that has a retail licence to sell surf clothes and hippie paraphernalia. She makes anklets and earrings and collects shells. Your friend is concerned about a proposed development a few kilometres further along the coast and the impact it will have on the marine environment and the town. She reads the local newspaper, the *Whailer*, but does not personally know the editor or any of the three reporters.

You work sixteen hours a day in a small public relations consultancy in Melbourne and the words *pro bono* have never entered your lexicon. Your friend texts you one day to see if you are coming down for a weekend soon. Because your boyfriend of three months recently sent you a text message to say that he was breaking off the relationship, you happen to have next weekend free. Plus Monday, because the boss says you have been working too hard. You drive down the coast, relax on the beach, and end up in a discussion about local politics because your friend is agitated. Without thinking about the consequences of your actions, on Sunday evening, over a few cool drinks, you volunteer to go into town the next day and visit the newspaper office to see what the position is regarding the development.

On Monday at around 11 a.m. you introduce yourself to the editor of the *Whailer*. You have a friendly chat, during which she tells you the newspaper has a policy to report objectively on all development applications but this one, her instincts tell her, is going to be really bad for the district. You have not revealed yourself as a city-based public relations person, simply as the friend of a local concerned resident. You drive back to the village and have coffee at your friend's shop. Your friend says the local paper always seems to take the side of the developers. But that's not what the editor told you.

You drive back to Melbourne late that evening, but you can't settle. You fire up your home computer and log onto the proprietary database that the consultancy accesses. You enter the *Whailer*. You enter *development*. You enter *environment*. You elect to gather material from the past ten years to coincide with the tenure of the editor. There are more than 250 articles that match your search. This means there is a possibility that the weekly newspaper has reported developments in more than half of its published editions. You do a quick coding and search the articles for specific content. You lean back from the desk and look out a rain-streaked window onto a grey Melbourne dawn.

Three hours later, in the office, you ring your friend. You confirm her suspicions. You add that there appears to be a strong emotional appeal from the material written by the editor to invite interest in all types of development, whether they are environmentally sustainable or not. Your friend says the local environmental group has planned to invite the media to an information night the following week. You offer to send her details of your investigation. You hang up and get on with work for your paying clients.

This is a simple example of how metrics can provide consistent evaluation of media, especially when there appears to be some ambiguity between what is said and what is published.

Message exposure

Message exposure is the most widely used form of evaluation in the subfield of media relations. It involves compiling **clippings** and **mentions**. This is also a good way to evaluate media acceptance of the message. Using this method we can evaluate message *content* against *exposure*.

According to US scholar Richard Perloff, exposure to all types of communication can influence stakeholders' attitude and behaviour (Perloff 2003). Perloff suggests exposure is a 'strong, robust persuasion phenomenon' and cites numerous advertising examples to support his argument. We can extrapolate Perloff's argument out of the advertising field and apply it to media messages, with an additional feature that neutral issues, those for which we have no strong opinion, are most likely to resonate because stakeholders have yet to develop an attitude or opinion about them. For message exposure to be effective as an evaluation method it needs to be linked to other forms of evaluation, such as focus groups and surveys. First, we collect all the material published and broadcast about our issue or event. In the past, this was sufficient for media relations practitioners to bill clients. It can still be used by practitioners as a measure of success. A campaign to have a political client's national issue or event published in the *Canberra Times* or the *Wellington Herald* will be successful if the material is published, but it will be measurably more successful if it is evaluated against a number of other criteria that might include style and tone of language. Its links to other forms of evaluation, such as focus groups and surveys, or opinion polls, as a secondary measure will reinforce the initial assessment of value. Message exposure, then, is a vital beginning for any type of evaluation.

> **clippings**
> material extracted from newspapers and other print sources that are relevant to a client's issue or event.

> **mentions**
> the number of times a client's issue or event appears in different media.

THE CHRONICLE: MEASURING ADVERSE EXPOSURE

How to measure bad press

Your client is a Sydney property developer with an interest in a highrise development and marina berths on the New South Wales and Victorian border. The proposed development is surrounded by bushland that is owned by the Crown and is designated wilderness. The small harbour and river on which your client is preparing to build the marina lies adjacent to a fishing village with a population of fewer than 1000 permanent residents. It is a popular holiday destination for Melburnians. The development application is being prepared for submission to the local council authority and the developer has commissioned your public relations agency to obtain favourable exposure of the event in the local media. The village has a sixteen-page, A4-sized, monthly newspaper published by volunteers. Within the region there is a bi-weekly newspaper owned and published by Rural Press, the largest media owner in regional New South Wales and Victoria. Two regional television stations—WIN and Prime—broadcast nightly local news, there is a local commercial radio station, and the regional office of ABC Southeast Radio, the public broadcaster.

While there are a number of stakeholders with whom it would be important to engage during such a campaign, the media are the primary stakeholders and the message has a specific content. The client is very keen for the village occupants to accept his planned level of development (which is far greater than anything previously attempted in the region) and for that to influence how three of the local councillors will behave when casting their vote on the development application. (There are nine elected councillors. Three have already been influenced directly by the developer and persuaded of the significant value in the proposal. Another three are opposed to the development. It is important to influence the three who have not yet formed an opinion, as one of the three opposed carries the weight of a mayoral casting vote.) Your task appears to be relatively simple—to find a positive angle on the development, write it up, and submit the material to local media stakeholders. The objective is to find a suitable angle around which to frame the client's event. The goal is to see the story published in and broadcast on the local media. The success of your campaign will lie in the publication and broadcast of material about your client's development. Or will it? There are a number of possibilities. Your client's development application could be reported:

- objectively
- positively
- negatively.

For it to be reported objectively the newspaper, radio station, or television station will take your material and report. It will not follow up with any investigation into the development's impact outside what you have outlined in your news release. To be reported positively, the story will need an angle that reflects its impact in some substantial way. The best angle for regional media in Australia is the economic impact.

Regional media support economic development in regional Australia and New Zealand because of high levels of investment drawn to the major cities. They see their role as partly to encourage economic development outside the major cities. But the economic rationalisation attached to media ownership and support for investment does not always attach itself to the individual reporter or broadcaster. In this, there will be other stakeholders that the newspaper reporter is interested in investigating so that a balanced story can be filed. Remember, this development is larger than any seen in the region and it backs onto a major wilderness area, so there will be environmental issues, existing services issues (rebuilding the sewerage system), and population density issues that come into play. There will be local conservation stakeholder groups and small business stakeholder groups who might be in opposition to the development and thus provide the newspaper reporter with colourful copy. It is your task—as the media relations expert—to provide the client with an evaluation of all the variables surrounding the event as well as acknowledging that the commission is to find an angle and write the story.

But submission of a news release without prior investigation might cause immediate grief. The monthly newspaper, for example, is opposed to all development in the region and is financially supported by an environmental group. This is not necessarily a bad thing as it functions as a counteraction to the orthodox economic rationalisation of the bi-weekly newspaper but it is important for research purposes to know this so you do not waste time engaging with the monthly medium. The monthly newspaper will undoubtedly frame the development in negative terms. Similarly, the leftist leaning ABC Radio might take a negative view, while the bi-weekly newspaper and the television news might look on the development more favourably because of its investment potential for the region. All this assumes an economic position, but it is the basis of a research profile on the media and on the way other stakeholders might view the event.

Media impressions

An impression is the measurement of the number of people who might realistically connect with the material in newspapers, on television, or on radio. It can be determined by circulation or audience numbers. If, for example, the *Courier Mail* claims a circulation of 500 000, then we calculate that, potentially, 500 000 people have been exposed to our message. If it also appears in the *Redcliffe Herald*, with a readership of 50 000, then the number of impressions is, potentially, 550 000. A following story a day later in the *SMH* totals a potential 1 050 000 impressions.

Now we might decide to use *gross impressions* as our method of analysis. We take the circulation figures for our publications and viewers and listeners for our television and radio broadcasts and multiply them by the number of times our material appeared.

Next we consider the percentage of the media coverage impressions that could be considered our target audience—say, 50 per cent of one hit in the *SMH*—and this becomes our total effective impressions.

Next we might measure the actual column centimetres appearing.

We can then assign a value to each piece relative to its position in the medium, where:

10 = front page, cover, or lead

9 = front page or section issue-appropriate

8 = front page of less important section

7 = prominent page position inside a section

6 = neutral position not immediately obvious

5 = short copy buried

4 = one par or less buried.

We can now calculate an average position value by adding individual placement values and dividing that total by the number of placements. This will give us an average position relative to our assumed values. Next, we assign a content value for each placement using some chosen scale.

In this case we might use:

10= three key copy points covered with pic

9 = three points without pic

8 = two points with pic

7 = two points without pic

6 = one point with pic

5 = one point without pic

4 = regardless of point coverage, negative angle.

We can calculate an average content value by adding individual content values and dividing that total by the total number of placements.

We can use similar methods to calculate average airtime by dividing the total minutes of airtime by the total number of placements.

As an additional overlap measure, we can calculate a total equivalent advertising value by multiplying the ad rate by the amount of space or time given to the placement.

We can then sum the individual ad values to reach a total equivalent ad value.

Assume that advertising space has the same meaning as editorial space in the mind of the audience. If the client wants an additional overlap, we can calculate a gross cost per impression by dividing the total cost of the campaign by the total gross impressions. We can calculate an effective cost per impression by dividing the total cost of the campaign by the total effective impressions. This is a post-campaign evaluation, but if we had conducted it pre campaign, we would have been in a better position to make a pre–post comparison and therefore in a better position to document the impact of the campaign. If we repeated this methodology each month we would have a time-series research design that would be even better. Equally important is to be able to measure failure so we don't repeat it.

Models of public relations evaluation that complement media relations

As well as the widespread use of Three M Evaluation in media relations, there is also the need for the media relations specialist to evaluate campaigns against other stakeholder expectations, attitudes, and behaviours. These stakeholders include communities, governments, activists, environmentalists, unions, employees, investors, and volunteers, among others. A variety of models are available to evaluate stakeholder interest, attitude, and behaviour towards client-sponsored issues and events.

Systematic tracking

Using a computer database, we can measure variables such as:

- market penetration
- type of publication
- tone of coverage
- sources quoted
- main copy points.

Some software will keep track of reporter bylines over a long period to see if the writer is being negative or positive about a campaign. The number of news stories sent with the number published and in what medium can also be compared. This gives us an idea of our return on investment.

Requests and 1800 numbers

Requests for further information is a good way to measure message response. Such requests can measure effectiveness and be evaluated against the types of stakeholder publics making the request. Media organisations invest in toll-free numbers to measure responses to their own promotions.

Attendance

Counting those who attend your event is a straightforward way to evaluate the success of a campaign—providing you have an event or activity. Galleries, libraries, and other institutions can measure the success of a media campaign against attendance at special events.

Internet hits

Internet hits are an electronic version of media impressions. What your client does with the hits is what counts. I know of one organisation that spoke with a talk-back host on early morning radio. In the two hours following the conversation, the client's website received a strong number of hits, but the client was unable to follow up directly because there was no mechanism within the site to take respondent details. It may be more valuable, however, to analyse the length of the session time that occurs, rather than the number of hits. The length of time someone spends on the site plays an important role in the evaluation process. You can add the cost of these into your budget if your assessment of the evaluation process requires it.

Focus groups

A focus group is a structured way of discovering what is liked or disliked about an issue or event. Focus groups are a supplement to individual interviews and provide a more substantial evaluative mechanism than the subjectivity of the individual. Focus groups have been appropriated by media relations practitioners as a model that can be used in formative and summative research evaluation. Focus groups are used as part of product marketing strategies but they have significance for media relations. An optimum focus group is made up of five to ten people who have characteristics that reflect the issue or event in question. While focus group data are qualitative in nature and are unable to be translated across an entire universe, their relevance to formative evaluation lies in their capacity to quickly provide opinions and attitudes that can be projected onto a campaign.

Telephone surveys

Another tactic that has relevance to formative, process, and summative evaluation in media relations are the research data collected from telephone surveys. Telephone surveys can be conducted cost-effectively across a wide or narrow universe and provide research data that can be extrapolated quickly in times of urgent decision-making. A telephone survey or poll used as research must identify its nature clearly so that it is not confused with product selling.

Models in disrepute

Two evaluation models that have been extensively used in the past but have shown themselves to be less worthy in the professionalisation of media and PR are set out below for comparison purposes. Neither the PRIA nor PRINZ endorses them.

Advertising equivalencies

This is a calculation of message exposure against the real cost of space in advertising terms. It is an interesting method that is not favoured by a lot of public relations practitioners. Some agencies multiply the space conversion to reflect a higher credibility for editorial content over advertising space, but this is fraught. The concept is difficult. It becomes a question of what is being measured. Should editorial be counted as equivalent ad space if it is negative? If an editorial mentions the name of your client's organisation once and an ad mentions it ten times, how do we measure equivalencies?

Production

An elementary evaluation method is to count everything that is produced on behalf of your client. This is one way to observe productivity, but it emphasises quantity instead of quality. It may be more cost-effective to write fewer pieces and concentrate on their newsworthiness. Six weeks on a *Courier Mail* piece may be more valuable than ten pieces in local weekly newspapers around Brisbane. Evaluation against expectations—how much material a person can get in any number of newspapers—is unrealistic because it is not the media relations person but the editor who makes decisions on content.

Approaches to media relations research methods

Research techniques that lead to evaluation

The theories that underpin media relations research are diffuse. While this book places importance on relationship building and framing as the basis of successful media relations, there are other extant theories that inform the research techniques employed in the field. The issue for most media relations practitioners is that they tend to follow what is known as the **Vienna Circle** argument of **logical positivism** when developing research (the idea that all things can, based on empirical evaluation, be measured for their significance). Like the journalist and reporter who must make judgments and evaluations on observable and available evidence, so the media relations practitioner makes similar pronouncements on what is observable and available. This also follows John Dewey's line of argument that truth is observable: *rebus sic stantibus*. But as a research technique observation alone will not reveal the truth in an issue or event as it is presented by media relations practitioners working on behalf of clients. In fact, most of them will be veiled and require deeper investigation.

> **Vienna Circle**
> an early twentieth-century group of individuals at Vienna University concerned with the notion of significance; the empirical study of issues and events and their utilitarian significance.

> **logical positivism**
> the proposition that philosophical problems can be solved through logical investigation, taking no account of emotional factors.

This is one of the most important aspects of research as an evaluation tool. It must have an ethical dimension that enables media to see the news value in an issue or event at both an empirical and a logical level. When media relations practitioners begin research, they are doing it for a specific purpose: to present the results of the research in an issue or event to journalists and reporters. So the research must take on the same profile as if the media relations practitioner were acting as a journalist or reporter. It must be investigated thoroughly and professionally. Researchers must think of themselves as media sources. A media relations practitioner must, therefore, understand the importance of primary and secondary research tools and what they bring to the issue or event.

Primary research

Primary research involves the media relations specialist in the same activities that occupy journalists and reporters. There is no difference in the undertaking. Media relations specialists use research to assist them to construct a specific message about issues and events and disseminate the message to a stakeholder—the media. Journalists and reporters use research to assist them to construct a specific message about issues and events and disseminate the message to a stakeholder—the public. Media relations specialists use the same primary research techniques available to the media:

- interviews
- focus groups
- surveys, polls
- direct observation.

The day a journalist begins work, they are told about the most important research tool at their disposal: the telephone book. Journalists build their own contact book from this basic resource and from hands-on contacts. The telephone is thus one of the most important technological tools available and, with the invention of mobile telephony, it has become indispensable. The same tool is crucial to the media relations specialist, but it is frequently used to disadvantage. As a primary research tool, media relations practitioners seem to feel an irrational need to use the telephone to badger journalists and reporters on a daily, if not hourly, basis. The ready availability of the technology is not justification for its abuse.

Technology and its availability has made the work of the media relations professional more accessible, but its access has reduced the individual's ability to use an important primary research tool: observation. Journalists and reporters are also guilty of failing to take advantage of this primary research tool. Reliance is placed on secondary sources and non-eyewitness or earwitness accounts, a condition that elevates the secondary source to an undeserved position of recognition. It is important for the media relations practitioner to learn to distinguish between the value in observation and the information obtained from secondary sources.

Secondary research

Secondary sources are not always unreliable. Most academic research is undertaken using secondary research principles. The importance of the secondary source is its reliability. Most academic books are considered to be reliable secondary sources. They are published after a long and arduous process that involves independent reading of draft manuscripts and extensive fact checking. So-called quality newspapers, such as the *New York Times*, the *Economist*, and *Le Figaro*, could be considered reliable secondary sources based on checks and balances that take place in their newsrooms. Some electronic databases (Lexis–Nexis, Factiva) are reliable and acceptable as secondary research sources while others, such as the world wide web, provide access to an enormous amount of material that could be considered, at best, unreliable. Many non-academic books also fit this category. It is important for a media relations practitioner to be able to distinguish easily between a reliable secondary source and an unreliable one, whether they are human or otherwise. Journalists and reporters learn by experience to distinguish between a reliable and unreliable source. The first time a source provides information that is checked and found to be inaccurate, the source becomes unreliable. So, too, the media relations practitioner must learn to quickly distinguish as to the level of reliability of the information supplied by clients.

A brief overview of qualitative and quantitative methods

As the names imply, qualitative and quantitative research are concerned with quality and quantity respectively. The distinction for media relations research, as for all other social and political science research, is that quantitative material is said to be more easily measurable than qualitative, as qualitative relies on subjective judgments. Research driven by either methodology is acceptable in different situations, thus, qualitative and quantitative can be considered situational. Quantitative measurement might appear easier to undertake because it is based on numbers, but as Stacks points out clearly in *Primer of Public Relations Research* (2003), as a formal process it enables research to be conducted with a precision not available in informal or qualitative research, and introduces the media relations practitioner to the complex world of descriptive statistical analysis. It also requires access to computer software such as Statistical Package for the Social Sciences (SPSS).

The question for media relations practitioners is in deciding when to use either methodology so that objectives and goals can be successfully reached. An orthodox approach is to suggest qualitative research is best used to inform a campaign so it is applied at the formative stage, as we have seen above. It is usually considered descriptive in nature. Qualitative research that informs a campaign at its inception might include interviews or conversations with employees of an organisation, observations of geophysical or other sites, and meetings and dialogue with constituents or other informed or uninformed stakeholders. At this stage of evaluation, qualitative research assists in roughing out the campaign.

Quantitative research at this stage might include content analysis of specific media, textual analysis of speeches and annual reports, or behavioural analysis of current affairs television program presenters. Quantitative measurements are observable but they require data to be accurate. We might, for example, want to know the gender of all entertainment reporters in Australia and New Zealand. First, we must define what we mean by 'entertainment' (the universe), then we must define what category of media we are interested in. These data are descriptive of one specific observation. Even though they may not be very useful in framing a campaign, they may assist in thinking about the relationship building process. With these data, we might then construct a survey to be distributed to entertainment reporters (as we have defined them) asking specific questions about their preferred method of receiving media material. This will provide us with additional descriptive data that will be useful in evaluating a client's entertainment event.

A more complex example of quantitative measurement might be the results of a survey of how reporters and journalists behave towards unsolicited media material. Let's say we have a client who, for whatever reason, provides the financial support to undertake a wide-ranging survey. We might broaden the requirements to include attitudes to media relations on a number of issues, including reception of news releases. Instinct and intuition work well in some circumstances but if we undertake a wide-ranging survey, we will have reliable data from which to measure any number of hypotheses. Let's assume a hypothesis: newspaper reporters on general news rounds reject media material that is not written in a style acceptable to their newspaper. Our survey will need to include a number of **Likert scale** type questions, which might be framed around specific steps a reporter takes when assessing press material (see chapter 6):

Likert scale

a scale used to represent attitudes; frequently from like to dislike, or approve through disapprove.

- Does a headline on a news release influence your attitude to its content?
- If a news release does not carry a headline does that influence your attitude to its content?
- Does a lead paragraph in a news release influence your attitude to the remainder of its content?
- If a news release does not have a distinguishable lead paragraph, does that influence your attitude towards its content?
- If a news release runs over more than two pages does that influence your attitude towards its content?

A Likert scale for these questions might range between *always* and *never*. Additional questions might relate to the reception of the material, and then move on to its content. One important question would be the inclusion of the name of the client's organisation. While it is not within the scope of this chapter to provide details about the process, the answers from returned survey questionnaires would be logged into a computer software program and the results tabulated to provide the required descriptive analysis. A number of valuable works have been written about the process of data gathering, investigation, and interpretation; many can be found in the bibliography.

A brief word about content analysis

One of the more popular quantitative methods in media relations evaluation is content analysis. It competes with rhetorical analysis, discourse analysis, semiotic analysis, conversation analysis, and critical analysis and, since as early as the middle of the twentieth century, it has been described as a valuable research technique for all types of communication (Berelson et al. 1954). More recently it has been defined by US scholar Kimberley Neuendorf (2002) as 'the systematic, objective, quantitative analysis of message characteristics. It includes the careful examination of human interactions, the analysis of character portrayals in TV commercials, films and novels; and the computer-driven investigation of word usage in news releases and political speeches' (2002: 1). Neuendorf argues that content analysis has been the fastest-growing technique in the field of mass communication in the past twenty years, a timeframe that neatly locks into the professionalisation of media relations since the 1980s, and demonstrates a correlation between the rise in popularity of the subfield and the method. Following Neuendorf, the process for undertaking a content analysis of an issue or event in media relations involves a number of steps. These include:

- establishing a rationale for the analysis
- defining the variables within the analysis
- defining the unit measurements for data collection
- developing a coding system, human or computer
- developing a sampling technique
- applying a coder reliability test
- tabulating and reporting the results.

The importance of content analysis to media relations lies in its ability to *test* and *validate* relationships and to augment other quantitative methods such as surveys. As Neuendorf suggests, the value of content analysis is pronounced when it supports other evaluative research. A content analysis of news, for example, will provide evidence of subjectivity in reporting, but it will be more valuable if it is cross-analysed with a survey of reporters generating the news. Content analysis is descriptive, inferential, and predictive. Its importance to media relations evaluation is unquestionable.

13

Conclusions

This concluding chapter is designed to offer a sense of place to students, theorists, and practitioners of media relations.

A generation ago US media studies scholar Joshua Meyrowitz wrote that a book is 'more than a medium of communication; it is also an artefact and a possession … it is a symbol of *self* and *identity*' (1985) (my emphasis). Meyrowitz was interested in the *old* technology of the book and the enormous cultural shift that was occurring in the early 1980s from print to electronic information and news gathering. He argued that an individual's sense of place was being eroded by media. To an extent, the practice of media relations, along with advertising and the wider field of public relations, contributed significantly to the erosion. At that time it was the province of organisations with the financial capital to invest in their campaign strategies and, as imagined by Habermas, an *in camera* consequence of Grunig's one-way asymmetrical model of communication, a secret business strategy known to the lucky few.

How things change. As I have argued in the preceding chapters, media relations now focuses on building two-way transparent relationships between stakeholders inside and outside the media, and is used and adapted by every conceivable type of organisation and individual to attract news attention to all types of issues and events. It is ethically derived and employed by organisations as highly placed as the United Nations and the World Health Organisation. It is now put to use in redefining a sense of place for individuals and organisations as global issues and events compete for space with local issues and events. But it is not yet mature.

Towards a mature media relations

Corporations, governments, and other large organisations that have traditionally played a hegemonic role in defining media relations are reassessing their relationships. Stakeholders who were once considered subversive, or at the very least, irritating, are seen more often in partnership, the result of a long and bitter struggle that has yet to be concluded. The first reason for the shift lies partly with the transformation of media relations from a shonky practice done by anyone who could string three sentences together, to an established tertiary education course. Second, its transformation towards a respectable profession is the result of all types of alternative organisations and groups adopting and successfully using strategies and tactics that were once the province of profit-based organisations. In the past, when corporations and governments used media relations campaigns to persuade and influence, they were perceived to be doing so for selfish reasons. The adoption of campaign strategies and tactics or, more importantly, the overt acknowledgment that not-for-profit organisations and environmental groups such as the Red Cross and Greenpeace employ full-time media relations experts, helped to alter the image and reputation of media relations. It could no longer be decried as a persuasive tool of big business. As smaller and less well-funded organisations and individuals began understanding and using media relations strategies and tactics for all types of stakeholder communication, including local government election campaigns and environmental awareness campaigns, the demonisation of the field could no longer be sustained.

But media relations has not yet reached a mature position. By this I mean it has yet to devise and develop all the theories and strategies that will be useful in the future. While relationship building and framing are two of the most important, further transformations in the media landscape will obviate the need for the development of new theories and practices. The internet, as imagined by US journalism scholar Todd Gitlin (2000), is at such an early stage in its life that we are yet to know what it will become as it shifts inexorably towards maturity. Part of its transformation is being revealed by the global acquisitions of internet media by traditional media corporations. This will have a profound effect on the way media relations theorists and practitioners approach the future, in the same way that it will impact on traditional news gathering precepts and practices. The circumvention of traditional media by media relations on behalf of clients will alter perceptibly. New campaign strategies will need to be designed.

Towards a mature news media

In 1976 the Western news media were reporting on conflict in the Middle East, particularly that between Israel and Lebanon, and on the closed economy of communist China. Thirty years later the Western news media are still reporting on conflict in the Middle East, the election of the militant Palestinian group Hamas and its trenchant opposition to the existence of Israel, the democratic election in Iraq, and the role of China in global politics and trade; they also report on the closed economy of North Korea. In 2036—another generation from now—the Western news media will still be reporting on political issues in the Middle East, possibly a conflict between Iran and Israel. It will also be reporting on the completed democratisation of China and the emerging democratisation of North Korea.

In 1976 the user-friendly Macintosh computer was still more than ten years from production, genetically modified mass consumption food was in its initial research stages, Europe was emerging from a thirty-year reconstruction program after the Second World War, and Japan was poised to become the first Asian tiger economy, building cheaper and higher-quality electronics and motor vehicles. Western news reporting, however, differed only slightly from its present shape. It was grounded in a set of values that were clearly identifiable: good rather than bad (today, bad has become evil), capitalism rather than socialism, and democracy rather than theocracy. Today's Western news reporting remains grounded in good, capitalism, and democracy. The structure of reporting remains constant and unchanged. It is this unchanging structure that reveals why the Western news media imagine news today much as they did in 1976 and as they will in 2036. But this does not mean that news reporting has reached maturity in the West.

Western news media at the beginning of the twenty-first century were ready to shift their news reporting focus so that global issues and events could be imagined outside the frame of localisation. Localisation relies for its effect on fear, threat, or punishment, or a combination of all three, to sustain it. Western news media had almost exhausted this model; alternative sources such as the internet have provided citizens with access to unprecedented levels of information—some good, some not so good—that they can imagine without engagement with orthodox news media. Western news media are now unable to create the paradigm shift that they need to sustain themselves, because a global issue of significance (think 9/11) forced them to continue using outdated methods and models. In this, they will continue to report global news issues and events of vast complexity by distilling them to become locally palatable, just as they have for the past 300 years.

The future for media relations

There are two separate registers within the subfield of media relations: how it is thought about and how it is gone about. Theory and practice in many fields exist as interlocking registers where the association of ideas and argument conflict and compete, but deliver a workable practice that consists of a reasoned position rather than an ideological dogma, despite the Nietszchian argument that practice is spontaneous error, productive blindness, and historical amnesia. Witness the biomedical field in which the investigation of the truth of a theory proceeds towards practical application at an enormously successful rate. Despite substantial efforts to create a **dialectic** in media relations, the client is the stakeholder who continues to shape practice. Imagine if a motor vehicle manufacturer asked customers what they wanted and then set about making the car, without recourse to engineering design theory? Or if a construction company, on the opinion of a few uninformed stakeholders, began to erect a very tall building without considering the theoretical implications of wind and other weather. For the media relations expert, history has been dominated by the client's perception of the subfield. Media relations has, therefore, been viewed as a marketing tool and, like other add-ons, with an inevitable cyclical downturn in business, it is one of the first elements to be cut from a budget. The field has been badly out of shape.

> **dialectic**
> the progression of a logical argument that will reveal one true theory as the embodiment of a field or sub field.

I have borrowed Habermas's notion of transformation to provide a glimpse of what the field of media relations will be as the twenty-first century evolves. As I outlined in the introduction, leading US scholars have acknowledged there is interesting and valuable work emerging from places other than the USA, among them Australia and New Zealand. By 2020, the profession will have been transformed by issues and events of its own creation. The most important of these will be the completion of the transfer of knowledge from the industry to the academy. By that time, like its journalism counterpart, almost all individuals working at management level within media relations will have earned tertiary qualifications specific to the field. The effect will be the circumscription of practice by particular theories. First, practitioners will become more specialised, developing more sophisticated evaluation techniques that provide greater transparency. Second, if they are to maintain credibility, theorists will be required to spend time practising. Additionally, many smaller boutique agencies will suffer the mergers and acquisitions that were the hallmark of the legal profession at the end of the twentieth century, but this will provide avenues for theorists who will act as adjuncts within the larger independent firms. There they will work closely with practitioner experts to develop more sophisticated technology and resources, such as global media databases and other software that will have the capacity to integrate economic, political, social, and environmental factors into seamless and transparent campaigns. They will develop strategies and tactics that, while arguably necessitating persuasion and influence as dominant communicative actions, approach a balanced dialectic in which all stakeholders share equally. The potential for a paradigm shift to occur will lie with the relationship that is built between theorists and practitioners. The relationship building will be complete when the frames that theorists and practitioners construct intersect.

Glossary

agenda
items to be considered at a business meeting.

agenda setting
a strategy that involves the placement of items in some chosen order.

agent
someone acting on behalf of someone else or an organisation in a matter.

aim
the conscious decision to take a direction and attempt to attain the objectives along the path of the direction taken.

asset stripping
the aggressive removal of items of value from a core business for the purpose of making a profit.

audience
a collection of individuals who listen to or watch some event or spectacle.

backstory
background information that assists in creating meaning, supplied to a journalist or reporter who assists in the interpretation of meaning of an issue or event.

bivalent
the idea that everything is either true of false, but in media relations terms the possibility that two stories can exist simultaneously in one narrative.

chronicle
a record or register; a narrative account of issues and events.

citizen
an inhabitant of a community.

client
a citizen or organisation who uses the services of another in a professional capacity.

clippings
material extracted from newspapers and other print sources that are relevant to a client's issue or event.

co-creational theory
the proposition that stakeholders in any communication will work together to achieve desired aims and goals.

community
a group of citizens; citizens organised into a political and/or social group.

comparative advantage
the ability to create something more or less valuable than an alternative.

competitive advantage
the ability to make an organisation more economically valuable when compared with similar organisations.

controlled media
any publication, broadcast, or communication that bypasses an agent or other force to reach its intended stakeholder.

controlled tactic
an action that does not rely on an agent or other force for its success.

core competence
the underlying assumption that an organisation or individual has a central ability and capacity to undertake the professional business in which they are involved.

corporate social responsibility
the awareness of organisations that there is more to their bottom line than profits and that to be sustainable in the long term they need to consider their social and environmental interests as well as their economic interests.

diachronic communication
any type of communication that can be tracked through time; especially with regard to language or culture.

dialectic
the progression of a logical argument that will reveal one true theory as the embodiment of a field or subfield.

dialogic
being in the nature of dialogue or conversation.

dialogic relationship
a relationship based on the importance of dialogue, or conversation; the idea that conversation or dialogue can act as a constructive communication between two parties at all levels of interest.

dialogic theory

the proposition that conversation or dialogue underpins actions and objectives.

discipline

an area of learning or scholarly endeavour.

economic capital

the accumulated assets of an organisation or individual from which profit is derived.

empirical

the act of observation and experiment; the use of experience rather than theory in achieving goals and objectives.

excellence theory

an argument developed by US scholar James Grunig that relies on four models of communication—press agentry, public information, two-way asymmetrical, and two-way symmetrical.

field

a sphere of action in which actors, agents, and other forces exercise theoretical and empirical arguments that contribute to the existence of the field.

force

power to control or influence some type of effect.

formative stage

the early stage of a campaign where ideas are being developed.

fractured paradigm

a break or crack in a particular view of the world.

frame

the preparation of a space so that it has boundaries.

framing

the act of shaping and forming a story so that it resonates with a particular viewpoint.

functional communication

any communication that can be related to an action or activity rather than to its form.

global

embracing the whole world, or a whole group such as a global internet search and replace technique.

goal

the finish of a campaign or action; the desired end to a media campaign, but less useful when considering the relationship building process.

hegemony
the dominance or influence of one thing over another.

historicism
the idea that social phenomena are determined by history.

historicist
an adherent of historicism.

knowledge gap theory
the proposition that interpretation and meaning can reduce gaps in knowledge among individual citizens or groups.

ideology
an idea or way of thinking that becomes the basis for a political, economic, or social system, and that continues its existence when not in the ascendancy.

independent variable
a thing that has the ability to change and that is not dependent on other actions or factors to make such changes.

informational objective
the communication of facts or information to individuals or organisations as an act in itself; the provision of information.

investor
one who supplies financial or other capital to the interests of an individual

landscape orientation
the placement of a page layout so that the width is greater than the height; derived from pictures of natural scenes.

Likert scale
a scale used to represent attitudes; frequently from like to dislike, or approve through disapprove.

listener
one who is attentive to a sound or speaker.

local
a sense of place that allows individuals to feel comfortable in their surroundings.

logical positivism
the proposition that philosophical problems can be solved through logical investigation, taking no account of emotional factors.

loss leader
something done for less than the real fee that will assist in making the object more appealing.

market capitalisation
the value of the material wealth of an entity as it is seen by stakeholders.

media
a vehicle that provides a means of communication; includes the instruments of communication, viz. newspapers, television etc, and the objects of communication, viz. journalists reporters, editors etc.

media release
the supply of information on issues and events to the media, usually in written form.

mediated communication
any form of communication that is undertaken by a third party on behalf of two other agents or forces.

mediation
the act or process of intervening on behalf of stakeholders.

mentions
the number of times a client's issue or event appears in different media.

motivational objective
the injection of enthusiasm into an individual or organisation through the exercise of persuasion and influence so an objective can be achieved.

multivalent
the possibility that a number of interpretations or meanings can be attributed to one narrative; taking three or more meanings from a single story.

news
information, whether published, broadcast, or communicated from one individual to another that has some bearing on issues and events.

news release
see media release.

news schedule
the timing and placement of news within a media organisation such as a newspaper or broadcaster.

nomenclature
a name, or the act of naming.

objective
the object of an action such as the communication of information.

other forces
interests, whether political, economic, or social, that are not part of a strategy.

paradigm
an example or pattern; a case that can be used as an example.

perfect binding
a way of joining together the pages of a publication such as a magazine or book; glued on the spine rather than stapled.

personality profile
as a backstory, a personality profile helps stakeholders shape their opinions about issues and events.

portrait orientation
a way of placing a page so that the height is greater than the width; see landscape.

press agentry
the action of seeking publicity through media and other sources on behalf of a client.

press release
see media release.

private
an individual acting in a non-official capacity; something removed from public access or view.

public
any number of individuals or citizens belonging to a community or nation.

public information model
the second of James Grunig's excellence models; the action of providing information, usually from government or other institutional sources, to wider stakeholder publics.

public opinion
an expression of social, economic, and political will after the point of mediation.

public sphere
the space in which citizens are freely able to gather to witness or discuss issues or events.

reader
someone who takes in information through observation.

redeemable tokens
forms of metaphorical currency that can be traded for votes; promises based on some future investment in political capital.

relationship building
the development of a connection or association, either emotional or rational.

reverse engineering
the dismantling of something in the reverse order that it was constructed.

rhetorical tokens
political promises.

ritual tactic
a tactic that has become embedded through convention or long-time use; a tactic that is habitually embedded in a campaign, for example, a candidate mug shot in a newspaper advertisement.

saddle stitched
a method of joining pages in a book or magazine by using a number of staples inserted in the spine.

shareholder
an individual, citizen, or organisation that has some financial or other interest in something.

situational analysis
the investigation of something in relation to its place or position relative to its place.

situational variable
the movement of the position of something in relation to its place.

social contract theory
the proposition that human society relies on mutual agreement for its continuation.

special interest groups
a group of citizens who form for a specific reason or action.

spike
the act of placing filed copy on a sharp metallic spike.

spin doctor
an interesting name for a public relations practitioner.

stakeholder
a citizen who has an interest, financial or otherwise, in the outcome of a media relations campaign.

stakeseeker
a citizen who is looking to have an interest, for whatever reason, in the process and the outcome of a media relations campaign.

strategic advantage
the ability to move ahead of or to outflank competitors.

strategic decision
a decision that directly relates to the design and development of a campaign.

strategy
a plan of action that takes advantage of core competencies to the detriment of competitors.

subfield
an area within a field that is taken up by specific theories and practices.

summative stage
the final part of a campaign where all the actions and objectives are added together.

symbolic capital
the investment in symbols and signs that are as important to an organisation as its financial capital.

symmetry theory
the proposition that communication, to be effective, must have as much input from one stakeholder as it does from a stakeholder in an opposing position—for example, a corporation and an environmental group.

synchronic communication
communication that occurs at a particular time in history; in particular with reference to language and culture.

tactic
the action taken to fulfil strategic intent and campaign objectives.

taxonomies
classifications, particularly in relation to certain principles.

triple bottom line reporting
the combination of reporting three elements of an organisation to stakeholders; profit, environmental sustainability, and social responsibility.

two-way asymmetrical
the third of James Grunig's models defined by the ability of a stakeholder to extract information from another stakeholder and to use it to some advantage without a concomitant advantage for the other stakeholder.

two-way symmetrical
the fourth of James Grunig's models defined by the ability of stakeholders to share extracted information to their mutual advantage.

uncontrolled media
news and other media providers who stand between a media relations campaign and the desired recipients of its aims and goals.

univalent
a story with one subject or theme.

universe
all the objects under investigation.

Vienna Circle
an early twentieth-century group of individuals at Vienna University concerned with the notion of significance; the empirical study of issues and events and their utilitarian significance.

yield
the return from a campaign relative to the maximum theoretical return obtainable.

Bibliography

Andsager, J (2000), 'How Interest Groups Attempt to Shape Public Opinion with Competing News Frames', *Journalism and Mass Communication Quarterly*, 77(3), 577–92.

Aristotle (1991), *The Art of Rhetoric* [Lawson-Tancred, H (ed.)] Penguin, London.

Bains, P, Egan, J & Jefkins, F (2004), *Public Relations: Contemporary issues and techniques*, Elsevier, Oxford.

Baudrillard, J (1998), *The Consumer Society: Myths and structures*, Sage, London.

Bennett, W (1998), 'The Media and Democratic Development: The social basis of political communication', in P O'Neil (ed.) *Communicating Democracy: The media and political transitions*, Lynne Reiner, Boulder.

Bennett, W & Entman, R (eds) (2001), *Mediated Politics: Communication in the future democracy*, Cambridge University Press, Cambridge.

Benson, R & Neveu, E (eds) (2005), *Bourdieu and the Journalistic Field*, Polity, Cambridge, MA.

Berelson, B, Lazarfeld, P & McPhee, W (1954), *Voting: A study of opinion formation in a presidential campaign*, University of Chicago Press, Chicago.

Bernays, E (1928), 'Manipulating Public Opinion: The why and how', *American Journal of Sociology*, 33, 958–71.

—— (1928), *Propaganda*, Liveright, New York.

Blumenthal, S (1992), *The Permanent Campaign*, Touchstone Books, New York.

Blumler, J & Gurevitch, M (1995), *The Crisis of Public Communication*, Routledge, New York.

Blyskal, J & Blyskal, M (1985), *PR: How the public relations industry writes the news*, William Marrow, New York.

Botan, C (1993), 'Introduction to the Paradigm Struggle in Public Relations', *Public Relations Review*, 19, 107–10.

—— (1997), 'Ethics in Strategic Communication Campaigns: The case for a new approach to public relations', *Journal of Business Communication*, 34, 187–201.

—— & Hazelton, V (eds) (1989), *Public Relations Theory*, Lawrence Erlbaum, Hillsdale, NJ.

—— & —— (eds) (2006), *Public Relations Theory II*, Lawrence Erlbaum, Mahwah, NJ.

—— & Taylor, M (2005), 'Public Relations: State of the field', *Journal of Communication*, 54, 645–61.

Bourdieu, P (1977), *Outline of a Theory of Practice* (trans. 1972), Cambridge University Press, Cambridge.

—— (2005), 'The Political Field, the Social Science Field and the Journalistic Field', in R Benson & E Neveu (eds), *Bourdieu and the Journalistic Field*, Polity, Cambridge.

Bowman, D (1988), *The Captive Press*, Penguin, Ringwood.

Bridgman, P & Davis, G (1998), *Australian Policy Handbook*, Allen & Unwin, Sydney.

Broom, G & Dozier, D (1990), *Using Research in Public Relations: Applications to program management*, Prentice-Hall, Englewood Cliffs, NJ.

Bryant, J & Miron, D (2005), 'Theory and Research in Mass Communication', *Journal of Communication*, 54(4), 661–704.

Calhoun, C (ed.) (1992), *Habermas and the Public Sphere*, MIT Press, Cambridge, MA.

Carson, L & Martin, B (1999), *Random Selection in Politics*, Praeger, New York.

Cavanaugh, J (1995), *Media Effects on Voters: A panel study of the 1992 presidential election*, University Press America, Lanham, MD.

Clayman, S & Heritage, J (2002), *The News Interview: Journalists and public figures on the air*, Cambridge University Press, Cambridge.

Converse, P (1964), 'The Nature of Belief Systems in Mass Publics', in D Apter (ed.), *Ideology and Discontent*, Free Press, New York.

—— (1974), 'Public Opinion and Voting Behaviour', in F Greenstein & N Polsby, *Handbook of Political Science*, Addison Wesley, Boston.

Cornelissen, J (2000), 'Toward an Understanding of the Use of Academic Theories in Public Relations Practice', *Public Relations Review*, 26(3), 315–26.

—— (2004), *Corporate Communications Theory and Practice*, Sage, London.

Crespi, I (1997), *The Public Opinion Process: How the people speak*, Lawrence Erlbaum, Mahwah, NJ.

Crouch, C & Marquand, D (eds) (1995), *Reinventing Collective Action: From the global to the local*, Blackwell, Boston.

Cutlip, S, Center, A & Broom, G (2000), *Effective Public Relations* (8th edn), Prentice-Hall, London.

Dahlgren, P & Sparks, C (1991), *Communication and Citizenship*, Routledge, London.

Dalton, R (1996), *Citizen Politics: Public opinion and political parties in advanced Western democracies*, Chatham House, Chatham, NJ.

Davidson, W P (1983), 'The Third Person Effect in Communication', *Public Opinion Quarterly*, 47(4), 1–15.

Davis, G, Wanna, J, Warhurst, J & Weller, P (eds) (1993), *Public Policy in Australia*, Allen & Unwin, Sydney.

Davis, G & Weller, P (eds) (2001), *Are you Being Served?: State, citizens and government*, Allen & Unwin, Sydney.

De Burgh, H (ed.) (2000), *Investigative Journalism: Context and practice*, Routledge, London.

Demetrious, K & Hughes, P (2004), 'Publics or Stakeholders? Performing social responsibility through stakeholder software', *Asia Pacific Public Relations Journal*, 5(2), 1–12.

Desario, J & Langton, S (1987), *Citizen Participation in Public Decision Making*, Greenwood, Westport.

Devlin, L (1987), *Political Persuasion in Presidential Campaigns*, Transaction, Somerset, NJ.

Dostall-Neff, B (1989), 'The Emerging Theoretical Perspective in Public Relations: An opportunity for communication departments', in C Botan & V Hazelton (eds), *Public Relations Theory*, Lawrence Erlbaum, Hillsdale, NJ.

Dozier, D, Grunig, L & Grunig, J (1995), *Manager's Guide to Excellence in Public Relations and Communication Management*, Lawrence Erlbaum, Mahwah, NJ.

Elwood, W (1995), 'Public Relations and the Ethics of the Moment: The anatomy of a local ballot issue campaign', in W Elwood (ed.), *Public Relations Inquiry as Rhetorical Criticism*, Praeger, New York.

Engel, M (1996), *Tickle the Public*, Gollancz, London.

Entman, R (1993), 'Framing: Toward clarification of a fractured paradigm', *Journal of Communication*, 43(4), 51–8.

—— (2003), 'Cascading Activism: Contesting the White House's frame after 9/11', *Political Communication*, 20, 415–32.

Esser, F, Reinemann, C & Fan, D (2001), 'Spin Doctors in the United States, Great Britain and Germany: Metacommunication about media manipulation', *Harvard International Journal of Press Politics*, 6(1), 16–45.

Etzioni, A (ed.) (1998), *The Essential Communitarian Reader*, Rowman & Littlefield, Lanham, MD.

Ewen, P (1996), *PR!: A social history of spin*, Basic Books, New York.

Fearn-Banks, K (2002), *Crisis Communications: A casebook approach*, Lawrence Erlbaum, Mahwah, NJ.

Ferguson, M (1990), *Public Communication: The new imperatives*, Sage, London.

Fishkin, J (1997), *The Voice of the People: Public opinion and democracy*, Yale University Press, New Haven.

Franklin, B (1994), *Packaging Politics*, Routledge, London.

—— (1997), *Newzak and News Media*, Arnold, London.

Fraser, N (1992), 'Rethinking the Public Sphere: A contribution to the critique of actually existing democracy', in C Calhoun (ed.), *Habermas and the Public Sphere*, MIT Press, Cambridge, MA.

Freeden, M (1996), *Ideologies and Political Theory: A conceptual approach*, Oxford University Press, Oxford.

Freidenberg, R (1997), *Communication Consultants in Political Campaigns*, Praeger, New York.

Fuller, J (1996), *News Values for an Information Age*, University of Chicago Press, Chicago.

Gamson, W (1990), *The Strategy of Social Protest*, Wadsworth, CA.

—— (1992), *Talking Politics*, Columbia University Press, New York.

—— (2001), 'Promoting Political Engagement', in W Bennett & R Entman (eds), *Mediated Politics: Communication in the future democracy*, Cambridge University Press, Cambridge.

Garnham, N (1992), 'The Media and the Public Sphere', in C Calhoun (ed.) *Habermas and the Public Sphere*, MIT Press, Cambridge, MA.

—— (2000), *Emancipation, the Media, and Modernity: Arguments about the media and social theory*, Oxford University Press, New York.

Gitlin, T (2000), *Inside Prime Time,* University of California Press, Berkeley.

Goffman, E (1974), *Frame Analysis*, Harper & Row, New York.

Gold, J & Ward, S (1994), *Place Promotion: The use of publicity and marketing to sell towns and regions,* John Wiley & Sons, London.

Goldman, E (1948), *Two Way Street: The emergence of the public relations counsel,* Bellman, Boston.

Goodnight, G (1992), 'Habermas, the Public Sphere and Controversy', *International Journal of Public Opinion Research,* 4, 243–55.

Graber, D (1988), *Processing the News: How people tame the information tide,* Longman, New York.

—— (2005), 'Political Communication Faces the 21st Century', *Journal of Communication,* 55(3), 475–507.

——, McQuail, D & Norris, P (eds) (1998), 'The Politics of News: The news of politics', *Congressional Quarterly,* New York.

Grant, W (1995), *Pressure Groups, Politics and Democracy,* Harvester Wheatsheaf, London.

Grunig, J (1992), *Excellence in Public Relations and Communication Management,* Lawrence Erlbaum, Hillsdale, NJ.

—— (2001) 'Two-way Symmetrical Public Relations: Past, present and future', in R Heath (ed.), *Handbook of Public Relations,* Sage, Thousand Oaks, CA.

—— & Dozier D (1992), *Excellence in Public Relations and Communication Management,* Lawrence Erlbaum, Hillsdale, NJ.

—— & Huang, Y (2000), 'From Organizational Effectiveness to Relationship Indicators: Antecedents of relationships, public relations strategies and relationship outcomes', in J Ledingham & S Bruning (eds), *Public Relations as Relationship Management: A relational approach to the study and practice of public relations,* Lawrence Erlbaum, Hillsdale, NJ.

—— & Hunt T (1984), *Managing Public Relations,* Holt Rinehart & Winston, New York.

Gunther, R & Mughan, A (2000), *Democracy and the Media,* Cambridge University Press, Cambridge, MA.

Habermas, J (1987), *Theory of Communicative Action,* Beacon Press, New York.

—— (1989), *The Structural Transformation of the Public Sphere,* Polity Press, New York.

Hague, D, Mackenzie, W & Barker, A (1975), *Public Policy and Private Interests: The institutions of compromise*, Macmillan, London.

Hallin, D & Mancini, P (2004), *Comparing Media Systems: Three models of media and politics*, Cambridge University Press, Cambridge.

Harris, T (1991), *The Marketer's Guide to Public Relations*, John Wiley & Sons, New York.

Hart, N (1987), *Effective Public Relations: Applying public relations in business and industry*, McGraw Hill, Maidenhead.

Hart, R (2000), *Campaign Talk: Why Elections Are Good for Us*, Princeton University Press, Princeton.

Heath, R (1992), 'Critical Perspective on Public Relations', in E Toth & R Heath (eds), *Rhetorical and Critical Approaches to Public Relations*, Lawrence Erlbaum, Hillsdale, NJ.

—— (1994), *Management of Corporate Communication: From interpersonal contacts to external affairs*, Lawrence Erlbaum, Hillsdale, NJ.

—— (1997), *Strategic Issues Management: Organizations and public policy challenges*, Sage, Thousand Oaks, CA.

—— (ed.) (2001), *Handbook of Public Relations*, Sage, Thousand Oaks, CA.

Hendrix, J (1998), *Public Relations Cases*, Wadsworth, Belmont CA.

Herman, S & McChesney, R (1997), *The Global Media*, Cassell, London.

Hindess, B (1989), *Political Choice and Social Structure: An analysis of actors, interests and rationality*, Edward Elgar, London.

Hirschman, A (1991), *The Rhetoric of Reaction: Perversity, futility, jeopardy*, Harvard University Press, Cambridge, Mass.

Hirst, M & Patching, R (2005), *Journalism Ethics: Arguments and cases*, Oxford University Press, Melbourne.

Hoffmann, J (2000), *Co-operation From a Distance: The relationships between journalists and the political élite in Germany*, International Association for Media and Communication Research (IAMCR), Singapore.

Hollingsworth, M (1997), *The Ultimate Spin Doctor: The life and times of Tim Bell*, Hodder & Stoughton, London.

Holtzhausen, D (1999), *Postmodern Values in Public Relations*, International Communication Association (ICA), San Francisco.

Hunt, T & Grunig, J (1994), *Public Relations Techniques*, Harcourt Brace, Fort Worth.

Hunter, F (1953), *Community Power Structure*, University of North Carolina Press, Chapel Hill.

Hurst, J and White, S (1994), *Ethics and the Australian News Media*, Macmillan, Melbourne.

Ihlen, Ø (2005), 'The Power of Social Capital: Adapting Bourdieu to the study of public relations', *Public Relations Review*, 31(4), 492–6.

Jamieson, K (1992), *Dirty Politics*, Oxford University Press, New York.

—— (1997), *The Interplay of Influence*, Wadsworth Publishing, Belmont, CA.

—— (2000), *Everything You Think You Know About Politics: And why you're wrong*, Basic Books, New York.

Janeway, M (1999), *Republic of Denial: Press, politics and public life*, Yale University Press, New Haven.

Johnston, J and Zawawi, C (eds) (2004), *Public Relations Theory and Practice*, Allen & Unwin, Sydney.

Jones, N (1995), *Soundbites and Spin Doctors: How politicians manipulate the media—and vice versa*, Cassell, London.

—— (1999), *Sultans of Spin*, Gollancz, London.

Jowett, G & O'Donnell, V (1992), *Propaganda and Persuasion*, Sage, London.

Katz, D (1960), 'The Functional Approach to the Study of Attitudes', *Public Opinion Quarterly*, 24, 163–204.

Kavanagh, D (1996), 'New Campaign Communications', *International Journal of Press/Politics*, 1(3), 60–76.

Keegan, W J & Green, M (1997), *Principles of Global Marketing*, Prentice-Hall, New York.

Keiran, M (ed.) (1998), *Media Ethics*, Routledge, New York.

Kelley, S (1956), *Professional Public Relations and Political Power*, Johns Hopkins University Press, Baltimore.

Kent, M & Taylor, M (2002), 'Towards a Dialogic Theory of Public Relations', *Public Relations Review*, 28(1), 21–37.

Kesey, K (1992), *Sailor Song*, Penguin, New York.

Kingdon, J (1995), *Agendas, Alternatives and Public Policies*, HarperCollins, New York.

Kingston, M (1999), *Off the Rails: The Pauline Hanson trip*, Allen & Unwin, Sydney.

Kitchen, P (1997), *Public Relations Principles and Practice*, Thomson Business Press, London.

Kruckeberg, D (1998), 'The Future of PR Education: Some recommendations', *Public Relations Review*, 24, 235–48.

—— & Starck, K (1988), *Public Relations and Community: A reconstructed theory*, Praeger, New York.

Kurtz, H (1998), *Spin Cycle: Inside the Clinton propaganda machine*, Pan, London.

Lane, R & Sears, D (1964), *Public Opinion*, Prentice-Hall, Englewood Cliffs, NJ.

Langer, J (1998), *Tabloid Television: Popular journalism and the other news*, Routledge, London.

Laswell, H (1927), *Propaganda Technique in the World War*, Knopf, New York.

Ledingham, J (2001), 'Government–Community Relationships: Extending the relational theory of public relations', *Public Relations Review*, 27, 285–95.

—— & Bruning, S (1997), 'Building Loyalty Through Community Relations', *Public Relations Strategist*, 3(2), 27–9.

—— & —— (1998), 'Relationship Management in Public Relations: Dimensions of an organization–public relationship', *Public Relations Review*, 24(1), 55–65.

—— & —— (eds) (2000), *Public Relations as Relationship Management: A relational approach to the study and practice of public relations*, Lawrence Erlbaum, Mahwah, NJ.

—— & —— (2000), 'Managing Community Relationships to Maximise Mutual Benefit: Doing well by doing good', in R Heath (ed.), *Public Relations Handbook*, Sage, California.

Leitch, S & Motion, J (2001), 'New Zealand Perspectives on Public Relations', in R Heath (ed.), *Handbook of Public Relations*, Sage, Thousand Oaks, CA.

Levin, D (2005), 'Framing Peace Policies: The competition for resonant themes', *Political Communication*, 22, 83–108.

Lindenmann, W (1997), 'Setting Minimum Standards for Measuring Public Relations Effectiveness', *Public Relations Review*, 23(4), 391–408.

Lippmann, W (1922), *Public Opinion*, The Free Press, New York.

Lipset, S (1960), *Political Man*, Heinemann, London.

Lloyd, (1985), *Profession: Journalist: A history of the Australian Journalists' Association*, Hale & Iremonger, Sydney.

Lucy, R (1968), 'The Liberal Campaign: How American?', in J Power (ed.), *Politics in a Suburban Community: The NSW state election in Manly 1965*, UNSW Press, Sydney.

Luntz, F (1988), *Candidates, Consultants and Campaigns*, Blackwell, London.

Mackey, S (2004), 'Crisis and Issues Management', in J Johnston & C Zawawi (eds), *Public Relations Theory and Practice*, Allen & Unwin, Sydney.

Manheim, J (1998), 'The News Shapers: Strategic communication as a third force in news making', in D Graber, D McQuail and P Norris, *The Politics of News, The News of Politics*, Congressional Quarterly, New York.

Marston, J (1963), *The Nature of Public Relations*, McGraw Hill, New York.

Martel, M (1983), *Political Campaign Debates: Images, strategies and tactics*, Longman, New York.

Mayer, H (1964), *The Press in Australia*, Lansdowne Press, Sydney.

Mayhew, L (1997), *The New Public: Professional communication and the means of social influence*, Cambridge University Press, Cambridge.

McChesney, R (1997), *Corporate Media and the Threat to Democracy*, Seven Stories Press, New York.

—— (1999), *Rich Media Poor Democracy*, University of Illinois Press, Chicago.

McElreath, M (1997), *Managing Systematic and Ethical Public Relations Campaigns*, Brown & Benchmark, New York.

McNair, B (2000), *Journalism and Democracy: An evaluation of the political public sphere*, Routledge, London.

Melleuish, G (1998), *The Packaging of Australia: Politics and culture wars*, UNSW Press, Sydney.

Meyrowitz, J (1985), *No Sense of Place: The impact of electronic media on social behaviours*, Oxford University Press, Oxford.

Michie, D (1997), *The Invisible Persuaders: How Britain's spin doctors manipulate the media*, Bantam, London.

Moloney, K (2005), *Rethinking Public Relations: The spin and the substance*, Routledge, London.

Negrine, R (1996), *The Communication of Politics*, Sage, London.

Neuendorf, K (2002), *The Content Analysis Guidebook*, Sage, Thousand Oaks, CA.

Nimmo, D (1970), *The Political Persuaders: The techniques of modern election campaigns*, Prentice-Hall, Englewood Cliffs, NJ.

—— (1978), *Political Communication and Public Opinion in America*, Goodyear, Santa Monica.

—— & Combs, J (1992), *Political Pundits*, Praeger, New York.

Novotny, P (2000), 'From Polis to Agra: The marketing of political consultants', *Harvard International Journal of Press/Politics*, 5(3), 12–26.

Packard, V (1957), *The Hidden Persuaders*, Longman, London.

Page, K & Hazelton, V (1999), *An Empirical Analysis of Factors Influencing Public Relations Strategy Selection and Effectiveness*, International Communication Association (ICA), San Francisco.

Paletz, D (1987), *Political Communication Research*, Ablex, Norwood, NJ.

Pan, Z & Kosicki, G (1993), 'Framing Analysis: An approach to news discourse', *Political Communication* 10, 55–75.

Papadakis, E & Grant, R (2001), 'Media Responsiveness to Old and New Politics Issues in Australia', *Australian Journal of Political Science*, 36(2), 293–309.

Park, H & Salmon, C (2005), 'A Test of the Third-Person Effect in Public Relations: Application of social comparison theory', *Journalism and Mass Communication Quarterly*, 82(1), 25–43.

Perloff, R (2003), *The Dynamics of Persuasion: Communication and attitudes in the 21st century*, Lawrence Erlbaum, Mahwah, NJ.

Phillips, P (1997), *Censored 1997: The news that didn't make the news—the year's top 25 censored news stories*, Seven Stories Press, New York.

Plasser, F (2000), 'American Campaign Techniques Worldwide', *Harvard International Journal of Press/Politics*, 5(4), 33–54.

—— (2001), 'Parties' Diminishing Relevance for Campaign Professionals', *Harvard International Journal of Press/Politics*, 6(4), 44–59.

Power, J (ed.) (1965), *Politics in a Suburban Community, Sydney*, University Press, Sydney.

Prior-Miller, M (1989), 'Four Major Social Scientific Theories and their Value to the Public Relations Researcher', in C Botan & V Hazelton V (eds), *Public Relations Theory*, Lawrence Erlbaum, Hillsdale, NJ.

Rawson, D & Holtzinger, S (1958), *Politics in Eden–Monaro: The personalities and the campaigns*, Heinemann, Melbourne.

Reisman, D (1950), *The Lonely Crowd*, Doubleday, New York.

Rosen, J & Taylor, P (1992), *The New News vs the Old News: The press and politics in the 1990s*, Twentieth Century Fund, New York.

Rosenbaum, M (1997), *From Soapbox to Soundbite*, Macmillan, London.

Sabato, L (1981), *The Rise of Political Consultants*, Basic Books, New York.

Sawer, M & Zappalà, G (2001), *Speaking for the People: Representation in Australian politics*, Melbourne University Press, Melbourne.

Schudson, M (1992), 'Was There Ever a Public Sphere? If so, when? Reflections on the American case', in C Calhoun (ed.), *Habermas and the Public Sphere*, MIT Press, Cambridge, MA.

—— (1995), *The Power of News*, Harvard University Press, Cambridge, MA.

—— (1999), *The Good Citizen: A history of American civil life*, Harvard University Press, Cambridge, MA.

Schumpeter, J (1976), *Capitalism, Socialism and Democracy*, George Allen & Unwin, London.

Seib, P (1994), *Campaigns and Conscience: The ethics of political journalism*, Praeger, New York.

—— & Fitzpatrick, K (1995), *Public Relations Ethics*, Harcourt Brace, Fort Worth.

Sekuless, P (1991), *Lobbying Canberra in the Nineties: The government relations game*, Allen & Unwin, Sydney.

Semetko, H, Blumler, M, Gurevitch, M & Weaver, D (1991), *The Formation of Campaign Agendas: A comparative analysis of party and media roles in recent American and British elections*, Lawrence Erlbaum, Hillsdale, NJ.

Seymour-Ure, C (1968), *The Press, Politics and the Public*, Constable, London.

Sharp, E (1999), *The Sometimes Connection: Public opinion and social policy*, Suny Press, New York.

Sharp, M (2000), 'Developing a Behavioral Paradigm for the Performance of Public Relations', *Public Relations Review*, 26(3), 345–61.

Shen, F (2004), 'Effects of News Frames and Schemas on Individuals' Issue Interpretations and Attitudes', *Journalism and Mass Communication Quarterly*, 81, 400–16.

Simms, M & Bolger, D (2000), 'The Australian Print Media and Partisan Bias in the Campaign', in M Simms and J Warhurst (eds), *Howard's Agenda*, University of Queensland Press, St Lucia.

Simms, M & Warhurst, J (eds) (2000), *Howard's Agenda*, University of Queensland Press, St Lucia.

Simons, M (1999), *Fit to Print: Inside the Canberra press gallery*, UNSW Press, Sydney.

Sinclair, A (1987), *Getting the Numbers: Women in local government*, Hargreen Publishing, Melbourne.

Sitton, J (2003), *Habermas and Contemporary Society*, Palgrave Macmillan, New York.

Smith, R (2001), *Australian Political Culture*, Pearson Education, Sydney.

Snooks, G (1998), *Longrun Dynamics: A general economic and political theory*, Macmillan, London.

Souter, G (1988), *Acts of Parliament: A narrative history of the Senate and House of Representatives Commonwealth of Australia*, Melbourne University Press, Melbourne.

—— (1991), *The House of Fairfax 1841–1990*, Melbourne University Press, Melbourne.

Sparrow, B (1999), *Uncertain Guardians: The news media as a political institution*, Johns Hopkins Press, Baltimore.

Sproule, J (2001), 'Authorship and Origins of the Seven Propaganda Devices: A research note', *Rhetoric and Public Affairs*, 4(1), 135–43.

Sriramesh, K & Vercic, D (2003), *The Global Public Relations Handbook: Theory, research and practice*, Lawrence Erlbaum, Mahwah, NJ.

Stacks, D (2003), *Primer of Public Relations Research*, Guildford Press, New York.

Stanton, R (2001), *Professional Communicators and the Means of Sociopolitical Influence*, Australian Centre for Independent Journalism, Sydney.

—— (2003), *Mezzanine Politics*, International Communication Association (ICA), San Diego.

—— (2004), *The Sociological Impact of Political Communication in Regional Australia*, Australian and New Zealand Communication Association (ANZCA), Sydney.

—— (2004), *The Impact of Political Communication on Regional Communities*, International Association for Media and Communication Research (IAMCR), Porto Allegre.

—— (2006), *Media Globalization: How the Western media imagines news*, International Political Science Association (IPSA), Fukuoka, Japan.

—— (2006), *Towards Public Relations Liberalization: An Australian Contribution*, 1st Asia Pacific Public Relations Conference, Seoul.

Stewart, R (1999), *Public Policy: Strategy and accountability*, Macmillan, Melbourne.

Stiff, J & Mongeau, P (2003), *Persuasive Communication*, Guildford Press, New York.

Stone, D (1997), *Policy Paradox: The art of political decision making*, W W Norton, New York.

Swanson, D & Mancini, P (1996), *Politics, Media and Modern Democracy: An international study of innovations in electoral campaigning and their consequences*, Praeger, New York.

Swanson, D & Nimmo, D (1990), *New Directions in Political Campaigning: A resource book*, Sage, Thousand Oaks, CA.

Taylor M, Vasquez G, & Doorley J (2003), 'Extending Issues Management: A case study of engagement between Merck and IADS activists', *Public Relations Review*, 29, 57–270.

Thayer, L (1968), *Communication and Communication Systems*, Irwin, Chicago.

Thompson, B (1995), *The Media and Modernity: A social theory of the media*, Stanford University Press, Palo Alto.

Thorne, R & Purcell, T (1992), 'Participation and Non Participation: Public meetings and surveys', in M Munro-Clark (ed.), *Citizen Participation in Government*, Hale & Iremonger, Sydney.

Thurber, J & Nelson, C (1995), *Campaigns and Elections American Style*, Westview Press, Boulder.

—— (eds) (2000), *Campaign Warriors: Political consultants in elections*, Brookings Institution Press, Washington, DC.

Tocqueville, A de (1835, 1840), *Democracy in America* (2 vols), R Heffner (ed.), 1956 edn, Mentor Books, New York.

Toth, E & Heath, R (eds) (1992), *Rhetorical and Critical Approaches to Public Relations*, Lawrence Erlbaum, Hillsdale, NJ.

Trent, J & Friedenberg, R (2000), *Political Campaign Communication: Principles and practices*, Praeger, New York.

Tuchman, G (1978), *Making News: A study in the construction of reality*. Free Press, New York.

Tumber, H (ed.) (2000), *Media Power, Professional and Politics*, Routledge, London.

Tunstall, J (1977), *The Media Are America: Anglo–American media in the world*, Constable, London.

Tye, L (1998), *The Father of Spin*, Crown, New York.

Tymson, C & Lazar, R (2006), *The New Australian Public Relations Manual*, Tymson Communications, Sydney.

Vasquez, G (1996), 'Public Relations as Negotiation: An issue development perspective', *Journal of Public Relations Research*, 8, 57–77.

—— & Taylor, M (2000), 'Public Relations: An emerging social science enters the new millennium', *Communication Yearbook*, 24, 319–42.

Walker, G (2006), *Sense-Making Methodology: A theory of method for public relations*, in C Botan & V Hazleton (eds), *Public Relations Theory II*, Lawrence Erlbaum, Mahwah, NJ.

Wattenberg, M (1992), *The Rise of Candidate-Centred Politics*, Cambridge University Press, Cambridge.

Weaver, D (1987), 'Media Agenda-Setting and Elections: Assumptions and implications', in D Paletz, *Political Communication Research*, Ablex, Norwood, NJ.

—— (ed.) (1998), *The Global Journalist*, Hampton Press, Cresskill, NJ.

——, Graber, D, McCombs, M & Eyal, C (1981), *Media Agenda Setting in a Presidential Election*, Praeger, New York.

Wilcox, D, Ault, P, Agee, W & Cameron, G (2000), *Public Relations Strategies and Tactics*, Longman, New York.

Wild, R (1974), *Bradstow: A study of status, class and power in a small country town*, Angus & Robertson, Sydney.

Wilson, G (1990), *Interest Groups*, Blackwell, Oxford.

Zoch, L & Molleda, J (2006), 'Media Relations', in C Botan & V Hazelton (eds), *Public Relations Theory II*, Lawrence Erlbaum, Mahwah, NJ.

Index